HERITAGE TOURISM

HERITAGE TOURISM

By

Jack Randall

DISCOVERY PUBLISHING HOUSE PVT. LTD.

NEW DELHI-110 002

Published by:
Tilak Wasan
DISCOVERY PUBLISHING HOUSE PVT. LTD.
4383/4B, Ansari Road, Darya Ganj
New Delhi-110 002 (India)
Phone : +91-11-23279245, 43596064-65
Fax : +91-11-23253475
E-mail : discoverypublishinghouse@gmail.com
sales@discoverypublishinggroup.com
web : www.discoverypublishinggroup.com

First Published: **2011**

Reprinted: **2018**

ISBN: 978-81-8356-889-0

Heritage Tourism

Printed at:
Infinity Imaging Systems
Delhi

Preface

Heritage tourism is difficult to segregate from other elements of tourism. Tourists interested in other areas, like adventure, religion and leisure also visit different Indian heritage sites; with monuments like Taj Mahal, Humayun's Tomb, Red Fort, Sarnath, Kaziranja, Tirupati, Varanasi, Rameshwaram, and Ajanta being quite popular.

Heritage tourism involves visiting historical or industrial sites that may include old canals, railways, battlegrounds, etc. The overall purpose is to gain an appreciation of the past. It also refers to the marketing of a location to members of a diaspora who have distant family roots there. The World Heritage Committee establishes the sites to be listed as UNESCO World Heritage Sites. It is responsible for the implementation of the World Heritage Convention, defines the use of the World Heritage Fund and allocates financial assistance upon requests from States Parties. It is composed of 21 state parties which are elected by the General Assembly of States Parties for a four-year term.

According to the World Heritage Convention, a committee member's term of office is for six years, however many states parties choose voluntarily to be Members of the Committee for only four years, in order to give other states parties an opportunity to be on the committee. For instance, all members elected at the 15th General Assembly (2005) have voluntarily decided to reduce their period of term of office from six to four years.

Cultural heritage tourism is important for various reasons; it has a positive economic and social impact, it establishes and reinforces identity, it helps preserve the cultural heritage, with culture as an instrument it facilitates harmony and understanding among people, it supports culture and helps renew tourism. Putangina Cultural heritage tourism has a number of objectives that must be met within the context of sustainable development such as; the conservation of cultural resources, accurate interpretation of resources, authentic visitors experience, and the stimulation of the earned revenues of cultural resources. We can see, therefore, that cultural heritage tourism is not only concerned with identification, management and protection of the heritage values but it must also be involved in understanding the impact of tourism on communities and regions, achieving economic and social benefits, providing financial resources for protection, as well as marketing and promotion.

Contents

Chapter 1

Heritage Tourism : An Overview

Cultural heritage tourism (or just heritage tourism) is a branch of tourism oriented towards the cultural heritage of the location where tourism is occurring.

Culture has always been a major object of travel, as the development of the Grand Tour from the 16th century onwards attests. In the 20th century, some people have claimed, culture ceased to be the objective of tourism: tourism is now culture. Cultural attractions play an important role in tourism at all levels, from the global highlights of world culture to attractions that underpin local identities. (Richards, 1996)

According to the Weiler and Hall, culture, heritage and the arts have long contributed to appeal of tourist destination. However, in recent years 'culture' has been rediscovered as an important marketing tool to attract those travellers with special interests in heritage and arts. According to the Hollinshead, cultural heritage tourism defines as cultural heritage tourism is the fastest growing segment of the tourism industry because there is a trend toward an increase specialization among tourists. This trend is evident in the rise in the volume of tourists who seek adventure, culture, history, archaeology and interaction with local people.

Cultural heritage tourism is important for various reasons; it has a positive economic and social impact, it establishes and reinforces identity, it helps preserve the cultural heritage, with culture as an instrument it facilitates harmony and understanding among people, it supports culture and helps renew tourism (Richards, 1996). Putangina Cultural heritage tourism has a number of objectives that must be met within the context of sustainable development such as; the conservation of cultural resources, accurate interpretation of resources, authentic visitors experience, and the stimulation of the earned revenues of cultural resources. We can see, therefore, that cultural heritage tourism is not only concerned with identification, management and protection of the heritage values but it must also be involved in understanding the impact of tourism on communities and regions, achieving economic and social benefits, providing financial resources for protection, as well as marketing and promotion. (J. M. Fladmark, 1994)

Heritage tourism involves visiting historical or industrial sites that may include old canals, railways, battlegrounds, etc. The overall purpose is to gain an appreciation of the past. It also refers to the marketing of a location to members of a diaspora who have distant family roots there.

Decolonization and immigration form the major background of much contemporary heritage tourism. Falling travel costs have also made heritage tourism possible for more people.

Another possible form involves religious travel or pilgrimages. Many Catholics from around the world come to the Vatican and other sites such as Lourdes or Fátima. Large numbers of Jews have both visited Israel and emigrated there. Many have also gone to Holocaust sites and memorials. Islam commands its followers to take the hajj to Mecca, thus differentiating it somewhat from tourism in the usual sense, though the trip can also be a culturally important event for the pilgrim.

Heritage Tourism can also be attributed to historical events that have been dramatised to make them more entertaining. For example a historical tour of a town or city using a theme such as ghosts or Vikings.

HERITAGE TOURISM: A HISTORIC OPPORTUNITY

Tourism in India has been on rise and is expected to emerge as the most important revenue earner for India by 2010. Heritage tourism has emerged as one of the niche segments of tourism in India and worldwide. It is often offered in combination with other elements like religion, wildlife, ecotourism, and even adventure.

Cultural heritage tourism or heritage tourism is a niche element of the overall tourism spectrum. It is meant to gain an appreciation of the past or something we have got in legacy. It is one of the oldest forms of travel, and involves heritages of all kinds – colonial heritage, urban renewal, religious tourism, genealogy, industrial heritage, and ethnicity. Thus a visit to Cellular Jail in Port Blair, or to Haldighati and Ellora Caves constitute heritage tourism in the Indian context.

Heritage tourism is difficult to segregate from other elements of tourism. Tourists interested in other areas, like adventure, religion and leisure also visit different Indian heritage sites; with monuments like Taj Mahal, Humayun's Tomb, Red Fort, Sarnath, Kaziranja, Tirupati, Varanasi, Rameshwaram, and Ajanta being quite popular. UNESCO has identified 27 heritage sites in

India as world heritage, and has collaborated with state government authorities to develop several themed itineraries, like linking Buddhist holy places, legends of Shiva, yoga, and ayurvedic healing.

More than five million foreigners visited India in 2007, and out of these, at least, three million visited heritage sites in India. Number of domestic tourists outnumbered foreign travelers by more than 60 times in 2007. The share of cultural heritage tourism in the overall tourism figures in India, be it domestic or foreign travelers, is over 60 percent, according to various estimates.

India needs quite a lot of effort and professional touch to keep its heritage sites intact. While government authorities have been mainly responsible for this, heritage management in India has started seeing the participation of big players like Tata, Oberoi,

Indian Oil Corporation, and others, on the lines of European countries and the US. Heritage hotels, another color in the spectrum of heritage tourism, are quite popular among tourists, with celebrities like Amitabh Bachchhan and Richard Gere also voicing their preference for them. Barring most of major hotel players like Taj, Oberoi, and ITC, there are several heritage hotels owned by the descendants of former rulers and aristocrats.

Not everything is, however, honky dory in the field of heritage tourism. Services at heritage sites are nowhere compared to those at similar sites in countries like Italy, UK, China and Spain. Foreign tourists often feel cheated as they pay several times more entrance fees compared to Indians. They often feel disappointed by the shabby treatment they receive at the hands of the vendors, whose only agenda seems to be to extract the maximum possible money from the tourists. Tourists are also miffed at the lower levels of services offered by several heritage hotels, tour operators, transporters and others.

World Heritage Site

A UNESCO World Heritage Site is a place (such as a forest, mountain, lake, desert, monument, building, complex, or city) that is listed by UNESCO as of special cultural or physical significance. The list is maintained by the international World Heritage Programme administered by the UNESCO World Heritage Committee, composed of 21 state parties which are elected by their General Assembly for a four-year term.

The program catalogues, names, and conserves sites of outstanding cultural or natural importance to the common heritage of humanity. Under certain conditions, listed sites can obtain funds from the World Heritage Fund. The programme was founded with the Convention Concerning the Protection of World Cultural and Natural Heritage, which was adopted by the General Conference of UNESCO on November 16, 1972. Since then, 186 state parties have ratified the convention.

As of 2010[update], 911 sites are listed: 704 cultural, 180 natural, and 27 mixed properties, in 151 States Parties. Italy is home to the greatest number of World Heritage Sites to date with 45 sites inscribed on the list. UNESCO references each World Heritage Site with an identification number; but new inscriptions often include previous sites now listed as part of larger descriptions. As a result, the identification numbers exceed 1200 even though there are fewer on the list.

Each World Heritage Site is the property of the state on whose territory the site is located, but it is considered in the interest of the international community to preserve each site.

History

Pre-convention

In 1954, the government of Egypt decided to build the Aswan Dam (Aswan High Dam), an event that would flood a valley containing treasures of ancient Egypt such as the Abu Simbel temples. UNESCO then launched a worldwide safeguarding campaign. The Abu Simbel and Philae temples were taken apart, moved to a higher location, and put back together piece by piece.

The cost of the project was US$ 80 million, about $ 40 million of which was collected from 50 countries. The project was regarded as a success, and led to other safeguarding campaigns, saving Venice and its lagoon in Italy, the ruins of Mohenjo-daro in Pakistan, and the Borobodur Temple Compounds in Indonesia. UNESCO then initiated, with the International Council on Monuments and Sites, a draft convention to protect the common cultural heritage of humanity.

Convention and background

The United States initiated the idea of combining cultural conservation with nature conservation. A White House conference in 1965 called for a 'World Heritage Trust' to preserve "the world's superb natural and scenic areas and historic sites for the present and the future of the entire world citizenry." The International

Union for Conservation of Nature developed similar proposals in 1968, and they were presented in 1972 to the United Nations conference on Human Environment in Stockholm.

A single text was agreed on by all parties, and the Convention Concerning the Protection of the World Cultural and Natural Heritage was adopted by the General Conference of UNESCO on 16 November 1972.

Nominating Process

A country must first take an inventory of its significant cultural and natural properties. This is called the Tentative List, and is important because a country may not nominate properties that have not already been included on the Tentative List. Next, it can select a property from this list to place into a Nomination File. The World Heritage Centre offers advice and help in preparing this file.

At this point, the file is evaluated by the International Council on Monuments and Sites and the World Conservation Union. These bodies then make their recommendations to the World Heritage Committee. The Committee meets once per year to determine whether or not to inscribe each nominated property on the World Heritage List, and sometimes defers the decision to request more information from the country who nominated the site. There are ten selection criteria - a site must meet at least one of them to be included on the list.

Selection Criteria

Until the end of 2004, there were six criteria for cultural heritage and four criteria for natural heritage. In 2005, this was modified so that there is only one set of ten criteria. Nominated sites must be of "outstanding universal value" and meet at least one of the ten criteria.

Cultural Criteria

1. "Represents a masterpiece of human creative genius"

2. "Exhibits an important interchange of human values, over a span of time, or within a cultural area of the world, on developments in architecture or technology, monumental arts, town-planning, or landscape design"
3. "Bears a unique or exceptional testimony to a cultural tradition or to a civilization which is living or which has disappeared"
4. "Is an outstanding example of a type of building, architectural, or technological ensemble or landscape which illustrates a significant stage in human history"
5. "Is an outstanding example of a traditional human settlement, land-use, or sea-use which is representative of a culture, or human interaction with the environment especially when it has become vulnerable under the impact of irreversible change"
6. "Is directly or tangibly associated with events or living traditions, with ideas, or with beliefs, with artistic and literary works of outstanding universal significance"

Natural Criteria

7. "Contains superlative natural phenomena or areas of exceptional natural beauty and aesthetic importance"
8. "Is an outstanding example representing major stages of Earth's history, including the record of life, significant on-going geological processes in the development of landforms, or significant geomorphic or physiographic features"
9. "Is an outstanding example representing significant on-going ecological and biological processes in the evolution and development of terrestrial, fresh water, coastal and marine ecosystems, and communities of plants and animals"
10. "Contains the most important and significant natural habitats for in-situ conservation of biological diversity, including those containing threatened species of outstanding universal value from the point of view of science or conservation"

Statistics

There are 911 World Heritage Sites located in 151 States Parties. Of these, 704 are cultural, 180 are natural and 27 are mixed properties. The World Heritage Committee has divided the countries into five geographic zones: Africa, Arab States (composed of North Africa and the Middle East), Asia-Pacific (includes Australia and Oceania), Europe & North America (United States, and Canada) and Latin America & Caribbean.

Russia and the Caucasus states are classified as European, while Mexico is classified as belonging to the Latin America & Caribbean zone. The UNESCO geographic zones also give greater emphasis on administrative, rather than geographic associations. Hence, Gough Island, located in the South Atlantic, is part of the Europe & North America region because the government of the United Kingdom nominated the site.

HERITAGE INTERPRETATION

Heritage interpretation is the communication of information about, or the explanation of, the nature, origin, and purpose of historical, natural, or cultural resources, objects, sites and phenomena using personal or non-personal methods.

Heritage interpretation may be performed at dedicated interpretation centres or at museums, historic sites, parks, art galleries, nature centres, zoos, aquaria, botanical gardens, nature reserves and a host of other heritage sites. Its modalities can be extremely varied and may include guided walks, talks, drama, staffed stations, displays, signs, labels, artwork, brochures, interactives, audio-guides and audio-visual media. The process of developing a structured approach to interpreting these stories, messages and information is called interpretive planning.

Those who practice this form of interpretation may include rangers, guides, naturalists, museum curators, natural and cultural interpretive specialists, interpretation officers, heritage communicators, docents, educators, visitor services staff, interpreters or a host of other titles.

Definitions of Heritage Interpretation

"Heritage interpretation is an educational activity which aims to reveal meanings and relationships through the use of original objects, by firsthand experience, and by illustrative media, rather than simply to communicate factual information."

Freeman Tilden for the US National Park Service

"Any communication process designed to reveal meanings and relationships of cultural and natural heritage to the public, through first-hand involvement with an object, artifact, landscape or site."

Interpretation Canada

"Interpretation is a mission-based communication process that forges emotional and intellectual connections between the interests of the audience and the meanings inherent in the resource."

The National Association for Interpretation.

The Definitions Project (consortium of over two dozen federal and non-profit organizations in the United States-.

John Veverka and Associates

"Interpretation enriches our lives through engaging emotions, enhancing experiences and deepening understanding of people, places, events and objects from past and present."

The Association for Heritage Interpretation.

"Interpretation is the process of communicating messages and stories about our cultural and natural heritage, providing the audience with inspiration and a wider understanding of our environment. Or quite simply, interpretation is about telling stories."

Scottish Interpretation Network

"Interpretation refers to the full range of potential activities intended to heighten public awareness and enhance understanding of cultural heritage site. These can include print and electronic publications, public lectures, on-site and directly related off-site installations, educational programs, community activities, and ongoing research, training, and evaluation of the interpretation process itself."

ICOMOS "Ename" Charter for the Interpretation and Presentation of Cultural Heritage Sites 2008 (see links below)

"Tilden's principles" of interpretation

In his 1957 book, "Interpreting Our Heritage", Freeman Tilden defined six principles of interpretation.

1. Any interpretation that does not somehow relate what is being displayed or described to something within the personality or experience of the visitor will be sterile.
2. Information, as such, is not Interpretation. Interpretation is revelation based upon information. But they are entirely different things. However all interpretation includes information.
3. Interpretation is an art, which combines many arts, whether the materials presented are scientific, historical or architectural. Any art is in some degree teachable.
4. The chief aim of Interpretation is not instruction, but provocation.
5. Interpretation should aim to present a whole rather than a part, and must address itself to the whole man rather than any phase.
6. Interpretation addressed to children (say up to the age of twelve) should not be a dilution of the presentation to adults, but should follow a fundamentally different approach. To be at its best it will require a separate program.

For the past 50 years, Tilden's principles have remained highly relevant to interpreters across the world. In 2002 Larry Beck and Ted Cable published "Interpretation for the 21st Century - Fifteen Guiding Principles for Interpreting Nature and Culture", which elaborated upon Tilden's original principles.

Natural Heritage Education

Natural Heritage Education is an educational program offered by Ontario Parks in some provincial parks in Ontario, Canada. It is designed to provide education focusing on the natural and cultural heritage of the park its surrounding area. Parks like Presqu'ile Provincial Park and Algonquin Provincial Park have very successful programs due to the use of multiple visitor centres, major park attractions, guided walks, children's programs, evening programs, night hikes, special event weekends and special event programs.

For instance, at Algonquin Provincial Park, visitors can enjoy the wolf howl led by park naturalists. At Presqu'ile Provincial Park, campers can enjoy a Canada Day program or a walk through the park at night with park naturalists.

Several other park agencies such as Parks Canada, Alberta Provincial Parks and state and national parks in the U.S. have similar programs.

World Heritage Committee

The World Heritage Committee establishes the sites to be listed as UNESCO World Heritage Sites. It is responsible for the implementation of the World Heritage Convention, defines the use of the World Heritage Fund and allocates financial assistance upon requests from States Parties. It is composed of 21 state parties which are elected by the General Assembly of States Parties for a four-year term.

According to the World Heritage Convention, a committee member's term of office is for six years, however many states parties choose voluntarily to be Members of the Committee for only four years, in order to give other states parties an opportunity to be on the committee. For instance, all members elected at the 15th General Assembly (2005) have voluntarily decided to reduce their period of term of office from six to four years.

World Heritage Committee Session

The World Heritage Committee meets many times a year to discuss the management of existing World Heritage Sites, and accept the nominations from countries. A session, known as the World Heritage Committee Session, takes place annually where sites are inscribed on the World Heritage List, after presentations made by the IUCN and/or ICOMOS, and deliberations made among the state parties.they meet once a year.

The annual session takes place in cities all over the world. With the exception of those held in Paris, where the UNESCO headquarter office is located, only state parties who are members of the World Heritage Committee have the right to host a future Session, pending approval by the Committee, as well as provided that the concerned State Party's term will not expire before it hosts the Session.

No.	Year	Date	Host city	State party
1	1977	27 June–1 July	Paris	France
2	1978	5 September–8 September D.C.	Washington, United States	
3	1979	22 October–26 October	Cairo & Luxor	Egypt
4	1980	1 September–5 September	Paris	France
5	1981	26 October–30 October	Sydney	Australia
6	1982	13 December–17 December	Paris	France
7	1983	5 December–9 December	Florence	Italy
8	1984	29 October–2 November	Buenos Aires	Argentina
9	1985	2 December–6 December	Paris	France
10	1986	24 November–28 November	Paris	France
11	1987	7 December–11 December	Paris	France
12	1988	5 December–9 December	Brasilia	Brazil
13	1989	11 December–15 December	Paris	France
14	1990	7 December–12 December	Banff	Canada
15	1991	9 December–13 December	Carthage	Tunisia

No.	Year	Date	Host city	State party
16	1992	7 December–14 December	Santa Fe	United States
17	1993	6 December–11 December	Cartagena	Colombia
18	1994	12 December–17 December	Phuket	Thailand
19	1995	4 December–9 December	Berlin	Germany
20	1996	2 December–7 December	Mérida	Mexico
21	1997	1 December–6 December	Naples	Italy
22	1998	30 November–5 December	Kyoto	Japan
23	1999	29 November–4 December	Marrakesh	Morocco
24	2000	27 November–2 December	Cairns	Australia
25	2001	11 December–16 December	Helsinki	Finland
26	2002	24 June–29 June	Budapest	Hungary
27	2003	30 June–5 July	Paris	France
28	2004	28 June–7 July	Suzhou	China
29	2005	10 July–17 July	Durban	South Africa
30	2006	8 July–16 July	Vilnius	Lithuania
31	2007	23 June–1 July	Christchurch	New Zealand
32	2008	2 July-10 July	Quebec City	Canada
33	2009	22 June-30 June	Sevilla	Spain
34	2010	25 July-03 August	Brasilia	Brazil

Convention and Visitor Bureau

A convention and visitor bureau (CVB) is the dominant form of destination marketing organization in the United States, but is found in other countries as well. Destination marketing organizations have many names – convention and visitors bureaus, visitors' bureaus, welcome centers, tourism bureaus, travel and tourism bureaus, information centers and more. Regardless of the name, these organizations offer many services to the traveling public. While each U.S. state has a department of travel and tourism, most counties and/or cities also have their own CVB, to promote a narrower geographical area.

Mission

Although there are many government and chamber of commerce bodies that have responsibility for marketing a destination to visitors and selling to conventions and meeting planners, most convention and visitors bureaus (CVBs) are non-profit organizations, working independently under the direction of a board of elected directors. The fundamental mission of a convention and visitor bureau is the promotion of the economic development of a destination through increasing visits from tourists and business travelers, which generates overnight lodging for a destination, visits to restaurants, and shopping revenues. Convention and visitor bureaus are the most important tourism marketing organizations in their respective tourist destinations, as they are directly responsible for marketing the destination brand through travel and tourism "product awareness" to visitors. While they primarily are funded through the collection of "bed taxes" on visitors, convention and visitors bureuas produce billions of dollars in direct and indirect revenue and taxes for their state and local economies with their marketing and sales expertise.

Services

Typically, a convention and visitors bureau provides information about a destination's lodging, dining, attractions, events, museums, arts and culture, history and recreation. Some even provide bus services, insider tips, top ten attraction and activity lists, blogs, photos, forums, free things to do, season-specific activity suggestions and more. The organization works with tourists and meeting planners to provide valuable information on their local area. Their goal is to help make a visitor's trip or a conference attendees' meeting a much more enjoyable and rewarding experience. In many locations, they work closely with a convention center that will offer large spaces for larger meetings, trade shows, and conventions than can be accommodated in a single hotel. Usually, these organizations also have a local office where one can find maps, brochures, travel professionals, local insight, visitors guides, souvenirs and more.

Marketing Initiatives

A convention and visitor bureau's marketing initiatives are typically achieved through the following: trade association marketplaces, web pages, advertising, distribution of promotional and collateral material, direct sales, hosting familiarization tours for journalists and travel industry personnel, and sponsoring other hospitality functions. The target decision maker of these marketing initiatives is not typically a resident in the community. Most often, if visitors are going to spend the night in a hotel, they reside at least 100 miles away. Thus, the marketing activity usually takes place or is directed outside the convention and visitors bureau's community. Convention and visitors bureaus in larger destinations often will market nationally and globally, while smaller cities may focus just on their state or region.

World Tourism Organization

The World Tourism Organization (UNWTO), based in Madrid, Spain, is a United Nations agency dealing with questions relating to tourism. It compiles the World Tourism rankings. The World Tourism Organization is a significant global body, concerned with the collection and collation of statistical information on international tourism. This organization represents public sector tourism bodies, from most countries in the world and the publication of its data makes possible comparisons of the flow and growth of tourism on a global scale. The official languages of UNWTO are Arabic, English, French, Russian, and Spanish.

Organizational Aims

The World Tourism Organization plays a role in promoting the development of responsible, ?sustainable and universally accessible tourism, paying particular attention to the ?interests of developing countries?.

The Organization encourages the implementation ?of the Global Code of Ethics for Tourism, with a view to ensuring that member ?countries, tourist destinations and businesses maximize the positive economic, ?social and cultural effects of tourism and fully reap its benefits, while minimizing its ?negative social and environmental impacts.

UNWTO is committed to the United Nations Millennium Development Goals, geared ?toward reducing poverty and fostering sustainable development.

History

The origin of the World Tourism Organization stems back to 1925 when the International Congress of Official Tourist Traffic Associations (ICOTT) was formed at The Hague. Some articles from early volumes of the Annals of Tourism Research, claim that the UNWTO originated from the International Union of Official Tourist Publicity Organizations (IUOTPO), although the UNWTO states that the ICOTT became the International Union of Official Tourist Propaganda Organizations first in 1934.

Following the end of the Second World War and with international travel numbers increasing, the IUOTPO restructured itself into the International Union of Official Travel Organizations (IUOTO). A technical, non-governmental organization, the IUOTO was made up of a combination of national tourist organizations, industry and consumer groups. The goals and objectives of the IUOTO were to not only promote tourism in general but also to extract the best out of tourism as an international trade component and as an economic development strategy for developing nations.

Towards the end of the 1960's, the IUOTO realized the need for further transformation to enhance its role on an international level. The 20th IUOTO general assembly in Tokyo, 1967, declared the need for the creation of an intergovernmental body with the necessary abilities to function on an international level in cooperation with other international agencies, in particular the United Nations. Throughout the existence of the IUOTO, close ties had been established between the organization and the United Nations (UN) and initial suggestions had the IUOTO becoming part of the UN. However, following the circulation of a draft convention, consensus held that any resultant intergovernmental organization should be closely linked to the UN but preserve its "complete administrative and financial autonomy".

It was on the recommendations of the UN that the formation of the new intergovernmental tourism organization was based. Resolution 2529 of the XXIVth UN general assembly stated:

" The general assembly believes that a formula that would allow agreement to be reached more readily among governments for the establishment of an international tourism organization of an intergovernmental, particularly to assist the developing countries would be:

(a) The conversion of the International Union of Official Travel Organizations into an intergovernmental organization through a revision of its statutes: (b) The establishment of operational links between the United Nations and the transformed Union by means of a formal agreement.

In 1970, the IUOTO general assembly voted in favor of forming the World Tourism Organization (WTO), based on statutes of the IUOTO, and after ratification by the prescribed 51 states, the WTO came into operation on November 1, 1974.

Most recently, at the fifteenth general assembly in 2003, the WTO general council and the UN agreed to establish the WTO as a specialized agency of the UN. The significance of this collaboration, WTO Secretary-General Mr. Francesco Frangialli claimed, would lie in "the increased visibility it gives the WTO, and the recognition that will be accorded to [it]. Tourism will be considered on an equal footing with other major activities of human society".

As of 2010, its membership included 154 member states, seven associate members (Flemish Community, Puerto Rico, Aruba, Hong Kong, Macau, Madeira, Netherland Antilles), two observers (Holy See, Palestine). 15 of these members have withdrawn from the organization for different periods in the past: Australia, Bahamas, Bahrain, Canada, Costa Rica, El Salvador, Honduras, Kuwait, Malaysia, Nicaragua, Panama, Philippines, Qatar, Thailand and Puerto Rico.

Additionally there are some 350 affiliate members, representing the private sector, educational institutions, tourism associations and local tourism authorities. The frequent confusion between the two WTOs – World Tourism Organization and the Geneva-based World Trade Organization – officially ended on 1 December 2005, when the General Assembly approved to add the letters UN (for United Nations) to the start of abbreviation of the leading international tourism body in English and in Russian. UNWTO abbreviation remains OMT in French and Spanish. UNWTO General Assembly concluded its work at its 16th session in Dakar, Senegal, on 2 December 2005.

Secretaries-General of UNWTO

1975–1985 — Robert Lonati (France)

1986–1989 — Willibald Pahr (Austria)

1990–1996 — Antonio Enriquez Savignac (Mexico)

1998–2008 — Francesco Frangialli (France)

2008–present — Taleb Rifai S.G ad interim (Jordan)

Structure

General Assembly

The General Assembly is the supreme organ of the Organization. Its ordinary ?sessions, held every two years, are attended by delegates of the Full and Associate Members, as well as representatives from the Business Council. It is the most important meeting of senior tourism officials and high-level representatives of the private sector from all over the world.

Regional Commissions

Established in 1975 as subsidiary organs of the General Assembly, the six Regional ?Commissions normally meet once a year. They enable member States to maintain ?contact with one another and with the Secretariat between sessions of the General Assembly, to which they submit their proposals and convey their concerns. Each Commission elects one Chairman and its Vice-Chairmen from among its Members ?for a term of two years commencing from one session to the next session of the Assembly.

Executive Council

The Executive Council's task is to take all necessary measures, in consultation with ?the Secretary-General, for the implementation of its own decisions and ?recommendations of the Assembly and report thereon to the Assembly. The Council meets at least twice a year. The Council consists of Full Members elected by the Assembly in the proportion of one Member for every five Full Members, in accordance with the Rules of Procedure laid down by the Assembly with a view to achieving fair and equitable geographical distribution. The term of office of Members elected to the Council is four years and elections for one-half of the Council membership are held every two years. Spain is a Permanent Member of the Executive Council.

Committees

World Committee on Tourism Ethics Programme Committee Committee on Budget and Finance Committee on Market and Competitiveness Committee on Statistics and the Tourism Satellite account Sustainable Development of Tourism Committee Committee on Poverty Reduction Committee for the Review of Applications for Affiliate Membership.

Secretariat

The Secretariat is led by Secretary-General ad interim Taleb Rifai of Jordan, who supervises about 110 full-time staff at

UNWTO's Madrid Headquarters. He is assisted by the Deputy Secretary-General. These officials are responsible ?for implementing UNWTO's programme of work and serving the needs of Members. The Affiliate Members are supported by a full-time Executive Director at the Madrid Headquarters. The Secretariat also includes a regional support office for Asia-Pacific in Osaka, Japan, financed by the Japanese Government.

Chapter 2

The Heritage Tourism Program

The Heritage Tourism Program provides consulting assistance in heritage tourism development, management and marketing. The program has developed a nationwide network of partners and resources - an unparalleled benefit to anyone seeking to enhance or develop heritage tourism programs.

The program staff includes national leaders in the field of heritage tourism with extensive experience at the local, state and national level. In addition to our core staff, the Heritage Tourism Program taps into a network of specialized national experts to create project teams to match the needs of our clients. No other heritage tourism consulting firm offers our unique blend of extensive hands-on heritage tourism experience at the local level combined with a national perspective on cutting edge trends and insights into the latest funding opportunities for cultural heritage tourism.

Our goal is to work with clients, building local capacity and encouraging long term sustainability. Our staff works to complement local expertise and build from existing work rather than "reinventing the wheel." Among our services are—

- Community assessment visits and recommendation reports
- Workshops on a variety of topics.

Since the program began in 1989, we have assisted hundreds of heritage and cultural sites, communities, regions and states in assessing resources and creating plans for sustainable heritage tourism programs. Past clients have included state tourism offices, state preservation offices, state Main Street programs, scenic byway organizations and other clients at the regional and local level. The Heritage Tourism Program can provide cultural heritage tourism assessments, project coordination, planning, facilitation, presentations and training workshops.

Introduction to Cultural Heritage Tourism

This half-day or one-day workshop provides a comprehensive introduction to cultural heritage tourism. The presentation includes an overview of cultural heritage tourism trends, demographics of cultural heritage travelers, and an in-depth look at the Five Principles and Four Steps of successful and sustainable cultural heritage tourism.

The workshop includes examples of success stories and best practices from across the country. The workshop also includes an opportunity for group discussion or breakout groups for participants to apply what they have learned in making plans for their own communities.

Interpreting Cultural Heritage in Your Community

Making sites and communities come alive is the focus of this one-day workshop. The workshop includes instruction on how to tell the story of your site or community, understanding interpretive methods and how to attract and engage visitors. Examples of various forms of interpretation will be given. Participants will learn how to choose appropriate interpretive tools – such as brochures, driving tours, walking tours, museums, exhibits, audiotours and tour guides—and will discuss plans for their own interpretive projects.

Marketing Your Community's Cultural Heritage

This one-day workshop helps participants learn how to collaborate with the tourism industry and to attract visitors to their community or region. Topics include an overview of current trends in cultural heritage tourism and instruction on the tools of marketing. Attendees participate in exercises to define their community's message and to develop strategies using public relations, advertising, tourism industry sales and other marketing tools. (To prepare for this workshop, Heritage Tourism staff will review current marketing activities and develop an agenda that will improve or enhance the existing plan. It is not necessary for a community to have a marketing plan as the workshop can also be a beginning point for plan development.)

Making Your Community Visitor Ready

Understanding and planning for the needs of visitors is the focus of this half-day workshop. The presentation will discuss why visitor-oriented customer service is important, how the needs of tourists differ from residents, operating visitor-friendly retail establishments and attractions and cultivating hospitable front-line tourism employees. Participants will receive materials and instruction to assist them in evaluating their community's visitor readiness.

Share Your Heritage: Strategic Planning

These 1½ to 2 day workshops are designed to address specific cultural heritage tourism issues facing participants in their communities or region. The workshop brings together 30-40 invited participants representing a variety of disciplines such as tourism, historic preservation, arts, environment, government and community planning. Sessions include cross-discipline training and interactive work groups developing strategic plans for their cultural heritage tourism program. Two expert national faculty members provide presentations and facilitate the work sessions. The lead faculty member, a member of the Heritage Tourism Program staff, also assists local organizers with pre-workshop planning and preparing a written action plan following the workshop.

Cultural Heritage Tourism Assessments

As noted in Four Steps for Successful and Sustainable Cultural Heritage Tourism, the first step your community or region should take in planning for a new or expanded cultural heritage tourism program is assessing your potential. Assessments include evaluating attractions, visitor services, organizational capacity, preservation of resources and tourism marketing.

The Heritage Tourism Program can assist by providing an objective, comprehensive assessment and making recommendations for development of your cultural heritage tourism program. In the past 15 years, the Heritage Tourism Program has conducted assessments in dozens of communities and regions across the country. Our approach is based on the Five Principles for Cultural Heritage Tourism Development and focuses on working closely with the community to identify challenges and opportunities and to craft effective strategies for program development.

Assessment Objectives

The main objectives of an assessment are:

- to gather a wide variety of opinions and suggestions from stakeholders
- to learn about the community's history and culture
- to evaluate the current visitor experience
- to evaluate current visitor services including signage, operating hours, hospitality, etc.
- to evaluate current local marketing efforts
- to assess the level of public and private support for tourism
- to meet with organizers and assess organizational capacity for program development

Planning an Assessment

Advance preparation is essential for a successful assessment visit. Steps in the planning process include:

1. Consultant selection. The Heritage Tourism Program will assign one of its staff members to conduct the assessment. If additional consultants are needed to address specific areas, the staff member will identify consultants with the necessary expertise.
2. Background materials. The local organizing committee will provide an information packet including (as available) visitor research, marketing plans, promotional materials, community histories and other materials to familiarize the consultants with the area in advance of the site visit.
3. Conference call. A call will be scheduled between local organizers and the consultants to identify issues, establish goals for the assessment and prepare a draft of key sites and meetings to include on the itinerary. Organizers will also determine if a public meeting is desired as part of the assessment.
4. Itinerary Development. Local organizers will develop and schedule an itinerary for the assessment:

   Schedule tours of all selected attractions.

   Schedule tours of sites that have potential for tourism development.

   Determine meeting locations for stakeholder interviews.
5. Organize Logistics. Local organizers will arrange and confirm assessment logistics:

   Obtain a contact person and contact number for each stop.

   Select a location for the public meeting. Provide LCD projector, screen (or blank wall), easels, flip charts and markers.

   Recommend overnight accommodations for consultants.

PLANNING THE ITINERARY

Assessments are generally two or three days depending on the size of the community, the number of communities involved, and the geographic area. If the area is very large, additional days may need to be added to adequately complete the assessment. The site visit will include several activities:

Consultant Reconnaissance

Upon arrival, the consultant spends several hours touring the community unaccompanied. This allows the consultant to gain an impression of how visitor ready the community is before meeting and touring with stakeholders.

Community or Regional Tour

This tour will be given by the local project leader and other stakeholders as needed to provide information about the area and sites that are included on the tour. Sites can include the following:

- Scenic drives
- Downtowns (walking and/or driving tours)
- Historic sites
- Cultural sites
- Parks or other natural resources
- Meeting facilities
- Hotels/motels/bed and breakfast inns
- Unique restaurants
- Unique retail shops or artists' studios
- Gateways or entrances into the community
- Visitor information centers

Stakeholder Interviews

Interviews allow the consultants to gather historical information, to understand residents' perceptions about tourism, and to explore residents' visions that can be developed for cultural heritage tourism. Interviews are generally no more than 45 minutes unless there is a large group participating in the interview. Interview categories may include:

- Convention and visitors bureau or chamber of commerce (tourism offices)
- Arts council directors (city agencies or community nonprofit arts groups)
- Historic site and museum directors, staff, board
- Event organizers
- Artists
- Historical societies
- Preservation organizations
- Cultural or civic organizations
- Local business owners
- Main Street staff and board members
- Parks and recreation (local and/or state)
- Government officials – mayor, county executive, council persons
- City or county economic development staff
- University or community college staff
- Local media
- Churches

Public Meetings

A public meeting can be scheduled as part of the assessment if desired by local organizers. The meeting site should allow easy access for participants. Depending on the timing of the meeting in the assessment visit, the meeting may include preliminary observations and recommendations for discussion. Meetings generally last approximately two hours and have the following format:

- Introductions of participants and consultants
- Powerpoint presentation by consultants explaining the assessment process

- National overview of cultural heritage tourism trends
- Discussion with participants about a vision for cultural heritage tourism
- Consultant team documents ideas and suggestions

The public meeting should be scheduled at a convenient time for target participants and should be publicized to attract the broadest participation possible including:

- Press releases to all local media two weeks in advance
- Emails or postcard notices to stakeholder organizations

Suggested Timeline for Planning an Assessment

Note: This proposed timeline is provided to give structure to planning for the assessment and to give an idea of the amount of time needed to prepare for the site visit.

- Week 1 - Planning committee formed. Choose representatives who are familiar with the community or region.
- Week 2 – Committee identifies sites for tour and identifies key stakeholders to interview; identify location for public meeting.
- Week 3 – Committee circulates list of tour sites and stakeholders to participants; make contacts to reserve facility for public meeting.
- Week 4 – Stakeholders submit suggestions, additions, etc. to the committee.
- Week 5 – Committee finalizes tour route and stakeholder interview list; begin making contacts to schedule tours and interviews; confirm arrangements for public meeting.
- Week 6 – Distribute press releases to all local media; mail or email invitations to public meeting; subcommittee reviews draft itinerary; make changes to itinerary as needed.
- Week 7 – Finalize itinerary for site visit; determine which committee member will provide transportation for each part

of the site visit; provide itinerary to consultants; committee member to visit public meeting location to outline set up needs and confirm availability of A/V, chairs, flip charts, etc.

- Week 8 – Contact each interview participant to confirm interviews; make any changes as needed.
- Week 9 – Provide finalized itinerary to consultants.
- Week 10 – Assessment visit – committee member should monitor schedule to keep interviews and touring on time; at each stop, contact the person at the next stop to update time schedules as needed. A committee member should arrive at the public meeting location in advance to oversee set up of the room, A/V, etc.

Conducting the Assessment

After becoming familiar with the community or region through advance preparation including materials review, internet research and committee conference calls, the consultants will be prepared to undertake the following activities as part of the assessment:

- Tour heritage and cultural tourism sites and evaluate the visitor experience for development and promotion opportunities.
- Identify opportunities for development of heritage and cultural resources to increase offerings to visitors.
- Assess visitor services including wayfinding signage and maps, guidebooks and other collateral materials, hospitality of frontline tourism employees, availability and quality of accommodations and restaurants, hours of operation of tourism-related retail businesses, etc.
- Meet with stakeholders such as attraction representatives, artists, festival planners, historical societies, preservation organizations, service providers, government officials and tourism promoters to discuss organizational capacity for program development and plans for the community's cultural heritage tourism program.

- Conduct a public meeting to explain the process of cultural heritage tourism program development and to hear residents' visions for their community and to assess the extent of broad-based community support for tourism.

Preparing an Assessment and Recommendations Report

Following the assessment visit, the consultants will prepare a written report including assessments and recommendations. The report will be provided to the community within 45 days of the site visit. The report will include a candid assessment of the community's cultural heritage resources and its organizational capacity for program development. Short and long-term recommendations will be included. The report can include:

- Assessment of cultural heritage resources and the experience currently offered to visitors.
- Recommendations for enhancement or improvement of existing cultural heritage resources.
- Identification of resources that have the potential for development as cultural heritage attractions.
- Evaluation and recommendations for visitor services such as signage.
- Recommendations for customer service/hospitality training for frontline tourism employees.
- Recommendations of needed action for preservation of cultural and historic resources.
- Recommendations for expanded or new programming opportunities such as festivals and events.
- Recommendations for expanding organizational capacity including new partnerships and communications systems.
- Evaluation of current marketing efforts and recommendations for new marketing strategies.

- Examples of "best practices" from other communities that could be applicable to the local community.

Report Presentation and Planning

The assessment process can also include a one-day follow up visit by the consultant(s). This follow-up visit would include a presentation by the consultants of the major findings and recommendations in the report and a work session with local organizers to determine next steps for program implementation.

More Information

For more information on scheduling an assessment visit for your community and to discuss assessment fees, contact Amy Webb at 303.413.1986, or Carolyn Brackett at 615.226.4078.

Cultural Heritage Tourism Program Staff

Amy Webb joined the National Trust's Heritage Tourism Program in 1993 and has served as the program's director since 1995. She is an active advocate for heritage tourism at the national level through her work with Partners in Tourism. She is a sought after presenter and has spoken at conferences in 41 states, two U.S. territories and Canada on national trends, success stories, and the principles of successful heritage tourism. Ms. Webb began the Share Your Heritage initiative in 1999, completing two success story publications, developing training materials and designing the Share Your Heritage training workshops. She helped to launch a new how-to website for cultural heritage tourism practioners at www.culturalheritagetourism.org in 2005.

Prior to coming to the National Trust, she worked as the Director of Tourism and Education for the Providence Preservation Society (PPS) in Providence, Rhode Island. During her eight year tenure she developed heritage education programs, organized an annual tour of historic homes, coordinated walking and motorcoach tours of historic Providence and created packaged itineraries and other collaborative marketing initiatives showcasing Providence's historic and cultural attractions.

Amy Webb holds a Master's degree in Architectural History and Historic Preservation from the University of Virginia and a bachelor's degree in Architectural History from Wellesley College in Massachusetts. Her Masters thesis focused on the interpretation of historic sites in America between 1850 and 1950.

Amy Webb is based in Boulder, Colorado. She can be contacted at amy_webb@nthp.org.

Carolyn Brackett, Senior Program Associate, Heritage Tourism Program

Carolyn Brackett has been a Senior Program Associate for the Heritage Tourism Program since 2002, providing heritage tourism consulting services to clients across the country. Ms. Brackett has conducted numerous assessment visits and assisted communities and regions in developing cultural heritage tourism plans. She also conducts workshops on various cultural heritage tourism topics and speaks about cultural heritage tourism at preservation and tourism conferences. Ms. Brackett's involvement in the tourism industry began in 1988 when she joined the Tennessee Department of Tourist Development.

From 1990-1992, Ms. Brackett served as the department's State Coordinator for the National Trust for Historic Preservation's Heritage Tourism Initiative. In 1993, Ms. Brackett served as Executive Director of Historic Nashville Inc., Nashville's nonprofit preservation organization. From 1994-1996, Ms. Brackett served at Director of Statewide Projects for Tennessee 200, Inc., the state's bicentennial organization. From 1997-2001, Ms. Brackett served as Director of Marketing for The Hermitage, Home of President Andrew Jackson. Ms. Brackett has a Bachelor of Science degree in historic preservation from Middle Tennessee State University in Murfreesboro.

Cultural Heritage Tourism Client List

Since 1989, the National Trust's Heritage Tourism Program has worked with a range of clients including state tourism offices, state preservation offices, state Main Street programs, scenic byway organizations and other clients at the national, regional and local level. A partial list of past clients includes:

- Alaska Department of Transportation and Public Facilities
- American Association for State and Local History
- American Express
- Appalacian Regional Comission
- Cane River National Heritage Area
- Colorado Scenic and Historic Byways Program
- Colorado Tourism Office
- Duluth, Minnesota Heritage Tourism Committee
- Federal Highway Administration
- City of Harrisburg, Pennsylvania
- Historic Southern Indiana
- Indiana Department of Tourism
- Indiana National Road Association
- Iowa Department of Travel
- Journey through Hallowed Ground (VA, MD, PA)
- Lancaster County Planning Office, Pennsylvania
- Lawrence County, Missouri (Old Trails Scenic Byway)
- Kentucky Department of Travel
- Maryland Heritage Areas Authority
- Mercer County, NJ (Upper Bellemont Farm)
- National Endowment for the Arts
- National Main Street Center
- North Carolina Cultural Heritage Tourism Partnership
- Ohio River Scenic Route

- Oil Heritage Region, Pennsylvania
- Panama City, Florida Downtown Improvement Board
- Pennsylvania Historical and Museum Commission
- Philadelphia Multicultural Affairs Council
- Preservation Development Initiative
- Rural Heritage Program
- Shenandoah Valley Battlefields Foundation, Virginia
- St. Mary's County, MD (Religious Freedom Byway)
- Tracks Across Wyoming
- USDA Forest Service
- USDA Rural Development, Office of Community Development

Chapter 3

Heritage Tourism in Delhi

Delhi has seen a number of dynasties to take birth and die in its soil for many centuruies. The monuments, cenotaphs and mausoleums of kings and queens fringed in the city still narrate the bloody heritage of the city. You will also be amazed to see the sky high forts and palaces depicting the grandeur of yore as you take tour in Delhi. Some famous destination which you should visit once you come in Delhi are -

Red Fort

Built in the red sandstone, the magnificent Red Fort or Lal Qila is yet another creation by the Emperor Shah Jahan after Taj Mahal which will be remembered by the people eternally. It is a part of the walled city of Shahjahanabad in Old Delhi. Within its fortifications are exquisite palaces, a finely proportioned mosque, the Moti Masjid or Pearl Mosque, the Diwan-i-Am or hall of public audience and the finely ornamented Diwan-i-Khas or hall of private audience, where the Mughal emperors held court seated on the bejewelled golden Peacock Throne. The small holes on the walls of Diwan-i-Khas and Diwan-i-Am narrate the vacancy of the jewels and stones that were used to decorate the facade. Recently, Red Fort has been recognised as a UNESCO World Heritage Site. Not only has this increased the number of tourists visiting the magnificent fort, it has also made the authority and travelers more conscious in preserving this unique treasure of histoy.

The Red Fort Archaeological Museum

The Red Fort Archaeological Museum is situated in the Mumtaz Mahal of the Red Fort. It flaunts a rare collection of Mughal artifacts. One part of the museum is dedicated to Emperor Bahadur Shah Zafar and exhibits the personal belongings of the Emperor. The silk robes embroidered with pearls and the silver hookah used by the emperor himself are the major attractions of the museum. The museum is open from 10 am to 5 pm and remains closed on Fridays.

Purana Qila - Reminiscence of Yore

The old fort with its massive walls and imposing gateways overlooks the modern city of New Delhi. It is located on what is possibly the site of the ancient settlement of Indraprastha - the city founded by the Panḍavas during the epic times of the Mahabharata.

It was the second Mughal emperor Humayun who embarked in 1538 on the construction of the fort and the city he named Din Panah. Sher Shah Suri who took control of the empire shortly afterwards completed the fort and built many of its fine structures including the octagonal sandstone tower and the Sher Manzil. An interesting hour long light and music programme takes the visitor through the history of the fort.

Qutab Minar Complex

Dominating the ruins of the earliest existing settlement of Delhi is the city's famous landmark- the Qutab Minar. The imposing victory tower 73 metre high was built by Qutbuddin Aibak (1192-98) the founder of the Slave Dynasty. The tapering, fluted structure has five storeys, each marked by intricately carved projections or balconies.

Elaborately carved pillars-which come from Hindu temples of the earlier setdement of Qila Rai Pithora embellish the courtyard of a nearby mosque. At the centre of the courtyard is the amazing Iron Pillar-the dhvaja stambha (flag pole) of a Vishnu Temple (4th-5th century AD). Cast in a process that is lost to the present world, the 7.2 metre pillar has not rusted through the centuries. Other interesting structures in die vicinity include die base of another unfinished tower - the Alai Minar

The National Gallery of Modern Art

Located in the stately Jaipur House the museum has a splendid collection of contemporary art. The gallery is open from 10 am-5 pm and remains closed on Mondays.

The National Museum

This prestigious institution houses artifacts from the time of the Indus Valley Civilization (2500 BC) to the present times. Bronzes from South The National Gallery of Modern Art India, an impressive collection of stone sculpture, miniature paintings, textiles, coins and tribal art form part of its extensive collection. Of special interest is the superb Central Asian Gallery that exhibits the silk banners, sculpture and wall paintings that form part of Sir Aurel Stein's collection - brought to India in the early part of the 20th century. Open from 10 am to 5 pm and Monday remains closed.

Ancient Tughlaqabad Fort

In the southern periphery of Delhi are the ruins of a massive fort. This was once the capital of the Tughlaq kings - an impregnable fortification built by Sultan Ghiyasuddin Tughlaq in 1321. The elegant tomb of the emperor, in red sandstone with its sloping walls and white dome, located near the fort, is considered to be one of the best examples of Tughlaq architecture.

Floral Beauty of Lotus Temple

Beautifully designed, the Baha'i House of Worship (also known as the Lotus Temple) is built in the shape of a lotus. Its petals constructed in concrete and faced with white marble have an extraordinary lightness. Nine pools of water around the structure add to the illusion of a lotus floating in water. It belongs to the Baha'i Sect and is dedicated to the oneness of all religions. People of all faith can come and pray in the sprawling prayer hall. The temple remains open everyday from 9:30 am to 5:30 pm.

Feroz Shah Kotla

The remains of the second city of the Tughlaqs is to be found between the Purana Qila and the walled city of Shahjahanabad. It was erected by Feroz Shah Tughlaq in 1354. Very little remains today but still standing rather incongruously on top of the ruins is an impressive Ashoka Pillar. Monolithic and over 12.8 metre in height, weighing 27 tonnes, it was brought by Feroz Shah and installed here.

Flourishing Mughal Gardens

Delhi has beautiful gardens around the city. The beautiful Mughal Gardens in the Presidential Estate is open to the public only in February and March (9.30 am. to 3.00 pm.). The Nehru Park with undulating lawns and a fine show of flowers in winter, is opposite the Ashok Hotel in Chanakyapuri. Another landscaped garden along the southern ridge is the Buddha Jayanti Park. The Kamla Nehru Park lies along the wooded northern ridge. At Kalindi Kunj (24 km) is an attractive park with green lawns and fountains. The Dhaula Kuan complex has an artificial lake, water falls and playgrounds.

Ancient Heritage of Hauz Khas

The Royal Tank (Hauz Khas) was excavated in 1300 AD by Alauddin Khaiji to supply water to his new capital Siri. Today the ruins of a madarsa are to be seen here. This theological college was built at a later date by Feroz Shah Tughlaq and his tomb also stands close by. The complex is surrounded by parkland and the little village of Hauz Khas is now an attractive shopping area.

Humayun's Tomb – The Royal Heritage of the Mughals

Another magnificent Mughal building, the tomb of the emperor Humayun was built by his wife in 1565-66. Set in a square enclosed garden, the finely proportioned structure in red sandstone and marble served later as a model for the Taj Mahal and many other Mughal tombs. It is open to all till 10 pm on all days of the week.

Splendours of Akshardham Temple

The exquisite Akshardham Temple situated on the bank of the serene river Yamuna is a wonder to the modern world. Embellished with 20,000 statues, floral motifs, arches and intricately carved pillars show the immense artistry that human hand can do. Spread over an area of 100 acres, the temple complex consists of exhibition halls, an IMAX theatre and a musical fountain besides the main temple. It has also got a restaurant portraying the architecture of the Ajanta-Ellora caves and an Ayurvedic Bazaar. The architectural style of the temple follows the famous Akshardham Temple in Gandhinagar, Gujarat. The entire temple compound is built in pink stone and pure white marble, where pink stone symbolizes bhakti (devotion) in eternal bloom and white marble of absolute purity and eternal peace. The temple is fast becoming one of the most favoured destination in Delhi. This splendid architectural marvel has also made it to Guiness Book of Wolrd Records for being the largest Hindu Temple Complex in the world. This is a much deserved recognition that Akshardham temple has recieved.

India Gate, The Majestic Arch

At the heart of the elegant capital city, laid out by the British, is the India Gate. This elegant 42 metre arch in buff coloured sandstone stands at the end of the ceremonial avenue, the Rajpath. The memorial is dedicated to the 70,000 Indian soldiers killed during the First World War and bears the names of more than 13, 516 British and Indian soldiers. The foundation stone of the memorial was laid by His Royal Highness, the Duke of Connaught in 1921 and was designed by Edwin Lutyens. Another war memorial Amar Jawan Jyoti was constructed in the premises after the independence and is dedicated to soldiers who died in the Indo-Pakistan War of December 1971. A flame burns under the arch day and night reminding the nation of the great sacrifice done by the Indian soldiers and their families.

Jama Masjid, The Royal Mosque

Located just opposite the Red Fort is the imposing Jama Masjid with its black and white striped onion domes and minarets is one of the largest and the most elegant mosques in India. The sprawling courtyard has a capacity to hold 25,000 devotees at a time. One of the major attraction of the mosque is the treasure room where a hair of the beard of Hazrat Muhammed, his used chappal, the canopy of his tombstone, the footprint of Muhammed on the stone and a chapter of Koran taken from its original holy book is kept. People following other religion are not allowed to enter the premises frm 12:30-2 pm.

Ancient Observatory, Jantar Mantar

This fascinating observatory, with enormous astronomical instruments constructed in brick and plaster, was erected by that intrepid astronomer and king, Sawai Jai Singh of Jaipur in 1724. He also built similar observatories in Jaipur, Ujjain, Mathura and Varanasi.

Lodi GardenA splendid landscaped garden surrounds the 15th century tombs of the Lodi kings. Ibrahim Lodi the last Lodi ruler was defeated in 1526 by Babur who established the Mughal Empire in India. A walk amidst the ancient, fat trees gives a true pleasure in the heart of Delhi. This is a favourite destination of the lovers of the city.

National Rail Museum

The fine outdoor museum has on view a range of locomotives and carriages ranging over the 150 years of the railways in India. A toy train takes children around the museum. CRAFTS MUSEUM The Crafts Museum with its fine collection of textiles and artifacts is set in a delightful rustic village complex in the Pragati Maidan grounds. Here rural craftsmen come every month from different parts of the country to demonstrate their techniques and sell their beautiful crafts.

Parliament House of India

The elegant circular design with 144 pillars, Parliament House flaunts excellent architecture by Sir Edwin Lutyens and Sir Herbert Baker. Built in buff and red sandstone, the beautifully proportioned structure has a circumference of nearly one third of a mile. There are chambers of Lok Sabha, Rajya Sabha and the library inside the sprawling building. Indian Nationals can apply at the Parliament Secretariat in order to have the visitor's pass whereas the Foreign Nationals have to apply through their respective Embassies or High Commissions.

Rashtrapati Bhawan – Residence of the Royalty

When set to build new British Capital, Edwin Lutyens and Herbert Baker chose the vacant land of Raisina situated at the south of Shahjahanabad for their project. Built atop Risina Hill, the 340-roomed Viceregal Lodge is now the residence of the President Of India and is known as 'Rashtrapati Bhawan'. Though Lutyens' claim the dome to be inspired from the Pantheon, Rome, the architecture of the palace bear much evidence to the Indian architecture. The Mughal Gardens designed by the Lutyens' inside Rashtrapati Bhawan premises is one of the major attraction of Delhi. The gardens are open to public from February to March every year. The entry to the gardens is allowed from 9:30 am-2:30 pm.

After a sojourn in Delhi you may find your whole world changing and when you compare your prior life with the new one, there is only one difference and that is you have visited all the unforgettable monuments and heritage sites of the Delhi where time has also forgotten to roll.

Chapter 4

Rajasthan Heritage Tourism

Rajasthan is a land of forts and palaces. Grand monuments stand proudly as living reminders of the rich history of this heroic land. You can see the Rajasthan forts and palaces when you visit the unique cities of Rajasthan. Jaipur, Jodhpur, Udaipur, Jaisalmer, Bikaner and Chittorgarh are just some of the places where Rajasthan Forts and Palaces abound. You can tour the fascinating Rajasthan Forts and Palaces on tours to Rajasthan with India Rajasthan Tours.

Amer Fort

This magnificent fort was built not by one but three rulers - Raja Man Singh initiated the project. Mirza Raja Jai Singh took over the cudgels from Raja Man Singh and the finishing touches were given by Sawai Jai Singh. This colossal fort took as long as two centuries to build, the major portion of the work was carried out in the 1500's.

The Amer Fort stands like a sentinel above the still waters of the Maotha Lake. The fort is a living testimony where the Hindu and Mughal architectural styles have merged in complete harmony to create a masterpiece of fusion architecture. In the days of yore, the Amer Fort used to be a palace, an administrative headquarter as well as a strategic military bastion.

One of the best ways to reach this imposing fort is by an enchanting elephant ride. Once inside, the fort reveals its majestic grandeur like a veil slipping from the face of a beautiful woman replete with medieval courtyards, exquisite temples, enchanting pavilions and gardens that seems to be a replica of Eden on earth.

The interiors of the fort has an amazing array of painted engravings and its parapets are adorned with intricate mirror and stone works. The initial courtyard of the fort is flanked by two stupendous edifices - Diwan-E-Aam built of red sandstone and the marvelous Ganesh Pol Gate. Further ahead, an array of walkways beautifully surround an archetypal Mughal garden around which there is the Sukh Niwas and on the other side is the Jas Mandir. However, the centerpiece of attraction is the magnificent Sheesh Mahal which is replete with ornate mosaics, tinted mirror and glass embellishments all of which makes it a place of stunning beauty.

The Fort's in-house Kali temple popularly referred to as the Shila Devi Temple is shrouded in mystery. The temple is conspicuous by its awesome silver doors and silver lions.

There is also the Zenana or the Women's Palace which has exclusive enclosures or chambers that are linked by a general walkway. The zenana is shrewdly designed to provide utmost seclusion and solitude to the Maharaja's queens.

The Fort also has remnants of its rich past and the oldest of ruins dates back to the 16th century. The fort can be divided into four segments and there are two ways of reaching - one is by climbing the daunting flight of steps and the other is by riding on elephant back through the expansive passageway. The intriguing Jaleb Chowk is the central courtyard and in the days of yore the victorious royal armed forces were received and greeted here and presented their war booty to the general public.

Bikaner Fort

Bikaner Fort is popularly referred to as the Junagarh Fort. It was built by Raja Rai Singh who was one of Mughal emperor

Akbar's trusted generals. There are as many as 37 citadels which protects the fort. This is one fort in Rajasthan which has never been annexed or conquered. There was one dubious instance though when Prince Kamaran laid seize to the fort, but could not keep it on hold for even 24 hours.

The fort's 37 bastions are nicely complimented with a number of palaces, towers, pavilions and temples. There is the exquisitely beautiful Chandra Mahal which is adorned with mirrors and art works. Other palaces worth seeing are the Phool Mahal, the Karan Mahal and the majestic Anup Mahal which used to serve as the assembly hall of the erstwhile rulers.

Inside the fort there is a museum, which has an astonishing collection of ancient manuscripts, gems and jewellery, exquisite carpets, treaties, arms and royal weaponry.

Apart from the museum, the Kanar Mahal is worth visiting which was exclusively built to commemorate the triumph over Mughal emperor Aurangzeb.

Chittorgarh Fort

The magnificent Chittorgarh fort located 175 kms. east of Udaipur is dedicated to Chitrangad Maurya Bappa Rawal. Who was the founder of the Sisodia dynasty. The fort is spread over 700 acres and houses regal palaces, temples and towers. This fort is rated as the foremost in embattlement tactics and is among the most impregnable forts ever built by the Rajputs.

The Chittorgarh fort rises like a mirage from the adjoining plains underneath and stands like a sentinel at a height of 180 meters. One has to cross several gates to reach Rampal which is the entry point to this impregnable fort. Legend has it that when Mughal emperor Akbar laid seize to the fort, two great Rajput warriors - Jaimull and Kulla fought till the last breath of their lives and in memory of the brave sons of the soil, two exquisite cenotaphs have been built within the ramparts.

The fort has several majestic palaces, each one more beautiful than the other. For instance the Rana Kumbha Palace, the Fateh

Prakash Palace, Rani Padmini's Palace to name just a few of the palaces that are housed inside the fort all exemplify with the saga of gallantry, courage and heroism of the redoubtable Rajputs.

The fort's piece de resistance from a purely touristy point of view are the two magnificent towers - Kirti Stambh and the Vijay Stambh. Apart from the towers, there are numerous palaces, temples and tanks which were built during the period from 9th to 17th century. The huge reservoir is believed to have been used by princess Padmini for bathing prior to her self-immolation in honor of her husband. There is also the Gaumukh which is made of rocks and shaped very much like a cow's mouth from where water gushes out.

The Vijay Stambh in particular is amazing and is built on a pedestal which is all of 10ft high. From the base, Vijay Stambh is 122 ft in height and 30 ft wide. This colossal tower is nine storied and one has to climb 157 circular flight of steps to reach the top from where one can enjoy the incredible vistas of the city of Jodhpur.

History points out that Chittorgarh Fort was captured thrice. The first annexation was by Ala-ud-din-Khilji. The second was by Sultan Bahadur Shah and the last attack and subsequent annexation of Chittorgarh Fort was by Mughal emperor Akbar who completely demolished the fort and reduced it into wreckage.

City Palace Jaipur

This former royal residence is an imposing blend of traditional Rajasthani and Mughal architecture and craftsmanship. Surrounded by walls, this piece de resistance of Jaipur's palace occupies one seventh of the walled city, comprising a string of minor palaces and imposing halls.

Of special significance is the Chandra Mahal which overlooks the breath-taking Jai Niwas Gardens and the highly revered Shri Govind Dev Temple. The museum within the palace has an array of galleries of rare painting, exquisite miniatures, scholarly manuscripts, artifacts and traditional treatises on architecture. The fine collection of guns and swords on display dates back to the 15th century and is one of the best in India.

The city palace was built by Raja Sawai Jai Singh and the royal family still uses a section of the palace. The exquisite 19th century Mubarak Mahal or The Palace of Reception which used to serve as the reception area of royal guests was built by Madho Singh and is now converted into museum which show cases a bewildering array of royal costumes of the charismatic prince Sawai Madho Singh. Apart from the royal costumes, on display at the museum are some intriguing 15th century royal armory that have been very well preserved.

There is also the Dewan-I-Aam which has now been converted into an art gallery and has unusual ancient Hindu manuscripts, exquisite work of art belonging to Persion, Mughal and Rajasthani school of art. The Dewan-I-Khas is conspicuous by its two large exquisite silver vessels, which were exclusively made for Maharaja Madho Singh. These vessels served the purpose of storing the holy Ganga water during the erstwhile ruler's much talked about trip to England.

The magnificent Chandra Mahal which is all of seven storied is now the residence of the present Maharaja of Jaipur. Needless to say, the palace with its exquisite paintings, flower - patterned décor, parapets that dazzle with mirrors and intricately carved ceilings makes this palace an enchanting abode. Each of the seven stories serves a distinctive purpose and are appropriately named. For instance, the Sukh Niwas or the hall of pleasure serves as the drawing cum dining room of the Maharaja while the Shova Niwas or the hall of beauty is conspicuous by its mirror coated parapets which dazzle with a million rays when lit up.

Hawa Mahal Jaipur

The Hawa Mahal or the Palace of Wind is a Jaipur landmark which was built by Maharaja Sawai Pratap Singh way back in the year 1799. The Hawa Mahal displays fanciful architecture and has been so named because the palace has specially latticed screens and arches for an unbridled flow of air currents in a set pattern with the passage of the sun.

Till the recent past, ladies of the court from within the palace positioned themselves by the balconies to watch processions passing through in the streets below without themselves being observed by the people.

The Hawa Mahal was designed by renowned architect Lal Chand Usta and is built of red and pink sandstone and is a living testimony of Rajput architectural grandeur. The Hawa Mahal is shaped like a pyramid and has a staggering 953 small windowpanes and all of them are conspicuous by their miniscule lattice work, miniature balconies and vaulted roofs all of which are exquisitely designed and engraved.

Hawa Mahal is accessible from where the City Palace is located and entry is via a majestic door which leads to the large courtyard and is clustered with two storied edifices on three sides.

Hawa Mahal offers breath taking views of Jaipur city, its palatial edifices and quarters. There is no sign of any ornate embellishments adorning Hawa Mahal.

Presently Hawa Mahal is managed by the Department of Archaeology, Government of Rajasthan. The most appropriate time to visit Hawa Mahal is early in the morning at the time of sunrise.

Jaisalmer Fort

Jaisalmer like other towns of Rajasthan is centered around a fort - the Jaisalmer Fort which is popularly referred to as Sonar Quila. The majestic fort is located to the south of Jaisalmer on the picturesque Trikut hill. The length of the fort is 457 meter and the breadth is 229 meters.

The Fort was built in 1156 and is one of the oldest forts in Rajasthan rising as it does like a mirage from the surrounding deserts. The Fort was built by Maharaja Jaisal who had the desire to set up a new capital since the former one located at Lodurva was susceptible to enemy incursions.

The fort has 99 towers some of which possess cannons even today. In the Chauhata Square the majestic palaces of Maharawals are located. To reach the palace, one has to climb a flight of steps. In close proximity is the Tazia Tower which is all of five stories and is conspicuous by its unusual roof. The external portion of the fort is well protected by lofty walls which has an exclusive corridor that leads to the first barricade.

In the days of yore, a majority of the population of Jaisalmer lived within the fort premises but with the burgeoning growth of population, people began living elsewhere from 17th century onwards. Nonetheless, even in the present times the fort is bustling with activity and there are a lot of people who still live within the ramparts.

The Fort has an unusual and weird device, which is set on top of the fort and was used to forecast the weather for an entire year. Legend has it that if it wafted in the northerly direction it was a sign of famine and if it wafted on the westerly direction it was a precursor to a fine monsoon.

All said and done, the magnificent Jaisalmer fort is one of the finest examples of Rajput architectural grandeur as far as the art of stone carving is concerned.

Mehrangarh Fort

The majestic Mehrangarh Fort is one of India's largest forts and located in the picturesque city of Jodhpur. The work of building the fort originally commenced in 1459 on the behest of the founder of Jodhpur - Rao Jodha but much of the fort as it stands today was built in the era of Jaswant Singh. This magnificent fort is spread over 5 kms. and is located on top of a hill which is all of 125 meters high.

To honor and memorialize momentous triumphs there are three stately gates to the fort. Once inside the fort visitors can't help marveling at some astonishing palaces which are a living testimony to the high standard of craftsmanship prevalent in those days.

The Moti Mahal which is made of elaborately carved stones is the dwelling place of the royal throne of Jodhpur which is popularly referred to as the Sringar Chowki in local parlance. There is also the majestic Umaid Villas that showcases some remarkable Rajasthani miniature art work. The Ajit Villa is conspicuous with its rich collection of musical instruments and regal attires while the gorgeous Phool Mahal is where the legendary Jodhpur Coat of Arms is preserved. The parapets of Phool Mahal are adorned with exquisite art works portraying various melodious scenes.

For some bravado, one doesn't need to go far. There is the well preserved Maan Villas which exhibits the arsenal and weaponry of the house of Rathores. The intriguing Tent Room is fabulous which has distinct Mughal features. Legend has it that it was once used by Mughal emperor Shah Jahan. The tent is richly embroidered with gold and is literally a treat to the eyes.

Mehrangarh fort has never ever been seized. The invincible fortifications are six meters thick. Some of the walls still bear cannon marks and today this magnificent Jodhpur fort is a living testimony that recounts the chronicles and legends of Jodhpur's rich past.

Rajasthan Heritage Hotels

Spread across the erstwhile princely state of Rajasthan are a large number of palaces and estates that were once home to families that ruled over India. These bastions of history, bristling with memories, some pleasant others less so, seats of intrigue, of coronations, royal residences where durbars were once staged, were abandoned with the passage of time as modern, independent India surged ahead on the road to progress. After India gained independence, maintaining these magnificent properties became a mammoth task, especially after the government of India abolished the privy-purse given to the royal families.

Many of these buildings were converted into heritage hotels, as much to maintain them as also a new means of livelihood. Despite the conversion however, most of these places have been able to retain the original flavour of medieval homes intact. Even the families, whose ancestors once served within these royal portals, have continued to find employment. And a slice of history that would otherwise have been irretrievably lost, continues to survive. With one major difference: You too can now be a part of it!

Heritage hotels can be clubbed into three main categories – forts and palaces, garhs and havelis.. On the top of the pyramid, the kings lived in opulent palaces with their family. The palaces usually sprawled over a huge area and included many manicured gardens, ponds and other facilities to cater to the royalty. The kings ruled over a number of thikanas or thakurs (feudal lords). The thakurs had their own area of control and lived with their families in palacial garhs. The garhs were imposing structures, usually built on a hilltop, and served the purpose of defense as well. Some of the larger kingdoms like Jaipur, had larger thikanas. And some of these thikanas were larger than or as big as some of the smaller maharajas in terms of money, power and wealth. Thikanas in Shekhawati like Mandawa, Mukundgarh, Dundlod and Dundlod were massive.

Besides the aristocracy, the merchant class too was extremely wealthy, some of them even richer than the maharajas themselves and financed wars and battles. They lived in huge havelis with a central courtyard. Usually located in crowded areas, in the heart of the city, havelis in Rajasthan exhibit its stunning architecture. The havelis in Bikaner, Jaisalmer and Shekhawati are fine example of these.

Besides the havelis of the merchants, some of the larger thikanas too had havelis at their capital as well. This acted as their residence when they were visiting the king.

Bhanwar Niwas Palace

The desert city of Bikaner in the Indian state of Rajasthan is one of those destinations that captivates the imagination of the visitors almost instantly. With its imposing forts, royal palaces and opportunities for exciting camel safari expeditions, Bikaner converts the vacation of any tourists into a vibrant one.

The old palaces or mansions of the city, specially are huge attraction. The Bhanwar Niwas palace is one of these palaces. Originally, a mansion built in the year 1927 by Bhanwarlalji Rampuria, the Bhanwar Niwas palace is a magnificent red sandstone building reflecting a wonderful blend of Indian and European style.

Today, the palace has been converted into a heritage hotel.

Bhanwar Niwas as a Heritage Hotel

Bhanwar Niwas Palace as as Heritage Hotel offers its guests a tranquility that is heartening. The palace hotel might not be as big as some of the best heritage hotels of Rajasthan, yet there is no lacking of the royal feeling that presents itself in every thing you see and do.

The Bhanwar Niwas palace, as a heritage hotel, unveils before its guests the glorious past with remarkable ease. There is a doorman at the gate and a Buick dating back to the time when the mansion itself was built. The Buick, at the very outset, seems to beckon the guests to get ready for a ride back into the royal era. A stay in the Bhanwar Niwas Palace Hotel is definitely a memory to cherish for life.

Facilities on Offer

Inside, the grand mansion hotel offers its guests 25 rooms for the purpose of accommodation. The rooms are each different from the other though a few things remain common in all - high ceilings, Belgian tiled bathrooms with huge tub and not to forget antique furnitures. Make use of these furnitures and feel yourself transported to an entirely different era.

The public rooms at the ground floor like the Little Drawing room and the Blue Drawing room are extremely lavish. The Dining Hall boasts of flower paintings that were personally made on the walls by the owner of the mansion. Admire the colours of the paintings while feasting on the vegetarian delicacies offered. The vegetarian items to choose from are not just restricted to Indian cuisine, rather Continental and Chinese cuisine also make brilliant alternatives.

Recreational facilities ensure that the guests get the best of both the traditional and modern era. Sipping in a cup of warm coffee brought specially from the 24 hours coffee shop, guests can either relax in the beautiful Blue Drawing room or listen to the music concert every evening in the brilliant courtyard. There is also a cloth bound book called An Indian Miscellany of Wise Nuggets for those who wish to catch up on the writings of a senior member of the Rampuria family.

Accessibility

The Bhanwar Niwas Palace is at a convenient distance of 2 km from the Railway Station and 1km from the Bus Stand. Nearest Airport is in Jodhpur which 250 km away.

Castle Mandawa

In the colourful region of Shekhawati, Rajasthan, lies a small remote town, Mandawa. It was a halting place for ancient traders who came down all the way from China and Middle East. The town itself came into existence after Thakur Nawal Singh built a fortress here. The fortress initially attracted numerous common people and later traders to settle down in the surrounding areas. Mandawa soon flourished though later with the dwindling in the caravan traffic business lost its earlier zeal. The merchants were forced to look into other options elsewhere in the country. Yet their love for the place encouraged them to build numerous havelis.

Today, the fort that gave life to Mandawa as a town has been converted into a heritage hotel while the other havelis form a major source of attraction.

Castle Mandawa as a Heritage Hotel

Castle Mandawa, which became a hotel in 1980, is every bit royal! From the moment guests step into the premises of the hotel, regality makes itself visible at every step forward. The hotel building is imposing and the entry of guests grand. On the back of a camel or horse, the guests make a dream entry with blowing trumpets and rhythmic beats of drum adding a regal sound effect. Traditional Indian welcome with tilak and garland add more charm to the colourful entry of the guests.

During their stay, the friendly staff ensures that the guests feel at home even while away from it.

Facilities on Offer

The rooms available for accommodation are 70 in number with total bed capacity of 140. The Royal Suites, Luxury Suites, Deluxe Rooms, Standard Rooms bear a distinct look each and reflect the taste of the erstwhile rulers. The elegant interiors of some rooms with a period look and modern touch are more pleasing than the others. There are some rooms that have been left untouched for a long time now including the ones that preserve the oldest frescoes. Most of the rooms open into a balcony. Guests are at a leisure to pick up a room of their choice.

Dining at Castle Mandawa is not just about enjoying a delicious meal. Rather, it is about enjoying the entire experience of dining in a wonderful setting. Every meal at the Castle - on the terrace with widespread views of temples and cenotaphs, in the dining room with its exquisite & colourful mural-paintings, in open air under the stars, in lawn with cool breezy air or around a bonfire in the rear courtyard - is a cherishing moment for guests. Adding more taste and fun to the meal is the performance by a folk artists and fire dancer that are almost as beautiful as thrilling. Both restaurant of the hotel, Jag Niwas and Bhagwat Niwas, offer Indian cuisine to the guests.

Fire dances and folk performances at dinner time are not the only means of entertainment in this heritage hotel. There is much more in store. Recreational facilities also include camel and horse rides, jeep safaris, gala dinners and a heritage walk of Mandawa. After all, the storybook town of Mandawa has to be given an opportunity to narrate its history through its havelis and paintings inside it! Puppet shows are a special attraction for the children too. And if relaxation is what brought you this hotel, then the Diwankhana, the formal drawing room decorated with family portraits and antique armour is just the perfect place.

A stay at Castle Mandawa is one of most colourful experience of life for the guests.

Accessibility

Castle Mandawa is located at a distance of 5 km from the Bus Stand and 14 km from the Railway Station. The nearest Airport is in Jaipur at a distance of 168 km.

Jai Mahal Palace

Jai Mahal Palace was originally developed around 1745 by Hargovind Natani, Military Commander and Prime Minister of Sawai Ishwari Singh of Jaipur. He initially fought from the side of Sawai Ishwari Singh's army and led it to a striking victory over Madho Singh's combined forces of Udaipur, Kota, Bundi, and the Marathas of Holkar states. However, later he ditched his own master and shook hands with Madho Singh which resulted in Sawai Ishwari Singh committing suicide. Later, after Natani's death, his property, including the Garden of Natani (on which the palace stands) was took over by the Jaipur state since he was deemed a traitor. From then, Jai Mahal Palace remained a princely property and continued so till the time Sawai Man Singh II (1922-1947) took over Jaipur State and converted Natani ka Bagh into the official residence of the Prime Ministers of Jaipur. After one year, the name Natani ka Bagah was changed with that of Jai Mahal Palace. It is said that the name could either be drawn from the name of the city itself or was a gesture of honour by Sawai Man Singh for his ancestor Sawai Jai Singh II or his son Jai.

After independence, Jai Mahal remained vacant till 1955 when finally the lack of accommodation facilities for ever- increasing tourists to Jaipur made jeweller Laxmi Kumar Kasliwal Man Singh transform this palace into one of the earliest palace hotels of Jaipur.

Jai Mahal Palace as a Heritage Hotel

The palace is today a luxurious hotel offering a stay of a lifetime. Positioned in the lush greenery of Mughal Gardens, the Jai Mahal Palace Hotel is a perfect place to enjoy the splendorous life of the erstwhile Rajput rulers. The architecture of the building, the spectacular surroundings, the interior designing and the colour scheme together present a picture postcard beauty.

The Taj Group of Hotels which manages the affairs of the hotel presently has ensured that the guests have an enjoyable stay in the Jai Mahal Palace. The guests are made to feel special during every second of their stay. Modern facilities have been kneaded finely with the traditional grandeur to provide the guests a classy feel.

Facilities on Offer

The hotel offers its guests 100 rooms for the purpose of accommodation which includes Special Suites, Superior Rooms and Deluxe Rooms. Superior rooms and Deluxe rooms, offering a choice of garden or pool facing rooms, are laced with all modern luxurious facilities. They also have a commodious sitting area to enable guests to feel free and comfortable while sipping a cup of tea or coffee. Deluxe rooms exude brightness with lively and colourful design. Staying in these rooms is like living a life at its prettiest self, however the star attraction of the Jai Mahal Palace are indubitably the 6 Suites which include Jaipur Suite, Topaz Suite, Gangaur Suite and Peacock Suite. The decor of these Suites, with a delightful mix of traditional and modern themes, is truly breathtaking and the luxury offered are enough to pamper any soul. In addition to amenities like choice of garden or pool views from the room, guests are provided a spacious living room and bedroom to feel more free and comfortable.

Dining in Jai Mahal Palace means plenty of options to choose from. The all day dining restaurant, Marble Arch serves its guests the best of traditional Indian delicacies specially Rajasthani cuisine apart from a range of European and Oriental dishes. As with the dishes, the interiors of this restaurant also offers a blend of traditional and modern with curved archways and impressive stoneware adding a touch of regality.

The Cinnamon is not an all day restaurant and opens only during lunch and dinner (12:30 hours to 15:00 hours and 19:00 hours to 23:00 hours). The speciality of this restaurant is that it offers some incredibly tasty Indian dishes influenced by Punjabi and Mughal recipes that are blend together by what is known as the Cinnamon - saffron tie up. Another appealing characteristic of the dishes offered here is that they are all prepared from fresh ingredients and genuine Indian herbs and spices which means that the guests have a real treat eating here.

For a more enjoyable dinner, there is Giardino serving traditional Italian cuisine in open air. Here guests can feast in a red brick courtyard with the pool closeby. The kitchen is also set in the open air making the entire experience of eating here more informal and tremendously fulfilling. The Pool Lounge and Terrace are excellent places to enjoy light snacks and refreshments whenever guests feel the need for one. The location of both these restaurant truly exemplifies the royal treatment offered. The Terrace, for example is set amidst beautiful Mughal Gardens which means an ambience redolent of a charm of the leisurely lifestyle.

Dining alone is little incomplete, atleast for those who love drinking. Jai Mahal Palace Hotel offers MariGold Bar for such guests. The bar is by all means modern and takes care of the sensitivities of the modern guests. International as well as Indian liquor and beverages are well stocked in this bar along with a single malts and cigar.

Like the accommodation and dining facilities, the recreational facilities in the Jai Mahal Palace hotel is abundant and superb. Take a splash in the cool water of the swimming pool, work out at the gymnasium, pick up exquisite Rajasthani items from the Shopping Arcade, take a deep breath during yoga sessions, sway along with the music of open air folk dances, immerse in the colours of puppet shows, hop around on a life size chess board, enjoy a camel buggy ride or horse riding trips, soak yourselves in the delightful theme parties..... the list of recreational facilities is endless.

Accessibility

The hotel is located at a distance of 14 km from Sanganer Airport, 3 km from Jaipur Railway Station and 1 km from Jaipur Bus Stand.

KHIMSAR FORT

Located in the Nagaur district of the Rajasthan, the Khimsar Fort was constructed by Rao Karamsiji (8th son of Rao Jodha, founder of Jodhpur) in the 16th century. Settled comfortably at the edge of Thar desert, between Jodhpur and Bikaner, Khimsar has a quintessential Rajasthani history of war and romance. Stories are rife as to how in earlier days, Khimsar endeavoured, though in vain, to free itself from the fiefdom of the Marwar empire and stabilize itself distinctly. Another story that captivates the imagination of the people is that the last great Mughal Emperor, Aurangzeb, himself paid a visit to this small village on request of a Thakur. However, the authenticity of this claim is highly dubitable.

The fort, that has been converted into a heritage hotel, is still inhabited by the direct descendants of its founder, and that also the 20th one! A ladies wing and a regal wing were added in the 18th and the 20th century respectively. Khimsar Fort has also been awarded the topmost recognition for a heritage property by Tourism Department of India in the form of 'Grand Heritage Award for Excellence'.

Khimsar Fort as a Heritage Hotel

The heritage hotel that is managed by the Welcom Group of Hotels offers a spectacular welcome to its guests with enthusiastic display of fireworks, as they enter its heavily studded gates. Right from here, guests get an inkling of the kind of lavish stay they will enjoy during their vacations.

The best part about the hotel is that it is located far away from the noise of big cities which means that guests have plenty of time to spend with themselves and family in solitude. Also, since the hotel is run by the direct descendants of the royal family and the staff too trace their links to the erstwhile courtiers, the hospitality is at its best. These people know how to treat their guests in a true regal manner and as such extend a warm welcome to everyone.

Facilities on Offer

The accommodation of 50 luxurious and well decorated deluxe rooms and suites swiftly carry guests back into a splendorous past. While some of the rooms exude traditional architectural form and furnishing, there are others that have an art deco look. The colours in the rooms range from bright red to more light shades of white and blue.

Dining in Khimsar fort hotel brings the guests out of the confines of a dining hall and offers them a one time opportunity to enjoy their meal in the ruins of Fateh Mahal, fort ramparts, on the rooftop of the dome, terrace gazebo or Khimsar dunes. Infact the venue for meals is changed keeping in mind the season and time. Quiet interesting! No wonder, the Rajasthani and the Continental meals taste even more delicious in these places. There is also a restaurant in case guests wish to dine inside. Here the portraits of 20 generations of ruling family look over as the guests enjoy and appreciate the delicious meal. The poolside bar Tabela and the Khimsar Lounge offers some really quality wine and beverages.

Recreation in Khimsar fort hotel means a varied lot. Starting from an in house museum that displays miniature paintings and the family antiques, guests can pay a visit to the nearby villages on the back of a camel or horse. A complete panorama of royal and simple lifestyle presents itself before the guests. A slightly better way for guests to explore the lanes of the village is to pedal a bicycle themselves. And for those, little unwilling to exert themselves, there are air conditioned limousines on hire. A perfect way to feel royal in a modern way.

The handicraft shop, with each of its items personally picked by the royal family is a must visit for a glimpse into the aesthetic taste of the members. After a day long entertainment on earth, Khimsar Fort Hotel takes its guests to view the sparkling beauty of the stars in sky. The inhouse telescope enables guests to watch the star studded sky on a clear night.

Folk dances (Kalbelia), puppet shows, snake charmer shows and magic shows keep up the spirit of guests throughout their stay.

Accessibility

Khimsar Fort is located at a distance of 40 km from the Railway Station and 0.5 km from the Bus Stand. The nearest Airport is 90 km away from the nearest airport in Jodhpur.

Lake Palace

This white marble structure rising out of the Lake Pichola has an irresistible charm that draws tourists from far and wide. The beauty of the Lake Palace is in a way responsible to bring Udaipur in the list of important tourists destinations of the world. Infact, the Lake Palace, along with two other palaces of Udaipur has also featured in the highly popular James Bond film, Octopussy.

The foundation of the Lake Palace was laid by Maharana Jagat Singh II in 1754. The palace covers the entire 1.5 hectares of the Lake Palace Island, earlier known as the Jag Niwas Island. Maharana Jagat Singh was pretty friendly with the Mughal contemporary, Shah Jahan, hence, his beautiful creation in Udaipur reflects some of the Mughal architectural influence. The palace served as summer residence for the Rajput rulers of Udaipur who loved to retreat to this magnificent palace in midst of a lake.

The rooms and apartments within the Lake Palace are all a classic example of sophisticated royalty. The beauty of the palace interiors is enhanced multifolds because of the presence of cusped arches, inland stones of pink, green lotus leaves and painted mirrors. The Bada Mahal, the Khush Mahal, Ajjan Niwas, Phool Mahal and Dhola Mahal are highly attractive. The upper rooms of the palace is perfectly round in shape. The courtyards have columns, pillared terraces, fountains and gardens which adds to the beauty of the palace.

The Lake Palace appears at its best during the dawn and dusk when the sun spreads its multihued shades in the water of the lake. Shimmering with every gust of wind, the reflection of the Lake Palace in the water is simply magical! A boat ride in the water of the Lake Pichola to or from the Lake Palace is an unforgettable experience for the tourists.

Lake Palace as a Heritage Hotel

The Lake Palace was converted into a heritage hotel in the 1960s by Maharana Bhagawat Singh and since then, the hotel is counted amongst the most beautiful & luxurious hotels of the world. The Lake Palace, operating under the Taj Group of Hotels, provides a perfect idyllic atmosphere for the guests to enjoy a cool stay amidst natural beauty.

Facilities on Offer

For the purpose of accommodation, the Lake Palace has in all 83 rooms including Standard Rooms, Deluxe Lake-facing Rooms, Luxury Rooms, Royal Suites and Grand Royal Suites. The air conditioned and spacious rooms are all elegantly decorated with different themes. The rooms have been renovated keeping in mind the taste of modern tourists, yet the opulence of the past seems to ooze from every nook and corner. For example, The Standard Rooms offer Lily Pond and terrace views, the Luxury rooms have spacious lounge area, the Lake facing rooms offer some really magical views of Lake Pichola and the Royal Suites beam with stained glass windows and traditional jholas (swings). The Grand

Royal Suites, as per its name, is a step ahead as far as its interior decor is concerned. high ceilings, ornate glasswork and miniature paintings together create a magical ambience within these rooms that transports the guests into an entirely different age where luxury made its presence felt at every step.

Dining in the Lake Palace Hotel is not just about enjoying a relishing meal. Rather it is an experience that makes the guests realize how the taste of the food enhances multifold the moment a beautiful environment is created around it. The Taj Lake Palace offers its guests 2 restaurant, the Neel Kamal and the Jharokha, to dine. Jharokha sets the atmosphere in its white marble interiors with hundreds of windows. A breakfast along with a hot cup of coffee viewing the lake provides a perfect start for the day. This restaurant is open throughout the day for guests to walk in any time they wish to have something.

Neel Kamal provides a completely different atmosphere with its wood-fired cooking and a show kitchen. Rajasthani specialities and a collection of quality wines served to guests with the backdrop of classical instrumental music lingers in mind even after the lunch and dinner is over.

Light afternoon meals can also be enjoyed at the Amrit Sagar while the Sadar Ghat Bar offers a pleasing opportunity to sit in an open air terrace facing the lake and sip in exotic champagne or iced tea.

The Lake Palace has a number of recreational option for the benefit of its guests. They can have a refreshing bath in the swimming pool of the hotel. For fitness freaks, there is a mini gymnasium to work out and maintain a good health. A spa, Jiva provides a combination of Indian as well as international health & beauty treatments for guests. Shopping Arcade provides the guests an opportunity to buy some ethnic Rajasthani goods. Adding more fun and entertainment to the stay of the guests are the folk music & dance performances by the local artists as well as the puppet shows.

Special arrangements for meetings, theme parties and cocktails are also available at the Taj Lake Palace. Mewar Mahal and the

Lily Ponds welcome guests for a memorable time. The meetings start off with traditional welcome with elephants and camels and culminate with beautiful fireworks. Similarly theme events means savouring delectable culinary cuisne of the region.

Accessibility

The hotel is at a distance of 25 kms from the Maharana Pratap Airport, 3 kms from the Railway Station and 2 kms from the State Roadways Bus Stand.

LALGARH PALACE

This palace was constructed by Maharaja Ganga Singhji in respect of his father Maharaja Lal Singhji. The palace is a pretty recent construction (1902) and lacks the sophisticated elegance of the earlier Rajasthani palaces. Still, this does not mean that the palace is not worthy of a visit. Infact, the palace reflects a wonderful blend of three different style, Rajput, Mughal and European, which definitely deserves an appreciative glance. The majestic red sandstone building with its overhanging balconies and sophisticated lattice work exudes a classic beauty.

The sight of lush green lawns with Bougainvillea bushes and peacocks rambling around the palace is simply fantastic. A carriage from Maharaja's royal train is instantly noticeable. Step inside the palace to discover grand halls, lounges, cupolas and pavilions. Today, the palace boasts of a library that is regarded as the fourth largest in the world and a musuem (Shree Sardul Musuem) that showcases a wide assortment of artefacts and personal possessions of Bikaner Maharaja. Some of the interesting items on display are empty wine and sherry bottles; brass vessels known as tokna used to connect revenue in earlier days; an old film projector; personal belongings of Maharaja Karni Singh like golf tees, electric tooth brush, swimming goggles, earplugs and even his sneakers. The library too has a commendable or rather largest collection of original Sanskrit manuscripts on parchments, copper and gold or silver plaques

Lalgarh Palace as a Heritage Hotel

Today, a part of the palace has been converted into a heritage hotel and is run by the famous ITC Welcom Heritage Group of Hotels. The palace provides its guests not only a comfortable stay but also an opportunity to feel the royal grandeur of the yesteryears. Guests to this hotel are welcomed in a traditional Indian style with a tika and aarti ceremony. The royal welcome also includes garlanding of guests and offering them welcome drink. A perfect beginning for a royal stay ahead!

Facilties on Offer

The accommodation of the hotel provides 42 rooms with a total bed capacity of 76. The rooms are decorated with period furniture - four poster beds, chaise-lounges and exquisite carpets. Guests can roam around in the palace and have a look at the royal reminders of the past that grace the walls of the palace like the vintage etchings, hunting trophies and old portraits.

The restaurant of the Lalgarh Palace hotel, known as the dining hall, offers its guests traditional Indian, Continental and Chinese dishes to relish. Rajasthani food is high on demand. The princely non vegetarian items are as delicious as the vegetarian items cooked in pure ghee. The aroma of the food itself arouses hunger in the most reluctant of food lover.

The hotel also takes care of the Recreational facilities of the guests. As such, light entertainment (Rajasthani folk performances and puppet shows) is offered on a daily basis by the hotel authorities. Shelling out a few extra bucks can also ensure a theme evening as well as camel safari trip in neighbouring areas. However, prior requests need to be made for this.

Accessibility

Lalgarh Palace is 3 km from the Railway Station and 1 km from the Bus Stand. Nearest Airport is in Jodhpur which is 250 km away.

NARAIN NIWAS PALACE

Narain Niwas Palace was built in the year 1928 by the Thakur of Kanota, General Amar Singh. He was also the commander of Jaipur and a close associate of Sawai Maharaja Man Singh, the then ruler of Jaipur. The actual building work of the palace, which was built as the countryside residence, was managed by Thakur Shivnath Singh, brother of Amar Singh. The name Narain Niwas Palace draws its name from their father, Thakur Narain Singh, who was equally renowned administrative personality.

Till half a century back, Narain Niwas was bordered by forest inhabited by wild boars, black bucks, panthers and birds. The forest provided an opportunity to Thakur Amar Singh to enjoy a shooting expedition.

Today, the palace serves as a heritage hotel and provides luxurious stay for its guests.

Narain Niwas Palace as a Heritage Hotel

Managed by the Kanota family till date, the Narain Niwas Palace Hotel offers its guests an opportunity to enjoy the traditional Rajput hospitality. The regal feeling seeps in deep as the guests examine the royal furnitures and decorative items in various parts of the palace. Staying at Narain Niwas Palace hotel is just perfect to start off and exploration of the pink city of Jaipur.

Facilities on Offer

The hotel offers 37 comfortable rooms including double rooms and suites for the purpose of accommodation. The rooms, with period furnitures, Rajasthani artifacts and colourful traditional frescoes and murals on the walls, have an ambience of old royalty. It offers its guests a royal retreat into that wonderful era.

With such wonderful aura of regality around the, dining becomes a pleasure in itself in Narain Niwas palace. The dining hall offers Indian, Continental and Chinese cuisine to satisfy the taste buds of its guests. There is also a bar to quench the thirst of the lovers of liquor.

Recreational facilities at the palace hotel ensures that the guests do not have to spend even a single monotonous moment. There is a swimming pool surrounded by big shady trees. Guests are free to either take a dip in the water or simply relax in the garden. Guests can also enjoy a game of billiards and table tennis at the palace hotel. The Ayurvedic massage centre of the hotel takes away all the worries of the body and soul of the guests. Furthermore performances by folk dancers and puppet shows add a distinctive charm during the stay.

Accessibility

The hotel is located at a distance of 11 km from the Airport, 5 km from the Railway Station and 4 km from the Bus Stand.

RAMBAGH PALACE

The Rambagh Palace was originally constructed in the year 1835 as a school for a young Ram Singh after his father, Sawai Jai Singh III died under mysterious circumstances. Initially, according to Rajput customs, Ram Singh, who was then just 15 months old, stayed inside in the Zenana, away from the influence of British. However, later, the experienced elders of Rajput clan felt that the young prince needed to move out of the Zenana in order to gain proper education. This laid the foundation of the Rambagh Palace. The garden in which the palace was built belonged to Kesar Badaran, the governess of Sawai Ram Singh and was also named after her. When, she died leaving behind no heir, her property was taken over by the state. Ram Singh had a soft corner for this garden and hence made it his hunting lodge, rest house and an official guesthouse. Ram Singh's son, Madho Singh added more rooms to this palace.

Later, history repeated itself, when Man Singh died in 1922 leaving behind an adopted son, Sawai Man Singh II. As before,

Man Singh's guardian Sir James Roberts decided that the young prince had to be trained properly away from the Zenana. Hence, Rambagh Palace again became a school, and very much like his predecessor, Man Singh too developed a liking for this palace. His fondness for this palace led him to declare it a royal palace. He spent quiet a lot of money to renovate and ornate and give it a befitting appearance of a royal palace. The palace gardens were once rated amongst the best in the world and the palace itself became the only one of its type having a polo ground attached to it.

After independence, being the ruler of the largest city of Rajasthan, Man Singh was appointed as Rajpramukh or Head of State of the Union of Jaipur, Jodhpur, Jaisalmer, and Bikaner for life and Rambagh palace became his official royal residence. However, things changed dramatically in 1956 when the scrapped his post to reduce the burden on official treasury. It was this sudden development that forced Man Singh to convert his home into a heritage hotel.

Rambagh Palace as a Heritage Hotel

Today, Rambagh Palace is one of the best heritage hotels in Jaipur. The Palace Hotel, sprawling in an area of 47 acres, is a terrific palace to stay at. Guests can easily slip back into an earlier era when kings and queens, in their exquisite ensemble, majestically drifted past the richly decorated palace halls and colourful gardens. The entire ambience of the palace hotel, the look, decor and the treatment offered, is completely adorable and mesmerizing.

The management of the hotel was taken over by the Taj Group in the year 1972.

Facilities on Offer

The Rambagh Palace Hotel offers 90 rooms including Luxury Suites, Historical Suites, Royal Suites and Grand Royal Suites for the purpose of accommodation. The royal rooms like the Prince's suite, Maharaja suites and the Maharani suite were earlier meant for the personal use of the royal family. The wide use of rich fabrics and silk drapes in the rooms remind guests of the colourful art and royalty of Rajasthan. Infact the Grand Royal Suites is truly a place to enjoy unlimited luxury. It has a large lounge overlooking the Rambagh Gardens that extends on to a terrace. Additionally, the suite also offers a royal dining room and a master bedroom with a dressing area. Even the Luxury Rooms exudes a wealth of colour and texture in its interior decor. The rooms at the hotel either provide a look into the courtyard with fountains or beautiful gardens. All the rooms are not only elegantly decorated with different traditional themes but are also equipped with modern facilities. Staying in the Rambagh Palace Hotel is like reliving the royal era in a more refined and modern way. The Historical and the Royal Suites have the services of a Personal Butler for the guests who can help them in planning their trip.

Dining at the Rambagh Palace Hotel means meals and refreshment that tickles the taste buds to the maximum extent. The Suvarna Mahal, the original dining room of the palace, remains open throughout the day and serves its guests delicious breakfast, lunch and dinner. The beauty of this restaurant is extremely awe inspiring. The hall is built in the French style and has a huge crystal chandeliers hanging from its ceiling to give it a royal look. Another restaurant by the name of Neel Mahal exudes a bluish charm and provides relishing light meals, snacks and refreshments. There is also the Steam which boasts of possessing the city's only wood fired pizza oven and a unique Mediterranean -Arabesque food bar. This place comes alive in the night (from 7 in the evening till early morning) when DJ's play the happening music forcing you to shake a leg on the dance floor. Between the period of October to April, every evening is a delightful treat for your gustatory senses with the Barbeque Exotica providing tasty grilled food. The Polo Bar has a stock of quality drinks for the guests including classic and contemporary cocktails, whiskies and single malts, wines, homemade iced teas, lemonades and ginger ales. The bar itself is decorated with polo memorabilia and trophies.

The recreational facilities at the Rambagh Palace Hotel is as regal as the accommodation and dining. Exotic steam bath &

massages, a round in the swimming pool and jogging track, a game of tennis and squash, high spirited folk dance performances and puppet shows, theme parties and banquets in a special venue called Panghat - all are meant to convey the regality of yesteryears to the modern guests craving for that beautiful life. A special game of Polo can be arranged on request in the palace hotel.

Accessibility

The hotel lies at a distance of 11 km from the Sanganer Airport. The Railway Station and the Sindhi Camp Bus Stand are both 4 km away.

Samode Haveli

Situated in the heart of the Pink City of Jaipur, the Samode Haveli is a classic reminder of the royal past. The haveli was originally built by Rawal Sheo Singhji who belonged to the Samode clan of Rajasthan. This clan claimed relation with Prithviraj Singhji, the famous Kachhawaha ruler. Rawal Sheo Singhji was the Prime Minister in the court of the Rajputs and this haveli served as the suburban manor house for him and his family.

Samode Haveli as a Heritage Hotel

The haveli was finally converted into a Heritage Hotel in the year 1988. Today, it offers its guests not only a comfortable stay but also an opportunity to take a virtual walk back into the royal era. One of the highlights of the haveli is the elephant ramp that was specifically built for the purpose of the marriage ceremony of Rawal Sahib's aunt. Personalized service for each of the guests, in an environment that merges history with modernity, ensures that the everyone gets what is preferred and wanted. Exploring the beautiful city of Jaipur while staying at the Samode Haveli is one worthwhile idea.

As a heritage hotel, Samode Haveli has earned quiet a few commendable mentions from reputed names. For example, the haveli found a place in the hotel hipster, Herbert Ypma's (writer of Hip Hotels Book series) top 20 all time favourites - Sunday Times May 2005 and also featured in the list of Tatler's 101 best hotels 2006.

Facilities on Offer

There are 29 rooms in total for the purpose of accommodation which include double rooms, deluxe rooms, suites and cottages. The interior of each of the rooms is a visual delight. Decorated with authentic antiques, fixtures and old family portraits, the rooms exude a classy elegance. The two suites, Maharaja and Maharani are lavish with every inch of the walls and ceilings covered with lovely paintings and exquisite mirror work. Staying in these suites are a one time experience for guests. Most of rooms have a separate dressing area. In brief, the accommodation of Samode haveli is as regal as it sounds.

Samode Haveli offers its guests Indian as well as Continental Cuisine. The dining hall of the haveli is richly decorated with hand paintings all over. There is also an open verandah where guests can enjoy a cup of tea in the afternoon. Special candle light dinners is also on offer. There is also a bar in Samode Haveli.

Recreational facilities for guests include an open air swimming pool with Moroccan design tiles, Jacuzzi and a wading pool for children. Here, guests can refresh their senses by splashing in the cool water. Refreshmnet can also be gained in the steam room and the ayurvedic massage centre. The green garden filled with colourful and fragrant flowers are a perfect place to relax and enjoy the beauty of nature. Cultural and puppet shows every evening enliven the entire atmosphere and the raises the spirit of the guests. For interested guests arrangements can be made to play golf at the Jaipur Golf Course as well.

More than all this, Samode Haveli offers its guests an opportunity to visit the local crafts bazaars which is situated quiet closeby. Items like blue pottery, hand block print, embroidery, jewellery and enamel work are worth seeing and shop for.

Accessibility

Samode Haveli is located at a distance of 17 km from the Sanganer Airport, 4 km from Jaipur Railway Station and 6 km from the Sindh Camp Bus Stand.

SARISKA PALACE

In the earlier era, when means of entertainment were limited to few options, members of royal family had to choose from the ones that suited their status and regal taste. The Rajput Maharajas associated themselves with courage and as such loved sporting entertainment like hunting. The hunting lodges were specially constructed by them in the forest regions so as to provide comfortable stay while their wild expedition. These hunting lodges even played host to other royal guests as well as foreign dignitaries.

The Sariska palace is one of these hunting lodges that was built by the Maharaja of Alwar, Jai Singh in order to welcome Queen Victoria`s son, the Duke of Connaught. It is said that in those days, the grandeur of the palace was simply outstanding. Moreover, the number of tigers and leopard were so great that the Maharaja and his guests could shoot them standing right in their balcony itself! Almost perfect for regal leisure!

Sariska Palace as a Heritage Hotel

Today, Sariska palace has been converted into a heritage hotel and the surrounding wild area has been declared a National Park and a Tiger Reserve. The 100 year old palace is not as lavish as some of the other palaces of Rajasthan, yet the Aravalli ranges in the backdrop and the Ruparail river flowing through the ground area make for some really charming setting.

Inside the palace, the decor constantly remind guests that they are staying in an erstwhile royal hunting lodge. There are a collection of stuffed beast, royal antiques, old photographs and paintings adorning every nook and corner of the palace. In brief, staying at

Sariska Palace Hotel is one fulfilling experience that is hard to forget by those who have stayed here.

Facilities on Offer

Amidst lush green environment, the Sariska Palace Hotel offers its guests 75 luxurious rooms with a bed capacity of 150 for accommodation. The palace wing undoubtedly is most imposing while the Queens Wing is more elegant. There is a haveli wing as well in the hotel which has its own distinct charm. The interiors of all the rooms are pleasing and provide the guests a perfect stay during their visit. The authentic Regency Victorian furnitures add a regal touch in every room.

The restaurant of the hotel known as the Dining Hall, decorated with antiques, serves its guests delectable Indian, Continental and Chinese cuisine. The Rajasthani cuisine, specially is a must try for all. Sariska Durbar I, II and III provide exceptional convention facilities as and when required.

With Sariska National Park in close vicinity, it is amply clear that the major recreational facilities for guests revolve round the wildlife. The heritage hotel makes available for its guests wildlife viewing by jeep safari, bird watching trip and nature walks.. Camel & horse safari and sightseeing tours to nearby villages are added attractions. Close to heritage, nature and life - recreation at Sariska palace is more exciting than you can think of. For a leisurely indoor entertainment, special events, theme parties and gala dinners are organised on request.

Accessibility

The Alwar railway station is at distance of 36 km from the Sariska palace and the bus station is 38 km away. The nearest airport is at Jaipur, 115 km away. A specia luxury train, Fairy Queen commences from Delhi and brings tourists to view the Sariska National park. The stay is arranged at Sariska palace again

UDAI VILAS PALACE

The Udai Vilas Palace is situated on the Brahmapuri island on the western side of Lake Pichola and spreads in an area of 30 acres of beautiful gardens lined up with decorative fountains and pavilions. The palace is a classic example of the architectural skills of the Mewar dyansty. The palace took nearly ten years to complete and served as a hunting resort for the royal family. Today, the palace has been converted into a heritage hotel.

Udai Vilas as a Heritage Hotel

Udai Vilas Heritage Hotel functions under the patronage of the famous Oberoi Group of Hotels. With the the Aravalli Hills in the backdrop and the shimmering waters of Lake Pichola in the front, the Udai Vilas Hotel enjoys a perfect setting amidst natural beauty. Moreover, the spectacular views of the Jagmandir and Jagniwas palaces, specially during sun rise and sun set adds to the feeling of being in a completely different world. Inside the palace hotel, the beauty of hand-painted mural, carved stone columns, landscaped terraces, lotus flowers carved in marble, brilliantly shinning gold-leaf cover of domes are a feast for eyes and joy for heart.

The luxury treatment accorded in the Udai Vilas Palace Hotel is comparable to the best in the country, Rajvilas, Jaipur and Amarvilas, Agra. Rambling around in the lush greenery of lawns, guests can feel the exhaustion of their body slipping out very fast and a renewed vigour replacing it with a remarkable ease. Guests have always found the true meaning of luxury after even a brief stay in this hotel. A stay in Udai Vilas Palace is truly an amazing experience that leaves guests asking for more. The love for the royal treatment offered here is pretty much apparent in the number of guests who decide to come back here for another round of stay.

Facilities on Offer

Udai Vilas Palace hotel has altogether 87 rooms for the purpose of accommodation including 63 Deluxe, 19 Superior Deluxe, 4

Deluxe Suites and 1 Kohinoor Suite. The Deluxe rooms have an area of 600 sq feet and offers its guests a private walled courtyard along with silken parasols, table and chairs. Guests are at a liberty to roam around a little bit in the courtyard or sit under the soothing shade of the silken parasol. The interiors of the rooms, heavily influenced by the Rajput style are a ready reckoners transporting the guests to the royal era. Additionally, the marble bathrooms too spell their charm on the guests and force them to spend more than usual time bathing.

The speciality of the Superior Rooms is that they all open into a semi private moated pool on a terrace. Views of Lake Pichola and a nearby wildlife sanctuary from the terrace instantly connects guests to the wondrous natural beauty around. The next level of rooms, the Deluxe Suites have an area of 1150 sq feet which means that the guest can move around more freely and comfortably. Staying in these suites is really special because apart from the basic amenities that are there in the above rooms, the Deluxe Suites offer its guests a private infinity pool and tented dining pavilion. Views from these suites, specially those of City Palace, are simply fantastic. There is also a telescope incase views of stars captures the imagination of the guests more than the City Palace. Infusing a sense of further royalty is the private staff - a personal butler who takes care of every requirement of the guests.

At the top of the level is the single Presidential Suite (Kohinoor) covering a massive area of 2650 sq feet. The rooms have a royal ambience that carry guests to the bygone era of grandeur and luxury. There is a fountained courtyard, massive private pool, sitting room with real fireplaces, and master suite with its own wooden sauna - nothing is amiss to make you feel at the top of the royal world.

Dining in Udai Vilas is really special because the chefs here have received a direct training from the few remaining royal chefs of Rajasthan. This means that the flavour and taste of the cuisine of the royal era will be yours to relish. Guests can visit the Udai Mahal, a restaurant offering traditional north Indian dishes for a special candlelight dinner or choose the Surya Mahal. The decor of the Surya Mahal reminds of the era of 1930's and Mediterranean and Thai style dishes give a a good alternative for the Indian dishes.

Chandani, the open air dining courtyard brings the guests out from the confines of the halls and allows them to enjoy their dinner with rhythmic beats of Rajasthani music and dance performances. For those guests who really find eating out an amazing experience, there are picnic lunch on private gondola. And then there is Bhagwanti Royal Barge for a private cocktail party. Floating around Lake Pichola, dinner on the barge is truly an awesome experience.

Recreational facilities in the hotel include a swimming pool whose cool water beckons many guests to take a refreshing dip. And for those who do not want to wet themselves yet enjoy the coolness of water, there are boat rides on beautiful Lake Pichola. Watch the sun rise and set from the horizon and appreciate the beauty that spreads at its arrival as well as departure.

There is a professionally run non clinical spa (Banyan Tree) in the Udai Vilas Palace hotel that offers its guests treatment ranging from Ayurveda to Aromatherapy. With a placid environment of mountains and lake in the backdrop of the hotel, this spa is hugely successful in alleviating the worries of mind and weariness of body.

Last but not the least, there is a library stocked with a selection of books, music and video discs. The library is a wonderful place to enjoy reading a book in complete isolation and silence.

Accessibility

The hotel is located 22 kms from the airport, 4 kms from the Railway Station and 3 kms from Bus Stand.

Umaid Bhawan Palace

The Umaid Bhavan Palace was built by Maharaja Umaid Singh during the period of 1929-34 when Jodhpur was struck with famine to provide food for work to a large number of suffering people. Located at the top of the Chittar hills, the palace is built of the Chittar sandstone. This has also earned it another name, that of Chittar Palace. The palace is a classic example of the Rajput architecture with extending balconies, large courtyards, huge terraces, blooming gardens and royal rooms. However, unlike the other palaces of Udaipur, this palace is devoid of the architectural finess.

The palace, which spreads over an area of 26 acres (including the one covered by lawns and gardens), is segregated into three distinctive part. The first one of the three parts is used by the royal family of Gaj Singh, grandson of Umaid Singh, for personal use while the second part has been converted into a museum. The third and the last part of the palace, today serves as a heritage hotel.

Umaid Bhavan Palace as a Heritage Hotel

This hotel belongs to the famous Taj Group of Hotels and provides its guests a chance to take a virtual walk down the royal era. The special aspect about the hotel is that some of the old retainers of the royal household themselves look after the needs and comfort of the guests. This is a unique experience that is hard to get in any other hotel. Also, every effort has been made in order to preserve the flavour of the grand royal residence despite making changes to fulfill the needs and taste of the modern tourists.

Facilities on Offer

The hotel offers 71 air conditioned rooms including Deluxe Rooms and Suites for the purpose of accommodation. Each room is beautifully decorated with original furnitures of the palace. The Maharani Suite, the Majaraja Suite, Regal Suite and Viceragal Suites have a royal charm that bewitches the guests in strictest of sense. The interiors, from pinkish to silvery are all completely regal and remind the opulence of age gone by even while offering all modern comforts.

The Maharani Suite was originally built for Umaid Singh's Maharani, Badan Kanwar and boasts of a commodious drawing room, dining room with attached kitchenette, a huge balcony providing glimpses of palace gardens, a dressing room with a wadrobe, and finally a bath carved out of a single piece of pink Italian marble. A mural of Goddess Kali dominates the entire suite.

Whilst the Maharani Suite exudes elegance par excellence, the Maharaja Suite is more robust in nature. There are murals of leopard, tigers, horses and popular Jodhpur sport of pig sticking. The sofas are covered with leopard skin and shelves filled with original artifacts of the palace. The highlight of the suite is the mirrored bar.

The Regal and the Viceregal Suites, once meant for catering to the royal dignitaries and guests, also reflect a royal beauty and charm, though the decorative themes and colour in each of them is different.

Dining at the Umaid Bhavan Palace Hotel is a real treat. The Marwar Hall of the Umaid Bhavan Palace is a perfect place to enjoy a variety of cuisine like Indian (specially Rajasthani) and Continental dishes. The Risala is a good alternative option to enjoy a delicious meal too. The walls of Risala are adorned with royal and martial portraits that highlights the victory of Jodhpur Lancers against the Turks at Haifa in 1918. The restaurant is open only during lunch and dinner time. The open vernadah of The Pillars provides a pleasant ambience wherein guests can have the pleasure of sipping in a light drink or enjoying light snacks while viewing some spectacular glimpses of the gardens, the city, the magnificent Mehrangarh Fort and not to forget the brilliant sun set. Cocktails, spirits, wines, beers and other beverages can also be enjoyed at the Trophy Bar where guests can sit at Elephant-foot stools with tiger skin cushions. Other decoration of the bar include large wild boar tusks, binoculars and a collection of fishing gear along with hunting, fishing and pig-sticking memorabilia.

For the entertainment of the guests, Hotel Umaid Bhavan Palace offers a number of recreational options. Guests can play a game of squash, billiards, croquet, tennis or badminton or take a splash in the water of the Zodaic, the underground swimming pool of the hotel. They can also feel refreshed walking in the sun drenched lawns or by taking exotic Kerala Ayurveda massage (at the edge of Thar Desert!). Rajasthani items can be picked up from the Shopping Arcade. The Umaid Bhavan Palace Museum with its commendable collection of antiques is worth seeing. Outside the palace hotel, village safaris and camel safaris to the sand dunes can also be organized.

Specially arranged theme lunch and dinner like the Baradari theme dinners, Flaming Torch dinners, Fountain courtyard dinnner, Mehrangarh Fort dinner (Daawat E Mehrangarh) and Sundeck lunches under Maharajas' tent are truly a once in a lifetime experience for the guests. All these are organized along with Rajasthani music and dance performances which adds colour and enthusiasm to the entire experience.

Accessibility

The Hotel is 3 km from the Jodhpur Airport, 5 km from the Jodhpur Railway Station and 3 km from the main Bust Stand.

Other Famous Heritage Hotels

Merwara Estate

Ajmer, a 7th century Rajput principality is also an important pilgrimage center for the Muslims. The Merwara Estate, just over a hundred years old was built to overlook Anna Sagar Lake. In the style of the period, it incorporated European influences into its architecture – Belgian etched glass, Italian marble floors, painted ceilings. Recently renovated, it has 50 guest rooms, a restaurant, swimming pool, and a conference hall.

Castle Awan

Established in the 15th century, and located between Jaipur and Bundi, in forested hills, Awan (150 km from Jaipur and 110 km from Sawai Madhopur) was a shooting preserve for the maharaja of Bundi, and later used by the complete princely order. Castle Awan is a palatial hunting lodge that's architecture is more reminiscent of the summer retreats of the most royal families. It has a total of 7 guest rooms, and a dining room.

Piramal Haveli

Located in Baggar, a Shekhawati town known for its late-style frescos, the Piramal Haveli was built in the early years of the 20th century. The haveli shows strong European influences in the manner of its verandahs and use of pillars, though the four courtyards are typically representative of the architecture in prevalence in this region. There are some whimsical frescos in the rooms that have been carefully appointed with period and Rajasthani furniture.

Fort Baghera

Located on the Ajmer-Sawai Madhopur road, about 100 km from Ajmer and 150 km from Jaipur, Baghera has a 17th century fort turned into a heritage hotel. The hotel hasfive double rooms and a charming, medieval ambience.

Balasamand Lake Palace

A lake resort, Balsamand was created in the 12th century by the Parihar Rajputs of Mandore, and was simply taken over by Jodhpur's Rathore rulers who converted it into a pleasure resort. Gardens were laid around the artificial lake along with a summer palace, the Balsamand Palace. The red sandstone palace was used for hunts and for royal excursions and today, it serves as a heritage hotel. It has 9 Suites and 26 deluxe rooms, all equipped with modern luxuries.

Royal Castle

The history of Balunda, a Merta village is strewn with remnants of its past – cenotaphs, stepwells, temples and other relics. The village which is ideal for exploring the region, is 128 km both from Ajmer and Jodhpur, and 45 km from Merta town. The 16th century Royal Castle fort was begun by the poet-princess Meerabai's brother, Rao Chanda, and has large chambers, an impressive entrance with painted walls and carved panels and towers. It has 6 rooms, and serves Indian meals on request.

Palace Bassi

Set in forested country, Bassi lay on the route of Mughal and Maratha invasions, and wears the scars of its history. Besides a shooting lodge, it has stepwells, cenotaphs, temples, and the Bassi Wildlife Sanctuary to offer as attractions. Bassi is 120 km from Udaipur. Palace Bassi is a part of a 16th century fort with its scarred battlements. The palace is a maze of domes, corridors, courtyards, apartment suites, arches and towering gateways, all at different levels. It has 8 rooms and serves simple meals.

Royal Rajwada

Bhadrajun has its own interesting mythological legend attached to it. When the Pandava prince Arjun eloped with Krishna's sister Subhadra, it was here they came to be married, and so the place was named: Subhadra plus Arjun, its distortion accepted as its present name. While prayers are still said at this holy site, Bhadrajun's past has a history filled with skirmishes and battles, as is evident from the forts and cenotaphs in the vicinity. Bhadrajun is 50 km from Jalore, 54 km from Pali, and 97 km from Jodhpur.The small palace, Royal Rajwada, dates back to the 16th century though most of the additions and changes are much more recent. The cupolas and balconies extruding off the surface are highlighted, so they appear more striking. There are 12 rooms, and a dining hall where a variety of cuisine is served.

Bhadrawati Palace

The Bhadrawati Palace is located in Bhandarej, a village that has had a crucial role to play in history. The village, 62 km from Jaipur, was a Badgujar settlement till the 11th century when the Kachchwahas won it for themselves, making Dausa their capital, much before they occupied Amber. Bhandarej and its surrounding countryside is ideal for jeep and horse safaris, and camel rides. One can visit Mina villages as well as some medieval stepwells. The Bhadrawati Palace is an elegant palace designed in the Mughal-Rajput style with a charbagh garden fronting it, its arched, pillared halls resound with its historical links. Ideal for visits to Bharatpur's bird sanctuary, it has 25 rooms and a restaurant.

Chapter 5

Agra Heritage Tourism

Agra is globally renowned as the city of the Taj Mahal. But this royal Mughal city has, in addition to the legendary Taj, many monuments that epitomize the high point of Mughal architecture and culture. In the 16th and 17th centuries, when the Mughal dynasty reigned the Indian soil, Agra was the capital of India. It was here that the founder of the royalty, Babar, laid out the first formal Persian garden on the banks of the river Yamuna. Here, Akbar, his grandson raised the towering ramparts of the great Red Fort. Within its walls, Jehangir built rose-red palaces, courts and gardens, and Shahajahan embellished it with marble mosques, palaces and pavilions of gem-inlaid white marble which are still immortal with their glory and will be so in the future.

The crowning glory of the city is obviously the Taj, a monument of love and imagination, that represents India to the world. But as you enter in the city you will discover some more hues of the city whose flavour reminds the glorious heritage of the Mughals in every step you take. Be it the sweet delicacy of 'Petha' (a sweet made of pumpkin) or the spicy Mughlai dishes, Agra is still dipped into the heritage. Agra shopping is something which seems to be a never ending affair where you can't help but having the exquisite miniature marble replica of the Taj or stylish Persian Carpets that too give Agra a world wide fame. The Government handicraft emporia in Agra are the best places to have these items.

Taj Mahal

Taj Mahal, where poet's words find an ultimate direction to articulate their emotion. It is a place where the artistry embraces the eternity and love attains divine salvation. The marble edifice situated on the bank of river Yamuna has suffered many ravages of time and with each sunrise and sunset, it has become immortal with its grandeur of heritage and legend. Taj Mahal was built by Mughal Emperor Shah Jahan to enshrine the remains of his beloved empress Begum Mumtaz Mahal which manifested the immortal love between, the two.

A Monument that Redefines Artistry

Designed by the Persian architect Ustad Isa, Taj Mahal is renowned for its architectural magnificence and aesthetic beauty. Resting on 313 square feet marble platform, Taj Mahal is guarded by four marble minarets that are embellished with intricate marble inlay work. The main dome is offset by four smaller domes; in fact, from whichever angle you look at it, the Taj presents a graceful configuration of lines, curves, colour and perspective. The graves of Emperor and Empress lie in the basement where no one is allowed to enter and a false grave structure is made for visitors which is enclosed by a screen of exquisitely wrought white marble, fine as lace. The jewel-inlaid cenotaph of the king and queen have the verses of the holy Quran inscribed on them. Intricately proportioned filigree work and scooping tiny excavations in the marble wall are nothing but masterpiece in itself. Touch the small holes in the wall which used to contain precious stones in the Mughal era and now holding the reminiscence of the past. Moreover, Pietra dura – the superb craftsmanship of inlaying semi-precious stones into the beautiful patterns are something that give Taj Mahal a unique look.

Taj Fascinates All Day Long

The Taj, which is nothing but a tender elegy in marble, blossoms with its marvelous beauty uniquely at different hours of the day. As the sun spreads its vermilion in the East, Taj blooms like a fine pink rose and its marble architecture seem to spread fragrance, but it takes no time to change its view to a sparkling diamond as the sun reaches the mid sky. In the evening, when the sun completes its journey for the day, and moon comes to heal the world, Taj becomes a mystery in itself. You may even forget to breathe or blink wondering it to be real or some illusion.

Myriad Colours of Taj Mahotsav

A non-stop ten days long carnival, Taj Mahotsav, held at Shilpgram near Taj Mahal in the month of February re-invents the great Mughal heritage of the city in large manner. An extravagant procession of beautifully caparisoned elephants and camels along with drum beaters, dancers and folk artists through the quiet roads of Agra takes it to re-live the royal memory of the Mughals. The festival brings a golden opportunity for the legendary artisans and master craftsman in order to display their exquisite work of art. With folk music , shayari (poetry recitation) and classical dance performance, Taj Mahotsav celebrates finest crafts and cultural nuances of India with Taj Mahal creating the majestic backdrop. Get engulfed in the multiple hues of Indian culture and craft and plan your Taj Mahal trip at the time of Taj Festival as nothing can be more exciting.

Tourist Information

Taj Mahal is open for public viewing from sunrise to 19 hours. The best time to make your plan in the year is from November to February. Being the one of the most renowned world heritage sites, you have to go through security checking and we suggest you co-operate with the guards. Any kind of food or baggage is not allowed inside and if you have any, you have deposit it to the counter. On payment of some charges you can use your camera inside the premises. Video cameras are restricted to the first platform inside the Taj entrance, 600 m away from the monument itself. Photography at the graves inside is forbidden. While entering in the mausoleum you will have to take off your shoes; you might also hire shoes that are put on rent or just go ahead bare footed.

Access

Agra is well connected to Delhi by Indian Airlines and other private airways operating flights on regular basis. One can also opt for train journey by the Shatabdi Express and the Taj Express running daily from Delhi Nizamuddin Station. Agra is only 204 km from Delhi and the excellent national highway caters smooth and luxurious journey by air-conditioned and deluxe coaches to Agra.

You must park at a short distance from the Taj premises and you may take the battery operated buses or horse carts to the entrance. Alternatively, you can walk the 2 km route also.

Where to Stay

Agra has a wide range of hotels and rest houses. The 5 star deluxe hotels provide luxurious accommodation in the city . UPSTDC`s tourist complex, Taj Khema near the Taj Mahal offers accommodation in tents and deluxe rooms. There is a UPSTDC Tourist Bungalow as well. Hotels and restaurants offer both Indian, Continental and Chinese cuisine with Mughlai cuisine, which is Agra's specialty.

AGRA FORT

Agra Fort, built by the successive contribution of three Mughal generations – Akbar, Jehangir and Shah Jehan – still fascinates the entire world with its majestic glory. The fort stared its journey in the days of Akbar under the supervision of Mohammed Quasim Khan, his commander-in-chief. Originally planned to build an invincible military structure by Akbar, the Agra Fort gained its elegance, lavishness and royalty of a palace at the time of Emperor Shah Jehan.

Splendrous Mughal Architecture

The remarkable architecture and the majestic fort complex stores the innumerable essence of the Mughal Emperors and you may fee like riding in the time machine. More like a city inside, the fort was built to fulfill the military purpose which spreads on the banks of Yamuna enclosing a humongous area of 3 km radius. Surrounded by a 70 foot high wall the fort houses the beautiful Pearl Mosque and numerous palaces including the Jahangiri Mahal, Diwan-i-Khas, Diwan-i-Am and Moti Masjid. The fort has four gates and is enclosed by a double barricaded wall of red sand stone. Many buildings were constructed within the fort of which very few remain till date. One of the most significant ones is the multi-storeyed Jahangiri Mahal built by Akbar for his wife Jodha Bai. The Mahal is reached through an impressive gateway and its inner courtyard consists of beautiful halls, profusse carvings on stone, exquisitely carved heavy brackets, piers and cross beams. Most of the panels in the eastern hall are decorated with the Persian styled stucco paintings in gold and blue.

It is believed that a century later, most of the structures were dismantled by Shahjahan and were replaced with white marble pavilions covered with intricate inlay work. Of which the most prominent ones are - the Diwan- i-khas, the Mausam Burj and the Shaha Burj. Away from the waterfront he built the Moti Masjid and the Diwan-i-Aam. If you check carefully you can find the dimples on the walls that were embellished with precious stones which could not survive in the ravages of time. Touch them and you will have a spine chilling experience. This is the place where Emperor Shah Jehan spent last days of his life after he had been imprisoned by his son Aurangzeb, seeing Taj Mahal, a symbol of eternal love where the heart-broken Shahjahan was subsequently buried and re-united finally with his beloved Mumtaz.

Tourist Information

Open on all weekdays from sunrise to sunset, the fort offers free visit on Fridays. Ample space of parking available just outside the fort makes it easily accessible by both cars and heavy vehicles. The best time to visit the fort is from November to February. The Son-et-lumiere show is performed at 7.30 pm in English and at 8.30 pm in Hindi on every weekday evenings.

Access

Agra is well connected to Delhi by Indian Airlines and other private airways operating flights on regular basis. One can also opt for train journey by the Shatabdi Express and the Taj Express running daily from Delhi Nizamuddin Station. Agra is only 204 km from Delhi and the excellent national highway caters smooth and luxurious journey by air-conditioned and deluxe coaches to Agra.

Where to Stay

Agra has a wide range of hotels and rest houses. UPSTDC`s tourist complex, Taj Khema near the Taj Mahal offers excellent sojourn in the deluxe rooms. There is a UPSTDC Tourist Bungalow as well. A number of 5 star deluxe hotels make accommodation facility in Agra comfortable.

Other Attractions in Agra

Itmad-ud-daulah

The Itmad-ud-daulah tomb stands in the centre of a grand Persian garden, an architectural gem of its times. It is the tomb of Mirza Ghiyas Beg, Emperor Jehangir`s wazir, or Chief Minister, and also his father- in- law. The structure was built by Empress Noorjehan, between 1622 and 1628 and is very similar to the tomb she constructed for her husband, near Lahore in Pakistan. This splendid garden tomb is believed to be the precursor of the magnificent Taj Mahal, and was the first Mughal structure to be built entirely of marble, and the first, again, to make use of pietra dura, the inlay marble work that came to be typical of the Taj. Near the Agra Fort, is Jami Masjid, built by Shahjahan in 1648. An inscription over its main entrance indicates that it was built in the name of Jahanara, the emperor`s daughter, who was imprisoned with the hapless emperor by Aurangzeb.

Sikandara - The Final Abode of Akbar

Situated at 8 km North-East of Agra, Sikandra is the place where the divine soul of great Mughal Emperor Akbar rests. Founded by Sikandar Lodi in 1492, Sikandra was re-constructed by Akbar as a site for his mausoleum, but before it could be completed, he died and was buried in a catacomb. You will find the tomb glorifying the centre of a large garden which is accessible by four excellent red sandstone gates designed by Jehangir, the son of Akbar. Flaunting a combination of Hindu and Muslim architecture, the tomb is a four storey high building with first three storeys built in red sandstone while the fourth one is entirely of marble. The crypt inside the tomb is decorated with dark blue plaster and gold leaf making it the appropriate place where royalty could rest finally. Four small windows high on the walls admit a dim light and you may find a torch useful here.

SHOPPING - THE MULTI HUED EXPERIENCE

Tourists coming to Agra make it a definite point to shop till they drop as the alluring marble souvenirs exhibiting an unique craftsmanship of Indian architecture are something that should not be missed. The Government emporia are the most authentic shops from where you can have the world famous marble miniature of the Taj in different sizes or even order for the marble furniture which are delivered at your desired destination in due time. Dazzling precious and semi-precious jewellery, exquisite Persian carpets and leather items are amongst the other popular buys in Agra. Shilpgram is a crafts village and an open-air emporium, stocking handicrafts from all over the country and is the ideal destination for lovers of Art. Also Sadar Bazar. Tajganj, Kinari Bazar, Munro Road, Pratap Pura, Gwalior Road which brush each other are the main bazaars of Agra towards the south. Take with you some sweets which are rare in taste like the Petha (sweet made of pumpkin) and Gazak (sweet made of sesame, jaggery and condensed milk) or something spicy snack like Dalmoth.

Tourists coming to Agra make it a definite point to shop till they drop as the alluring marble souvenirs exhibiting an unique craftsmanship of Indian architecture are something that should not be missed. The Government emporia are the most authentic shops from where you can have the world famous marble miniature of the Taj in different sizes or even order for the marble furniture which are delivered at your desired destination in due time. Dazzling precious and semi-precious jewellery, exquisite Persian carpets and leather items are amongst the other popular buys in Agra. Shilpgram is a crafts village and an open-air emporium, stocking handicrafts from all over the country and is the ideal destination for lovers of Art. Also Sadar Bazar. Tajganj, Kinari Bazar, Munro Road, Pratap Pura, Gwalior Road which brush each other are the main bazaars of Agra towards the south. Take with you some sweets which are rare in taste like the Petha (sweet made of pumpkin) and Gazak (sweet made of sesame, jaggery and condensed milk) or something spicy snack like Dalmoth.

After a tour in Agra, you may not find your life very same again. With handful of exquisite handicraft items and a miniature Taj on your desk, the colourful memories of Agra tour will always accompany you.

Chapter 6

Chennai Tourism

Located on the stretch of Coromandel coast, some 60 metre above sea level, Chennai, the capital of Tamil Nadu, is the gateway to south. This 350 year old city flourished around Fort St. George and slowly and steadily took over the nearby town and villages. The fourth largest city of India now has a population of around 6.4 million with maximum of them speaking Tamil and Malayalam. English and Hindi are also widely spoken and understood languages. The Knowledge of these languages make Chennai an easily tour able city for the international tourist. The land of Bharatnatyam is one of the four metro capitals of India and is considered to be the fastest city in terms of growth. Chennai also has the distinction of being called the automobile capital of India. With around 40% of automobiles giants having a plant in Chennai and more than 75% of total car production rolling out of Chennai, the city is surely on an overdrive. The fusion of tradition and modernity is something that you will notice in almost all aspects of Chennai life.

The cost of living in Chennai is among the lowest in the country, and that means you can go on a shopping spree and come back keeping your pocket relatively full. Options of what to shop for are ample in Chennai. In fact Chennai is a heaven for shoppers like you. Ready made clothes including international brands and traditional wear, contemporary and antique artworks are few of the major items that you can buy here. You can also enjoy the city's distinct culture and warm hospitality, which are also quite famous world over. International tourists have never found it difficult to get used to the environment of this vibrant city. Chennai, with the kind of enthusiasm it has, perfectly reflects the true colors of India.

Kollywood, the Tamil film industry is another energetic aspect of the people of Chennai. The actors in this industry are considered nothing less than Demigods and you will see larger than life hoardings having their cut outs bigger than any you will find in the whole country. As trend suggests, people of Chennai are so affectionate towards their superstars that they choose them to even head the government. The passion and dedication towards this industry is surely something to be seen in real life.

Pilgrimages - Purity For Soul

Chennai is home to people of all religion and its pilgrim sites are on top of any tourist itinerary. These pilgrim sites are especially famous for their sacredness and architectural splendor. Temples like Shri Parthasarthy and Kapaleeswarar Temple are one of the oldest temples and are known as one of the most divine destinations in southern part of India. They are also famous for the holiness and sanctity that is maintained inside the temple. Chennai also has many Chuches like St. Mary's church and Mosques like Thousand Lights Mosque that are acknowledged as important pilgrim sites for people throughout the country.

Beaches - Straight Out of A Picturebook

Chennai is visited a lot by tourist just to savour the exasperating beauty of these beaches. There are three main beaches in this city of which Marina beach is the most beautiful and most visited. Marina beach is the second longest beach in the world with a stretch of around 4.5 kms. As you take a walk on the seafront, you will come across statues of famous people like MGR, Anna and many other great leaders. The other famous beaches are Elliot beach, also called the night beach, ideal for sea bathing and Covelong beach which is famous for a 17 century fort built by the Nawab of Carnatic.

Bharatnatyam - Divine Defination of Dance

Bharatnatyam is one of the most popular forms of classical Indian dance. Its exact time of origin is not known, but it has undergone several noticeable transformations in its several hundred-year history. Bharatnatyam is so full of poise and grace, that when you see it in real life, it seems as beautiful as poetry in motion. By tracing its origins in the Natya Shastra, written by the great sage, Bharata, it comes to be known that it is a highly traditional and stylized dance form. Earlier known as Dasi Attam and Sadir, it was only practiced by Devadasis of the South Indian temples. For a long time, it was not considered a reputed profession, until Rukmini Devi worked towards it and brought it to be one of the most sought after dance forms in the world of performing arts.

Cuisine - Delight For Tongue

South Indian cuisine from Chennai could be the best memory that you take away from here. From the idlis and vadas, to idiyappam and dosa, Chennai is so full of different delicacies that once you have a taste of them, you will be left asking for more. Having your lunch on a banana leaf might not be on your wish list before you come to Chennai , but after one experience, it will definitely be there on your favorite's list, right on top. For the best in town vegetarian, you can go to Madras Cafe or Raj Restaurant. And for sumptuous non-vegetarian Chettinad cuisine which is considered to be a specialty in Tamil Nadu, Sea food restaurant-Kayal is a great option. Tamil Nadu, especially Chennai, is famous for its filter coffee called as 'Kaapi' without which your trip to Chennai is not complete.

Chennai Attractions

Popularly known as the Gateway To South, Chennai is the most lively city in the whole of South There is a distinctive charm about the city that separates it from other big cities. The moment you set foot on this stunning part of South India, you will be captivated by the warmth in the hospitality of the people of

Chennai. The capital of Tamil Nadu is also famous for the options that it provides in the domain of sightseeing. The city is saturated with buildings with their walls full of carvings. Visit the temples, and you are bound to find new definitions for spirituality and Purity. The beaches in the city are equally mesmerizing with Marina beach leading the way. So just Wander out into the city and you will experience how past heritage so remarkably blends into the present traditions.

Marina Beach

Marina beach is considered to be the jewel in the crown of Chennai. Adjacent to the Bay of Bengal, this ravishing piece of land is the second longest beach in the world. You will come across the statues of Mahatma Gandhi, MGR, Anna and many other great leaders when you take a walk along the Stretch of a distance of 4.5 km. The view of sunsets and sunrise from Marina Beach are such a splendor that, even the best man made marvels stand no comparison. Evenings on the beach are really colorful with many stalls lining up on the beach and a large number of enthusiastic tourist starting to show up.

Fort St. George

Fort St. George is the first British fort in India in the year 1644. The construction of the fort started the activity of people settling around the fort and commencement of trade with other states. This is why it is said that Chennai (formerly Madras) started its evolution around this fort. The fort is a well sculpted citadel with a 6 meter wall that withstood a number of sieges in the 18th century. Today the fort renders its services as the administrative headquarters for the legislative assembly of Tamil Nadu. There is a museum that holds many relics from the days of Raj, including many portraits of the governors.

Kalakshetra

Kalakshetra is the apex institution for classical dance, music and the fine arts, established in 1936 which is the brainchild of

Late. Rukmini Devi. A Proteges of Annie Besant, was deeply influenced by the progressive views of the Theosophical Society. She defied tradition by learning and performing the classical dasi attam, which was considered to be in the sphere of devdasis (Temple Dancers). Covering an area of 100-acre in Thiruvanmiyur in South Chennai, Kalakshetra has enrolled students from around the world who have the flair for learning the best. Over the years, Kalakshetra has been associated with the betterment of the ancient cultural traditions of India. The auditorium within the Kalakshetra is built according to the Natya Shastra. The institute also conducts research into works of several renowned Sanskrit scholars to stage dance productions, not only for Indian audiences but also for major world theaters.

Guindy National Park

Guindy National Park, is a major attraction for all true wildlife enthusiasts. It is situated on an area of 2.82 sq. km. The distinctive feature of this park is that it is actually located within a city, unlike all other national parks in the country. It has a small population of animals that include Black bucks, Bonnet Macaques, Spotted deer, Mongoose and Jackals. Among the birds seen here are - Yellow wattled lapwings, Partridges, Bulbuls, Babblers, Mynas, Cuckoos, Pittas and occasionally a Baza.

Snake Park

Situated in the Guindy National park, Snake park has become a major attraction among the visiting school children but it also is a hit among visitors of all ages. It has a huge variety of snakes, venomous and non-venomous, small and huge turtles and tortoises, various species of Crocodiles, Caimans and Gharials. It also has an interesting enclosure with four chameleons which are quite difficult to spot because more often than not, they stay hidden in the small bushes. The park also holds hourly lecture sessions to educate people about these wonders of wildlife. And specially for the daredevils, they will have the rare opportunity to handle snakes during these demonstrations.

Parthasarathi Temple

The temple dedicated to Lord Krishna is a creation of Pallavas in the 8th century. Although this is considered to be one of the oldest temples in the region but it definitely has the most visually appealing structure. The temple is spread over an area of 1.5 acres and is a Triplicane. The temple finds its mention in the ancient Vaishnavite works of Alwar saints and is one of the 108 sacred center of the Vaishnavites. Vaikunth ekadashi is the main festival celebrated in this temple. There are special prayers that are offered to the deity on every Saturday in the Month of Purattasi.

Kapaleeswarar Temple

Kapaleeswarar temple is an ancient temple around 350 years old devoted to Lord Shiva. Situated at Mylapore, this temple is the biggest in the city. The structure of the temple is purely in Dravidian style and is a great example of their wizardry in architecture. Inside on the walls, you will find inscriptions which date back to 13th century. The gopuram in the center has carvings illustrating tales from Hindu Mythology and with a towering height of 37 meters, it has an impeccable presence. The Teppam festival(float festival) is an annual event which attracts a large number of devotees. The Paradosham Festival which is held after every two weeks is also a crowd Gatherer.

So if you are planning to visit the Southern India or somewhere even close, do not forget to explore the innumerable fantasies in Chennai that are waiting to mesmerize you and give you the time of your life on the journey of a lifetime

Madurai Tourism

The very ancient city of Madurai is one of the oldest cities of India and dates back to several centuries before Christ. Situated some 472 km from Chennai, Madurai is located on the banks of River Vaigai. Madurai is also the second largest city of Tamil Nadu after Chennai and covers an area of 109 sq km. Madurai was home to the ancient Tamil Sangam and also hosted the literary summit that produced the first Tamil epic and many other famous literary works. Madurai is also one of the most sacred temple towns of India. The presence of Meenakshi Temple, around which the city evolved, has made Madurai one of the most widely visited pilgrim as well as a tourist destination. The city is not overly crowded and has a population of around 1 million. Major part of the population speaks the native language Tamil but English is also used. The people here are friendly, caring and have a deep respect for their culture and heritage which indeed is very rich. In the present world, it is a fast paced commercial center taking the competition head. The city is mainly famous for the hand loom products and tourists can purchase the local apparels and items as a memorabilia of their visit to Madurai.

Attractions - The Pearls of History

Madurai is purely a pilgrimage center and all the city attraction are generally temples and palaces. But that does not in any way mean that a casual travelers will not find anything that will interest them. In fact these temples are the best way to experience and explore the ancient and exceptional man made marvels which can easily be put among the best human creation of all times in the whole world.

Sri Meenakshi - Sundareshwar Temple

It is said that Sri Meenakshi Sundareshwar temple and Madurai city both originated together, this shows how much importance this temple holds in the history and present of Madurai. The complex of Sri Meenakshi temple is huge and covers an area of around 65000-sq m. the construction of this temple dates back to more 2000 years. The complex of the temple grew with contributions from many dynasties that once ruled over Madurai. There are four gigantic gateways enclosing two shrines that contains splendid art and sculpture works. But the most important feature of the temple is the thousand-pillared hall in which each pillar has a big and brilliant statue sculpted on it. Rest assured, you will not leave the temple without being spellbound. The temple is open everyday from 4.30 am to 12.30 pm and from 4.00 pm to 9.30 pm.

Mariamman Teppakulam

Mariamman Teppakulam is a magnificent square tank built by King Thirumalai which is located 5 km east of Meenakshi Temple. The tank covers an astonishing area of almost 16 acres. The temple is the venue of the resplendent float festival held in the month of January and February to celebrate the birth anniversary of King Thirumalai. Towards the northern side of the tank, there is a temple dedicated to Mariamman who is a famous village deity.

Thirumalai Nayak Palace

Situated just 1.5 km from Meenakshi Temple, the Thirumalai Nayak Palace is a classic and rare example of Nayak Architecture. It was constructed in the year 1523 by King Thirumalai Nayak . It was built under the supervision of an Italian Architect. The structure used to be four times bigger than what it is now. A huge portion of the magnificent palace was destroyed by the grandson of King Thirumalai. In 1866-72, by the orders of Lord Napier, the then Governor of Madras, the palace was restored and today you can see an entrance gate, a main hall and a dance hall, all treat to eyes. There is also a half hour show about life, passions and victories of King Thirumalai which is very inspiring and is a must see for tourists who want to know how past age kings used to live in royalty.

Gandhi Museum

Situated in the old Palace of Rani Mangammal, the Gandhi Memorial Museum is one of the most important place to be visited in Madurai. This museum is a memorial of "Father of India" Mahatma Gandhi. The Gandhi Museum showcases th main highlights of the freedom struggle and contains a picture gallery of the Gandhian movement. The museum also houses a gallery of relics, Khadi and village industries section.

Accommodation

Hotels in Madurai offer facilities that suit every kind of traveler. There are star rated hotels as well as budget hotels that are all situated close to the tourist attractions. Hotel Taj Garden Retreat and Madura park Inn are the star category hotels that cater to every luxury wish of their guests. For a slightly less luxurious stay, you can opt for Hotel Supreme and Germanus Days In.

Getting There

By Air

Madurai has its own Domestic airport which is around 10 km from Madurai city. It has flights coming in daily from Chennai, Bangalore and Coimbatore.

By Rail

Madurai is considered to be a major railway station in the South. It is well connected to all the other major railway stations and there are trains that run directly to these important stations.

By Road

NH-7 and NH-45 connect Madurai ti all parts of India. From all big cities of Tamil Nadu, there are State transport buses and Luxury coaches that ply to and from Madurai.

Local Transport

Buses and auto rickshaw are the major players in local transportation. Taxis are also there in good numbers that ferry people inside the city walls and to other nearby towns and cities.

Kanyakumari Tourism

Kanyakumari, lying on the southernmost point of peninsular India, is the meeting point of three oceans-the Bay of Bengal, the Arabian Sea and the Indian Ocean. Apart from being a famous tourist destination, it is also considered as an important Hindu pilgrim destination for the presence of some of the most sacred temples in south India like Kanyakumari temple. Famous for its beautiful views of sunrise and sunset over the horizons, Kanyakumari has been enticing tourists for ages because of its breathtaking location. The multicolored sand is a unique feature of the beaches here. The city is also blessed with almost all kinds of ecosystems that a tourist sets out to experience, one can see graceful beaches, gorgeous mountain valleys, evergreen forests and rubber and clove plantations in the deep interiors - all creates a perfect ambience to take-up a trip to Kanyakumari.

Situated by the shore, Kanyakumari enjoys a pleasant climate and can be visited throughout the year. During summers, the temperature can rise to mid thirties, while it can dip to a low twenty during winters. A tourist can indulge in a lot of adventure activities here like trekking, biking, swimming and surfing. So when you decide to spend your vacation in Kanyakumari, don't forget to pack your full traveling gear right from the swimming suit to trekking equipment all of which are sure to come in handy.

Attractions - Find It All Here

Kanyakumari is a successful tourist destination not just because of its location, but also due to the options that Kanyakumari offers its guest a tour of mesmerizing sights and relaxations. The town is full of natural splendors and man made attractions that have always beckoned travelers from around the world to experience the feeling that one possibly cannot get at any other destination.

Kanyakumari Beach

The Kanyakumari beach with multi-colored sand and rocky shoreline is definitely one of the most beautiful beaches in south India and offers a great change from all other beaches. The waves that hit the shore are quite strong and frequent, that means that one does not get to enjoy a step into the shallow water or a sea bath. The shore being rocky makes it more dangerous to venture out to the sea, so people are asked to stay within the prescribed zone. You can shop for shells that are on sale on the Kanyakumari beach. There is a lighthouse on the beach from where one can get a ravishing view of the sea.

Kanyakumari Temple

The Kumari Amman Temple also known as Kanyakumari Temple is located on the shores and is dedicated to a Goddess the incarnation of Goddess Parvati, the virgin goddess who did penance to obtain Lord Shiva as her husband. The main attraction for tourists from around the world is the scintillating view of the temple and the adjoining ghats, which are sitting pretty on the shoreline. The diamond nose-ring on the statue of the deity adds an enchanting glow to the already shining statue. Famous for its sparkling gleam, it is said to be visible even from the mid of sea.

Gandhi Mandapam

This is the place where the urn containing the ashes of Mahatma Gandhi was kept before a portion of which was immersed in the three seas. The exemplary temple is located near to the Kumari Amman Temple and is one of the most picturesque spots in Kanyakumari. The temple is build in such a way that on October 2nd, the birth date of Mahatma Gandhi, the rays of sun fall exactly on the spot where the urn containing the ashes is kept. So if possible choose this day to visit this splendid monument and witness the magical moment right in front of your eyes.

Vivekananda Memorial Rock

Situated some 500m away from the mainland Vivekananda Memorial Rock attracts a large number of tourists and was built in the year 1970 in memory the great Swami Vivekananda. It is built on the same spot where Swami Vivekananda spent some of his time meditating. Keeping this in mind, the temple also has a meditation hall. So if you want to get rid of all the worldly tensions, take some time out and sit in the hall meditating all your problems away. From ancient times, even before the temple was built, the rock was considered a sacred place and was known as 'Sripada Parai' meaning that the rock is blessed by the touch of feet of 'Devi Kumari'. Feel the spirituality of the place by sighting the divine footprints of the Goddess, which is visible on the rock.

Accommodation

Choosing an accommodation in Kanyakumari could be the easiest thing that you do in Kanyakumari. The number of hotel and lodges in the city is really astonishing. There are hotels that fit everybody choices and everybody's pocket. Pick any budget, luxury, beach resort, or a star category hotel and rest assured you would leave Kanyakumari satiated to your deepest. Hotels like Fishermen's cove, Temple Bay Ashok Beach resort and MGM Beach Resort are few that stand out in all areas of hospitality.

Getting There

By Air

The nearest airport is Trivandrum, which is some 80-km away from here. The airport is frequented by flights from all the major cities of India.

By Rail

Tirunelvelli is the nearest rail head around 80 km away. Trains from stations of Delhi, Mumbai and Trivandrum come to Kanyakumari through a broad gauge railway network.

By Road3

Kanyakumari is very well connected to all the major cities in the Southern India. Tourist buses, both luxury coaches and state transport buses ply in and out of Kanyakumari with good frequency.

Rameswaram Tourism

Rameswaram is an island on the tip of Indian Peninsula and is connected to the mainland at Mandapam by rail. The town is in the Ramanathpuram district. It also known as the 'Varanasi of the south'. The city is a major pilgrimage center for Hindus, both Shaivites and Vaishnavaites. It is here Lord Rama offered thanks to Siva. The main attraction of the town is the Ramanathaswamy Temple,which is one of the most important temples in southern India. The temple happens to be one of the twelve Jyotirlingas. It is also connected by one of India's engineering wonders, the Indira Gandhi Bridge. It took 14 years to build and was opened by Rajiv Gandhi late in 1988. Travelers will not have to face any problems as English is widely understood and spoken.

Rameshwaram has become a great tourist destination due to the presence of few of the most known architectural wonders of South India. Tourist throng to this city to witness the magnificent Ramanathaswamy Temple and Kothandaraswamy temple. Another place that attracts tourist is the Adam's bridge that is said to be created by Lord Rama and his Army to cross to Lanka. Its a chain of small islands that almost connect India to Sri Lanka. Tourist can also have a great time shopping as Rameshwaram is full of different and exquisite items. You can find a variety of ornamental items made up of palm leafs and sea shells. To appreciate the real beauty of these marvels, you have to see them all in front of your eyes.

One of The Four Dhams of Hindus

The great Sage and reformer of 8th century, Sri Shankaracharya(Adi Shankara), grouped the four most important temples towns of India and named them 'The Char Dham' (the four abodes). These four temple towns are Puri in east, Dwarka in West, Badrinath in north and Rameshwaram in South. It is said that one who travels to all these Dhams in a single tour, attains the ultimate salvation and is freed from the chain of rebirth cycle. These towns are considered to be the most sacred by Hindu religion and visiting them is considered a must for everyone before they set upon the final journey of their life. Rameshwaram with temples like Sri Ranganathaswamy Temple, and Kothandaraswamy Temple is definitely the most important of all the four. People from all over the world and of all religion come to Rameshwaram to make their lives relieved of all the sins of their past lives.

Attraction - Allures of Past Culture

Ramanathswamy Temple

Ramanathswamy Temple is a prime example of Dravidian architecture, the Temple has the largest temple hallway in India. Started in the 12th century, the construction of temple has contribution from many rulers who ruled this city at some point of time. The main attraction of the temple is the huge twenty-two wells. It is said that the water in these twenty-two wells all have different taste and even have curative properties. Take the golden opportunity and taste the water from the wells and experience it for yourself. Festivals like Maha Shivarathri, Thirukalyanam, Mahalaya Amavasai and Thai Amavasai all are celebrated with great energy and enthusiasm.

Kothandaraswamy Temple

Kothandaraswamy Temple is around 12 km away from town. The temple is dedicated to Lord Rama, Goddess Sita, Lakshmana, Hanuman and Vibhishna. This is the only structure that withstood the cyclone of 1964. It is said that it was here that the brother of King Ravana surrendered to Lord Rama.

Dhanushkodi

A place called Dhanushkodi is located at the eastern end of the island. It is named after Lord Ram's bow and is at a distance of 8 km from Rameshwaram. The chain of small islets and reefs in the sea between Sri Lanka and Dhanushkodi collectively are known as Adam's bridge. It is believed that Lord Hanuman and his army laid boulders and used them to reach across to Sri Lanka.

Erwadi

At a distance of 24 km from Rameshwaram, Erwadi is an important Muslim pilgrim spot. It is famous for the tomb of Ibrahim Sahid Auliya, which is located at Erwadi. Muslims from across the globe visit Erwadi, especially during the month of December to participate in the annual festival held to pay tribute to this saint.

Where To Put Up

There are ample hotels in Rameshwaram, both world class and budget. These hotels look after the needs of business travelers as well as vacationers with equal ease and quality. The hotels that stand out are Hotel Venkatesh, Hotel Maharaja and Tamil Nadu Hotel.

Getting There

By Air

The nearest airport is at Madurai around 163 km away. It takes around 3 hrs to reach Rameshwaram from Madurai. The transportation from airport to city center is not a problem.

By Rail

Rameshwaram is well connected by rail to cities of Tamil Nadu like Chennai, Madurai, Trichy and other major cities. Two important trains run daily in and out of the city from Rameshwaram to Chennai.

By Road

Buses to all cities of Tamil Nadu are frequent from Rameshwaram. Apart from State transport buses, Luxury coaches by Private operators also operate to and from the city.

Local Transport

Inside the city walls, you can hire a jeep or an auto rickshaw to visit all the major tourist attractions of Rameshwaram.

Thiruchirappalli Tourism

Situated at a distance of 320 km from Chennai and 150 km from Madurai, Tiruchirapalli, popularly known as Trichy, is a land of rich history and culture. Tiruchirapalli, the once fortress of Chola dynasty has retained its aura and exuberance that it used to enjoy earlier. The beautiful, massive temples dots this land, stand as icons and edifices of a prolific past. One sight of these temples is good enough to transport tourists into charismatic charm of its bygone era and experience the enchanting allure. Apart from temples, Trichy is also known for the famous and the fascinating Rock Fort, an architectural marvel that is built on a 83 m high rock, rising amidst the plains. This fort with a towering presence over the city has become a landmark that attracts a huge chunk of tourists into Tiruchirapalli. Undoubted, the center of attraction is Sri Ranganathaswamy Temple situated on an island in mid river, the temple complex covers an areas of whopping 250 hectares that makes it the largest temple in India.

With passing time, Trichy has developed itself into a dream destination for travelers. The helpful and caring people of the city and the pleasant climate add beauty to this already stunning city. Tourists who come to Tiruchirapalli never leaves this wonderful city without picking memorabilia and memories that can be savored for the rest of their lives.

Major Attractions - Abundance of Splendor

Tiruchirapalli is a temple town and its major attractions revolve round its magnificent temple architecture that have withstood the test of time and still have the same appeal and effect. The tourist with an eye for architectural beauty will have their time worth in gazing the largest Sri Ranganathaswamy Temple architecture and landmarks like Rock Fort Temple. Tiruchirapalli has surely made up its mark on international world map.

Rock Fort Temple

This temple sits pretty atop a mammoth piece of rock which rises from the plains, soaring to a height of 83 meters. The Rock fort temple is a combination of three temples, of which The Sri Thayumanaswamy Temple dedicated to Lord Shiva - halfway up is the most famous and visited temple complex by the devotees. The temple has a 100-pillared hall, and a Vimana completely covered with gold, which more often than not captures the imagination of the onlookers. There are several remarkable rock-cut cave temples on the southern face of the rock, dating back to the Pallava period, which perfectly compliment the resplendence of the Rock Fort. This temple site is also the chosen venue for the famous Carnatic wars between the French and English, which was fought around this rock.

Sri Jambukeshwara Temple

The Sri Jambukeshwara Temple is located 5 km from the town, dedicated to Lord Siva. The legend has it that an elephant worshiped Lord Shiva near the Jambu tree, hence the temple was named Jambukeshwara. There are seven gopurams and 5 concentric walls, which are completely covered with splendid carvings. These carvings are so life-like that they virtually transport the beholder into the past realm. It is built around a Siva Lingam, which is completely submerged in water that comes from a spring in the sanctum sanctorum. Although non Hindus are not allowed inside the temple, but such tourists can experience the structural beauty of the complex from outside which also is worth the time. The temple is open daily between 6 am to 1pm and between 4pm to 9.30pm.

Samayapuram Mariamman Temple

Samayapuram Mariamman Temple is located 12 km north of the city junction on Trichy-Chennai highway. The Maariamman Temple is one of the most visited shrines in Tamil Nadu. The temple is dedicated to Maariamman, who is a form of Goddess Shakti associated with prosperity and health. Locals believe that the deity cures diseases such as Small Pox and Chicken Pox. The walls of the temple have carvings of Goddess Shakti in her various manifestations and also other heavenly sculptures of various Gods.

Srirangam (Sri Ranganathaswamy Temple)

The temple of Sri Ranganatha is the largest temple in India. It is of great importance to all Hindus as it is considered to be the supreme temple dedicated to Lord Vishnu. The temple is located some 6 km from Trichy and is on the banks of River Kaveri. This 13th century temple is surrounded by seven scintillating rectangular courtyards and has 21 spectacular gopurams, among which Rajagopuram is the largest in India. The walls and surroundings of the temple are rich in brilliant carvings and wonderful paintings that have proved to be a great attraction for the tourists.

Accommodation

Trichy provides accommodation for all kinds of travelers. Hotels ranging from star category loaded with all modern facilities to budget lodges that cater to the basic needs with reasonable price. Hotels that stand out from the rest of the crowd are Hotel Sangam, Hotel Jenneys Residency, Hotel Aristo and Hotel Chitra.

Getting There

By Air

Tiruchirapalli has its own airport which is around 5 km from the city. All major cities of India have direct flight connection with Tiruchirapalli (Trichy). Flights to Colombo and Gulf countries also operate from here.

By Rail

Trichy is considered to be an important station of South India. It has trains running in and out of the city to all the main cities of Tamil Nadu and India.

By Road

Trichy has highways that connect the city to all major parts of Tamil Nadu. State transport buses regularly ply in and out of the city.

Local Transport

No problems in getting around Trichy. You will find ample of buses, taxis auto rickshaws and rickshaws that will take you to all the destination of your choice.

UDHAGAMANDALAM (OOTY) TOURISM

Situated at a distance of 105 km from Coimbatore, this Queen of Hill Stations is located in the Nilgiri Hills at an altitude of 7,347 feet above sea level. The weather being pleasant all rounds the year, attracting tourists through out the twelve-month period. The landscape of this beautiful land is dotted with rolling hills and plateaus completely covered with thick blanket of vegetation, tea gardens and different beautiful trees. This hill station was developed by the British as a summer retreat for them. The train ride to Ooty is another feature that has gained popularity among locales and international tourists alike. The ride on one of the few running steam trains will definitely take longer than other modes of travel like a bus or a cab, but the leisure journey in the train from Mettupalayam will definitely be the most scenic of all train travels that you have ever done. A must to do, while you are touring the Ooty hills. Apart from sightseeing, you can also indulge in many adventure activities like trekking and hiking through the woods.

Places To Visit - Nature At Its Most Generous

Ooty is called the 'Queen of Hill Stations' for very obvious reasons. This is the most naturally gifted part of Tamil Nadu and the most scenic of all hill stations in the whole country. Ooty offers plethora of attractions to keep tourist on their toes exploring, experiencing and enjoying the charismatic lure of this panoramic beauty. To be honest, the whole of Ooty is so ravishingly beautiful that there is no specific place that you can pin point as a tourist attraction, every ninch of the city is so mesmerizing that tourists keep turning their heads again and again towards whatever they see once. Most visited spots in Ooty are the Rose Garden, Government Botanical Garden and Doddabetta Peak.

Rose Garden

Maintained by Department of Horticulture, this is a must visit site for all nature lovers. The garden is at an elevation of around 2200-m above sea level and covers an area of 4 hectares. The garden has five terraces that have more than 2800 varieties of roses, the largest collection among any Indian garden. You are allowed to take photos inside the garden but you will have to pay extra for that.

Coonoor Sim's Park

This is a botanical park which is situated in the Coonoor town around 19 km away from Ooty. The park is located at a height of 1858 meters above sea level and covers an area of 12 hectares. The park showcases more than 1000 species from 85 families few of which, you will only find in this park like the rare species belonging to Eucalytus, Acacia and Cinnamomum. There is also a glass house that has many ornamental plants and flowers.

Ooty Lake

This artificial lake was built in the year 1825 by Mr. John Sullivan, the then district collector. The lake, around 2.5-km in length and 40 feet deep, offers options for both boating and fishing. Before you go for a boat ride, take care of your safety and get a life jacket. And if you are interested in fishing as well, don't forget to take prior permission from the officials.

Doddabetta Peak

The Doddabetta Peak is situated some 10 km from Ooty. It is at a height of 2623 m and is famous as the highest peak in Nilgiris.

It offers few of the most breathtaking views of the Nilgiri peaks that have made it one of the most visited spots in Ooty. Trek to the top peak as it is not very challenging, and at the same time provides views that are worth every step you take through the jungles.

Government Botanical Garden

This Botanical Garden is maintained by Government of Tamil Nadu, department of Horticulture. The Garden which was started in the year 1848 covers an area of 22 ha and is located at a height of 2250 m above sea level. The garden has been decorated with trees that have been collected from all over the world. It is home to rare species of trees like the Lily Pond and the Italian garden that bear colorful flowers. It also has the Cork tree, which is one of its kinds in India. Other attractions are the monkey-puzzle tree, called so because monkeys can't climb it and a 20 million year old fossil tree trunk.

Where To Put Up

Accommodation facility is good in the city with hotels ranging from five star to economy class being present here. All travelers are bound to find a hotel or a lodge that are according to their needs and tastes. Even the most basic hotels are priced aptly and take good care of their guests. Few hotels that can be recommended are Hotel Sinclairs, Hotel The Monarch, Sullivan Court and Sterling Holiday Resorts.

Getting There

By Air

The nearest airport is in Coimbatore around 100 km away. Coimbatore receives flights from all major airports in the country.

By Rail

Ooty is connected to Chennai by Nilgiri Express that takes tourist till, Mettupalyam. From there, you can either take a bus or a steam train. The surroundings on both the routes are breathtakingly attractive.

By Road

Ooty is well connected to all the major cities of Tamil Nadu and few cities of Karnataka. There is regular public and private bus services to and from Ooty.

Local Transport

Local buses, taxis and rickshaws are easily available that you can hire to roam around in the city.

Chapter 7

Orissa Heritage Tourism

Konark Tourism

Konark is one of the better known names that comes to our mind when we talk of Orissa. It is a small town in the district of Puri. Situated at a distance of 65 km from Bhubaneswar and 35 Km from Puri, Konark is easily accessible by all modes of transport. Konark is most famous for the magnificent Sun Temple that makes this small town, a really big name in the world of tourism. Though Konark is visited by tourists throughout the year, it still has a very clean and unhampered environment. The climate is also quite favorable throughout the 12 month period. The Konark beach also is a major attraction of the town.

Konark is host to an annual dance festival that is held here every December. Here, you will witness all classical dances of India like Bharatnatyam, Odissi, Kathak in all their glamour and poise. The performances are given by eminent dancers. The festival is held having the brilliantly floodlit Sun Temple as its background. Konark Dance festival beckons classical dance lovers from all parts of the world. Another festival that is held here is the Sun Festival or Magha Saptami. During the festival, devotees take holy dip in the sea before sunrise and worship Sun God at the Sun Temple.

Attractions - Magic Carved on Stones

There are not many attractions in Konark, but the few that are there, are among the best in Orissa. Apart from the famous Sun Temple, pilgrims also come to see the Mayadevi Temple which stands not too far away from Sun Temple. Tourists are not only attracted to these magnificent temples, they visit Konark to enjoy the beauty of nature on Konark Beach and to explore the history of Konark in the archaeological museum.

Major Attraction of the City : Sun Temple

Sun Temple, located in Konark, is probably the best known attraction that is there in Orissa. The temple was build by King Narasimhadeo in the 13th century. Sun Temple is also referred to as 'Black Pagoda' as it is build of black granite. The temple dedicated to Sun God was build as a chariot to him with wheels on all sides of the temple. It is one of the earliest places where Sun God was worshiped. Although few sections of the temple are now in ruins, but still the aura and the elegance of the temple is retained. Konark was once a busy port and many ships came and went. To Europeans, it served as a landmark who started calling the temple Black Pagoda. Sun Temple is considered a marvel among other temples and has been the inspiration for many writers and poets. Numerous books and articles related to its history and architecture have been written. Looking at the temple. Rabindranath Tagore, once said, "Here the language of stone surpasses the language of man".

HISTORY OF SUN TEMPLE

It is said that Sun Temple is built on the place where Samba, the son of Lord Krishna worshiped Sun God for liberation from a curse put upon him by his father. Legend has it that Samba was arrogant about his beauty and once made fun of a great sage Narada. Sage Narada planned to take revenge. He once lured Samba to the side of the lake where his step mothers were taking bath. Lord

Krishna came to know of this unacceptable act by his son. Infuriated, he cursed his son with Leprosy. When Lord Krishna realized that his son was tricked by Sage Narada, he asked Samba to worship Sun God, who is the healer of all diseases. Samba Worshiped Lord Surya on the sea coast. He spent 12 years of penance worshiping Sun God. After long, Surya God appeared and asked Samba to take a holy dip in Konark. As soon as he was relieved of Leprosy, he planned to built a temple dedicated to Sun God at the very same place where he appeared.

Architecture of Sun Temple

Few sections of the temple are now in ruins, but still major portions are still intact. The temple is an unparalleled example of medieval temple architecture. Sun Temple is a form of Vahana (vehicle) style as it is in the shape of a chariot. There are many such temples in India, however none come close to the magnificence of Sun Temple. The main temple structure stands on a platform. There are 12 wheels carved on the two sides of the platform. Each wheels is more than 10 feet in height. The spokes of the wheels work as sundials predicting the exact time of the day. Just stand under one of the wheels and feel the grandness of them. To complete the chariot, there are structures of 7 galloping horses at the entrance of the temple. These seven life size horses are a major attraction of the temple. Once you are close to the walls of the temple, notice the intricate carvings that have been done on the walls. There are images of God and Goddesses, men, women, warriors and scenes from day to day life. It is said that the temple was not build how it was envisioned. But some say that it was build exactly the way it was planned. The magnetic dome was removed from the top as it was causing many ships to crash around the shores. It is kept in the ASI (Archaeological Survey of India) museum for display.

Other Information

Sun Temple in Konark is close to both Bhubaneswar (64 Km) and Puri (35 Km). So it makes a easy reach to the temple by any mode of transportation. Closest airport is at Bhubaneswar whereas nearest railhead is in Puri. And if you are visiting Konark around December, do not forget to be a spectator at the electrifying Konark Dance Festival which showcases all Indian classical dances like Bharatnatyam, Odissi, Kuchipudi and many more. They are performed by dancers who have earned great appreciation for their work from around the world. You can visit Konark any time of the year, as it has a favorable climate throughout the 12 month period.

Sun Temple is one of the most celebrated temples in India. It has been the pride of Orissa since the day it was constructed. Considered as a marvel in temple architecture, Sun Temple is the most stunning structure on the shores of Orissa.

Other Attractions of the City

Mayadevi Temple

Situated to the southwest of Sun Temple, Mayadevi is an important attraction of Konark. It is not entirely clear as to whom the temple is dedicated. Some people believe that the temple is dedicated to one of Sun God's wives, while there are some who say that the temple belongs to Sun God himself. The walls of the temple have erotic sculptures carved on them. Also look at the precise carvings of dancing nymphs, court scenes, floral motifs and hunting scenes that adorn the walls of the temple. Two lion structures stand at the entrance and on either side of the temple you will see two gigantic elephant images. The structure of war-horse also increases the attraction of the temple remains.

Archaeological Museum

The museum in Konark belongs to Archaeological Survey of India (ASI). The present museum was started in the year 1968. You will find the sculptures and parts of Sun Temple that came apart from the main temple building. The museum has four galleries that showcase 260 antiquities that were found in and around Sun Temple. The galleries display sculptures like various incarnations of Lord Vishnu, image of Surya God in sandstone and many celestial nymphs. The other attraction of the museum are a huge structure of head of a crocodile, reconstructed temple wall and the Khandolite built reconstructed wheel. You will get to see images of numerous monumental sites of Orissa which are displayed in the corridors. You can visit the museum on all days except Fridays. The timing for the visit are 10 AM to 5 PM.

Konark Beach

The Beach in Konark is among the best on the eastern coast. With clear sands and shimmering blue ocean, Konark Beach which is named as chandrabhanga, is an absolute visual treat. The waterfront is an apt place to relax and unwind. The famous Konark Sun Temple is just few paces away from the beach and you take a walk and visit the temple. Though the scope for water sports is not much on the beach, but an evening walk on the beach is really soothing. Or you can just lie down on the golden sands and enjoy a sunbath while watching the local fishermen do their daily chores.

Where to Stay

Konark is one of the most visited towns in Orissa but still there are not many places to stay. It is probably because of its closeness to Puri which is a major city of the state. Though limited, there are good hotels to stay in. Main hotels in Konark are Panthanivas Tourist Bungalow, Sunrise Lodge, Yatri Niwas and Konark Lodge.

How To Reach Konark

By Air

Bjju Patnaik Airport in Bhubaneswar is the nearest airport which is at distance of 65 Km. Flights from all major cities of India are regular to and from Bhubaneswar. From airport, you can hire a taxi or take a bus for a one hour ride.

By Rail

Nearest railhead is at Puri which is at a distance of approximately 35 Km. Puri is connected to all parts of India with regular trains. Hiring a taxi is the best way of commuting between Puri and Konark.

By Road

Puri and Capital city of Bhubaneswar are both at close proximity from Konark. There are good number of transport buses as well as private coaches plying from both the cities.

Local Transport

Auto rickshaws, taxis and cycle rickshaws are there for roaming around in the city. Bus service is also good in Konark.

PURI TOURISM

Situated right by the side of Bay of Bengal, Puri is one of the oldest cities in eastern side of India. The city is at a distance of around 60 km from the capital city of Bhubaneswar. Puri is one of the four Dhams (Sacred places) in India along with Dwarka, Rameshwaram, and Badrinath. The presence of Lord Jagannatha Temple is probably the reason it is considered such an important pilgrimage destination. One thing that comes as a surprise is the appearance of many monasteries here. It is said that this port city once acted as the place from where thousands of devotees of Lord Buddha carried his message to far off places like Philippines and Java and these devotees built the monasteries.

Apart form the Lord Jagannatha Temple, Rath Yatra is another religious attraction of the city. Held in the month of July, it is a procession of Lord Jagannatha and his siblings from the temple to Gundicha Mandir which is at a distance of 3 km. One more thing that makes tourist visit Puri is the Puri beach festival. With many performances and classical dance shows, it is a perfect representation of culture of Orissa.

Major Attraction of the City

Lord Jagannatha Temple

Puri is one of the most visited cities of Orissa and Jagannatha Temple is its greatest attraction. The temple is an important pilgrim destination for Hindus. Jagannatha Temple is one of the four Dhams (most sacred places) in India along with Badrinath, Dwarka and Rameshwaram. The temple is dedicated to Jagannatha (Lord Krishna). The word Jagannath in Sanskrit means 'Lord of Universe'. There are three main deities in the temple, Lord Jagannatha, Goddess Subhadra and Lord Balabhadra. It is visited by devotees throughout the year but during Rath Yatra, the number increases many folds. It is probably the most exuberantly celebrated event of Orissa. Though only Hindus of Indian origin are allowed entry into the temple, one can admire the exceptional beauty of the temple from outside as well.

History of Jagannatha Temple

The construction of Jagannatha Temple started during the reign of Anantavarman Chodaganga Dev who was a famous ruler of Kalinga. Few of the portions were completed during his reign itself. However it was King Ananga Bhima Deva who reconstructed it and brought it to the shape it is in today. The rituals were carried on in the temple till 1558 when an Afghan General Kalapahad attacked . After sometime, when Ramachandra Deb formed an independent kingdom at Khurda, the images were reconsecrated. The Legend that goes with it is that Dharma found the original image of Lord Jagannatha near a fig tree. It was in the form of a Blue Jewel. The image was blindingly bright so he wanted to hide it in earth. King Indradyumna of Malwa wanted to find the image. And for that he performed penance for long and hard. Lord Vishnu then appeared and told him to look for a log on the coast in Puri. As advised, he came to Puri and found the log. There, Lord Vishnu and Lord Vishwakarma appeared as artists and carved images of Lord Krishna, Lord Balarama, and Goddess Subhadra from the log. These were the images that were consecrated in the Jagannatha temple.

Architecture of Jagannatha Temple

It is among the finest architectural works that still stand in Orissa. The temple is walled by a 20 feet high wall. The premises covers an area of around 40000 sq. feet and has more than 120 small temples inside the temple. Most of these temples are built in the Orrisan style of temple architecture. The main shrine is around 214 feet tall and is in a curvilinear shape. What will amaze you the most will be the 11-m high pillar, which is, located right at the entrance. This pillar has 16 sides to it and some magnificent carvings on it. The premises is divided into four parts, Bhogmandir, Natamandir, Jagamohana and Deul.

Other Information

Being situated in Puri, which is one the major cities in Orissa, Jagannatha Temple easily accessible. Puri is at a distance of 93 from the capital city of Bhubaneswar. For staying, there are many hotels and dharamshalas (low budget accommodations) around the temple. Only Hindus of Indian origin are allowed inside the temple premises. One can visit the temple throughout the year although best time is during the Rath Yatra in July when the festive mood in Puri is at its peak.

RATH YATRA

It won't be wrong to call this 'Festival of Chariot' the grandest festival to take place in India. Held at Puri every year in the month of July, it is one of the most important and awaited festival of Hindus. Full of colors and spectacle, the nine day festival never fails to mesmerize all who witness it. During the festival, Lord Jagannatha, Lord Balabhadra and Goddess Subhadra, who are the main deities of the Jagannatha Temple, are taken out on three gigantic chariots to Gundicha Mandir. This probably the only time when the main idols of deities are taken out of temple anywhere in India. Since the time the festival has started, it has amused not only Indians but foreigners as well. It is said that when Britishers first observed Rath Yatra, they were so intrigued by its atmosphere and energy, that they termed it 'Juggernaut'. Even today, people from all over the world, both Hindus and Non-Hindus, visit Puri to be one among the millions standing on the sidelines and behold the magnificent event.

Significance of Rath Yatra

'Rath' means chariot and 'Yatra' means procession or travel. There are many legends related as to why Rath Yatra is celebrated. Some say that Lord Jagannatha desired that he wants to visit his birthplace, Gundicha Ghar, once every year. Another story goes that, Lord Jagannatha once took his sister, Goddess Subhadra to show the beauty of Dwarka in a chariot, and this day is celebrated as Rath Yatra. There is one more legend according to which, Lord Krishna and his brother Lord Balabhadra went to Mathura on a chariot, accepting the invitation of his Uncle Kamsa. It is said that, one who sees the deities in the chariot will attain salvation.

Celebrations of Rath Yatra

The energy and enthusiasm with which Rath Yatra is celebrated is simply outstanding. It all starts when the idols of the three deities, Lord Jagannatha, Lord Balabhadra and Goddess Subhadra, are taken out in a procession. Listen to the sudden increase in the prayer chants of the people as the idols are brought to the three magnificent chariots waiting outside the temple. The chariots themselves are one of the main attractions of the festival. Humongous in size, the chariots are decorated extravagantly. Chariot carrying Lord Jagannatha is called Nandighosh Rath, chariot carrying Lord Balabhadra is called Taladvaja Rath, and chariot carrying Goddess Subhadra is named Padmadhvaja Rath. The chariots are not similar in build either. The number of wheels and the size of the chariots differ.

After seating all the idols, which itself takes hours, the traditional king sweeps the chariot with a golden broom. With this starts the pulling of the chariots by thousands of devotees. The chariots are taken to Gundicha Mandir which is located 3 km from Jagannatha Temple. All along the way, the devotees stand wherever they can find space, to get a glimpse of the deities. The atmosphere is simply magical and will take you deep into the feeling of devotion. After 8 days, the images of the deities are taken back to Jagannatha Temple from Gundicha Mandir in the same way they were brought here.

Tourist Information

Commuting to Puri during the festival time is not easy. Book yourself a ticket way in advance as crowd coming into the city is huge. Same is the case with accommodation as well. Most of the hotels would be full during the season. So it is better to make arrangements as early as possible.

Rath Yatra is one of the few festivals that beckon devotees from across the continents. The excitement and enthusiasm of the event is something that has to be witnessed to be felt completely. So become a part of this unique celebrations that will definitely be the most enthralling experience of your life.

PURI BEACH

Beaches in Puri are probably the best of all that are there on the eastern side of India. Tourists flock to the beach almost throughout the year, but the best time to visit the beach is during the famous Puri Beach Festival which is held early in November. This five day festival is a lot like the Goa festival with fashion shows and Rock concerts continuing throughout the night. There are also classical dance performances. In fact, the Puri Beach Festival turns out to be a perfect mirror of Orissa culture.

Sun Temple

Sun Temple, located in Konark, is probably the best known attraction that is there in Orissa. The temple was build by King

Narasimhadeo in the 13th century. Sun Temple is also referred to as 'Black Pagoda' as it is build of black granite. The temple dedicated to Sun God was build as a chariot to him with wheels on all sides of the temple. It is one of the earliest places where Sun God was worshiped. Although few sections of the temple are now in ruins, but still the aura and the elegance of the temple is retained. Konark was once a busy port and many ships came and went. To Europeans, it served as a landmark who started calling the temple Black Pagoda. Sun Temple is considered a marvel among other temples and has been the inspiration for many writers and poets. Numerous books and articles related to its history and architecture have been written. Looking at the temple. Rabindranath Tagore, once said, "Here the language of stone surpasses the language of man".

History of Sun Temple

It is said that Sun Temple is built on the place where Samba, the son of Lord Krishna worshiped Sun God for liberation from a curse put upon him by his father. Legend has it that Samba was arrogant about his beauty and once made fun of a great sage Narada. Sage Narada planned to take revenge. He once lured Samba to the side of the lake where his step mothers were taking bath. Lord Krishna came to know of this unacceptable act by his son. Infuriated, he cursed his son with Leprosy. When Lord Krishna realized that his son was tricked by Sage Narada, he asked Samba to worship Sun God, who is the healer of all diseases. Samba Worshiped Lord Surya on the sea coast. He spent 12 years of penance worshiping Sun God. After long, Surya God appeared and asked Samba to take a holy dip in Konark. As soon as he was relieved of Leprosy, he planned to built a temple dedicated to Sun God at the very same place where he appeared.

Architecture of Sun Temple

Few sections of the temple are now in ruins, but still major portions are still intact. The temple is an unparalleled example of medieval temple architecture. Sun Temple is a form of Vahana (vehicle) style as it is in the shape of a chariot. There are many such temples in India, however none come close to the magnificence of Sun Temple. The main temple structure stands on a platform. There are 12 wheels carved on the two sides of the platform. Each wheels is more than 10 feet in height. The spokes of the wheels work as sundials predicting the exact time of the day. Just stand under one of the wheels and feel the grandness of them. To complete the chariot, there are structures of 7 galloping horses at the entrance of the temple. These seven life size horses are a major attraction of the temple. Once you are close to the walls of the temple, notice the intricate carvings that have been done on the walls. There are images of God and Goddesses, men, women, warriors and scenes from day to day life. It is said that the temple was not build how it was envisioned. But some say that it was build exactly the way it was planned. The magnetic dome was removed from the top as it was causing many ships to crash around the shores. It is kept in the ASI (Archaeological Survey of India) museum for display.

Other Information

Sun Temple in Konark is close to both Bhubaneswar (64 Km) and Puri (35 Km). So it makes a easy reach to the temple by any mode of transportation. Closest airport is at Bhubaneswar whereas nearest railhead is in Puri. And if you are visiting Konark around December, do not forget to be a spectator at the electrifying Konark Dance Festival which showcases all Indian classical dances like Bharatnatyam, Odissi, Kuchipudi and many more. They are performed by dancers who have earned great appreciation for their work from around the world. You can visit Konark any time of the year, as it has a favorable climate throughout the 12 month period.

Sun Temple is one of the most celebrated temples in India. It has been the pride of Orissa since the day it was constructed. Considered as a marvel in temple architecture, Sun Temple is the most stunning structure on the shores of Orissa.

Chilka Lake

Chilka lake is the greatest endowment that nature has bestowed upon Orissa. Chilka Lake is the largest brackish water lake in Asia covering an area of around 1,100 sq. km. Although in dry seasons, the area of the lake comes down to 906 sq. km. Formed due to the silting action of River Mahanadi, the lake is separated from Bay of Bengal only by a small sandy ridge. There are 52 rivers and rivulets that drain into Chilka Lake. Chilka Lake is dotted with some wonderful small islands that make the lake more picturesque. Nalabana Island, Honeymoon, Island and Breakfast Island are the most famous of all. He Island of Kalijai is an important pilgrimage place as the Temple of Goddess Kalijai is situated here. The temple is the venue of a huge fair that attracts not only locales but tourists as well. The fair is held on the day of Makar Sakranti which falls in the month of January. The pear shaped lake has the richest and most unique range of flora and fauna. For this reason, Chilka Lake was recognized as a Ramsar Site, which means it has been designated as a wetland of international importance.

Flora and Fauna Attractions

Chilka Lake is one of the largest nesting grounds for migratory as well as residential birds in India. It also has one of the richest bio-diversity as well. The Nalabana Island has been classified as a Bird Sanctuary under the wildlife protection act. It is named as Chilka Bird Sanctuary. There are more than 150 species of migratory and residential birds here. It is said that, around a million migratory birds nestled here during the winter season. If you are an enthusiastic bird watcher, then winter season is the best time for you to visit Chilka Lake. Many rare and endangered birds are also in the list of birds that regularly visit Chilka. Migratory avi-fauna come here from as far as Siberia, Afghanistan, Iran and Himalayas. Few species of birds that have been found here are Flamingos, Egrets, Gray and Purple Herons, Storks and White Ibis, Spoonbills, Brahminy Ducks, Shovellers and Pintails. Avifauna is not the only type of life form that you are going to see here. Chilka lake is equally rich in aquatic life as well. More than 225 species of fishes have been recorded here. Irrawady Dolphins are also found here which are the most famous among tourists and kids.

Chilka Lake is also home to numerous aquatic as well as non aquatic plants. In a recent survey, more than 710 species of plants are found in and around the Chilka Lake. Such a huge variety of flora and fauna including numerous rare and endangered species of all forms has been the main reason for considering Chilka Lake as Ramsar site.

Tourist Information on Chilka Lake

To enjoy the beauty of Chilka, one needs to choose the best time to visit the lake. It is definitely during the months of October to June. It is during this period that the arrival of migratory birds is at its peak. The nearest airport to the lake is in Bhubaneswar around 120 km away and the nearest railway station is in Balugaon and Rambha. Cruising in the lake is the most indulged in activity by the tourists. Take a boat ride to all the islands which is definitely going to be a wonderful experience.

Staying Options In Puri : Toshalisands Hotel

Toshali sands Resorts has become a name synonymous with Puri. Located close to all the major tourist spots in Puri, the resort covers an area of around 30 acres. Toshali sands is the first 4 star hotel that has been approved by Department of Tourism in Orissa. The surrounding area of the resort is absolutely scintillating. Overlooking the panoramic Balukhanda Forest Reserve, the sights will surely leave you mesmerized. The resort has gradually become the most sought after place to stay in Puri. Here, you have the option of choosing to live in extremely lavish rooms or spend some high quality time in subdued yet remarkably decorated ethnic cottages. Though the outlook of the resort makes you think of it as a paradise for leisure travelers but the amenities that are there for business travelers and the service they get, simply leaves them stunned and on top of the world.

Accommodations

Toshali sands has given great care in appointing every room and cottage. There are many options that you can choose from here. Accommodation has been divided into different types, Deluxe cottage, Villa, Deluxe Rooms, Deluxe Suite, and Presidential Suite. For traditional stay, go for any of the 50 Deluxe cottages and for extremely lavish comforts, opt for any other accommodation. Room facilities that you will find in almost all types are TV, day long room service, telephones, mini bars, AC and most of all huge open spaces. The recreational facilities are also of top notch. In Toshali sands, you can enjoy the facility of gym, Ayurvedic massage center, outdoor games like tennis and badminton, water sports in the privately owned Balighai Beach. If you think that having kids along with you will hamper the enjoyment, do not worry. There is a separate kids section in the resort that will keep your kids engaged and happy, no matter how naughty they are. Puri is sometimes referred to as commercial center in Orissa. That means, the city receives quite a few business travelers as well. And with facilities like largest conference center in Orissa, ultra modern communication facilities, Internet service, well stocked library, secretarial service, Toshali sands has wooed every business traveler to the land of Lord Jagannatha. There are three different conference halls with different seating capacity. Indraprastha, which is the largest of all, can accommodate up to 400 people. Panchayat and Mantrana are other two large convention halls. A board room for 15 people is another luxury that the hotel offers.

Dining

Expect nothing less than the best for your stomach in Toshali Sands. It has one of the most celebrated restaurants in Puri. Named as Phulpatana, it is a multi cuisine restaurant. Get to taste the best of Continental, Chinese, Indian and Orissan cuisine. Phulpatana is largely famous for successfully experimenting. They offer dishes that you will not get anywhere else. It has a well stocked bar as well called Madhuban. It serves a range of Indian as well as foreign brands.

Tourist Information

Toshali Sands is situated right in the heart of Puri. It is at a distance of 20 km from the Jagannatha Temple 8 km from the Railway station and 3 km from magnificent Puri Beach. The hotel offers facilities to take you to day long excursions to Konark Sun Temple. It also offers trips inside the city as well.

Toshali Sands has set new standards for luxury, lavishness and services among the hotels of entire Orissa. The resort provides facilities that will make your holiday the moments to be remembered for the lifetime. Toshali sands will prove to be your home away from home with the difference of being a little more pampering, a little more mesmerizing.

Getting There

By Air

The nearest airport to Puri is in Bhubaneswar which is situated at a distance of around 56 Km. Indian Airlines and all major private airlines have regular flights to and from Puri. It receives flights from all important cities of India like Delhi, Mumbai, Kolkata, Bangalore and Chennai. From the airport, there is regular bus service to Puri. You can also hire a taxi.

By Rail

Puri has its own railhead which is one of the most important stations in East India. It has connections from all major cities of India. The station is situated close to the heart of the city and is accessible from all corners of the city.

By Road

Puri has good road network and is connected to all the major cities of Orissa. Bhubaneswar, the capital of Orissa is just 56 Km from Puri. State transport buses ply to and from all parts of the state.

Local Transport

Apart from buses, Puri has the facilities of taxis, cycle rickshaws and auto rickshaws to move around in the city.

Chapter 8

West Bengal Tourism

Storehouse of Myslical Splendors

A dream destination for vacationers, West Bengal is a gift of nature unlike any other. Nestling on the eastern side of India, West Bengal is bordered by Jharkhand and Bihar to the west and Nepal to north east and extends from Himalayas till Bay of Bengal. With such varied geography, West Bengal has some of the best hill stations crowning its head and exquisite beaches washing its foot. The most famed of all is Darjeeling; arguably the best tea producer in the world. Overlooking the mighty Mt. Kanchenjunga, it offers breathtaking views of sun rise on Eastern Himalayas. Along with the splendid Darjeeling tea, what brings glory to this jewel of East India is the Darjeeling Toy Train. Run by Darjeeling Himalayan Railways, the train has been operating for almost a century now and has been recognized as a World Heritage Site by UNESCO. Darjeeling is surrounded by many other scintillating hill stations like Kalimpong, and Siliguri.

Nature did not restrict its endowments to north of Bengal only. One of nature's best wonders lies abreast with Bay of Bengal. The world's largest mangrove forest and India's largest national park, Sunderbans, lies on the Gangetic plains. Sunderbans National park is famous for the mysterious Royal Bengal Tigers, coined the man eaters. The wildlife park has the highest number of Royal Bengal Tigers in India. This ecological giant is has been awarded the status of a World Heritage Site by UNESCO.

More than anything else, West Bengal flaunts its history and culture as its most prized possessions. Like anywhere else, West Bengal too is a mix of its past and present. However, there are not many places like Bengal where past glory is more prominent and stands with the same glory and aura. Especially the capital city of Kolkata, where century old buildings stand shoulder to shoulder with the flashy new glass buildings. The former capital of British India, Kolkata was earlier called as Calcutta. The greatest attractions of Kolkata are its heritages like Victoria memorial, Town Hall, the famous Indian Museum and Rabindra Setu (Howrah Bridge). The strategic position of west Bengal made it an important gateway into India. Not only did British come to India through here, many others like Portuguese and French too used Bengal as their settlement. They too left their mark on West Bengal which can still be seen. History of West Bengal is incomplete without a mention of legendary personalities that made the history so special. Noble Laureate Rabindranath Tagore, Bankim Chandra Chattopadhyay, and Satyajit Ray have all taken West Bengal to the world.

The state is called the cultural and intellectual capital of India. And if you wish to know the reason why, visit West Bengal during the five day Durga Puja celebrations held during September-October months, precisely during the Navaratris. The energy, enthusiasm and devotion will take you to a different dimension of experiencing. Religion of West Bengal is not the only aspect this festival shows us. It brings forth the exquisite cuisine, rich art and crafts, music and dance, traditions and creativity of Bengali people.

West Bengal is a state with uncountable attractions to see and even more things to do. A lifetime in West Bengal seems less to experience this one of a kind state in all its colors and fervors. Start your journey in West Bengal from any corner and by the time you are through with attractions of the state, you will crave to start it all over again.

West Bengal Heritage Trail

It would be a pleasant experience to travel down the corridors of history. The tour may begin with the historical remains of the ancient capital of Bengal -Gourand Pandua and seeing Bara Sona Mosque, Dakhil Darwajah, Qadam Rasul Mosque, Lattan Mosque, Gumti Gate, Firoz Minar, Adina Mosque and Ekiakhi Mausoleum.

Next comes Murshidabad, the seat of the Nawabs of Bengal, the prominent attractions being Nimak Haram Deohri, Khushbagh, Hazarduari, Great Imambara, Moti Jheel, Katra Mosque, Medina Mosque and WasifManzil. Krishnanagar, Bethuadahari, the Chandrodaya Temple at Mayapur and the Sonar Gouranga Temple at Nawadip attract tourists in Nadia District. The majestic Curzon Gate, now known as Vijoy Toran, the tomb of Sher Afghan and Golapbagh in Burdwan and the famous terracotta temples of Kalna, particularly the 108 temple complex dedicated to Lord Shiva, are amongst the chief attractions in Burdwan district.

The Viswabharati University at Santiniketan, established by Rabindranath Tagore, Sriniketan, a centre for traditional handicrafts and Bakreswar, famous for its hot springs are amongst the most famous in Birbhum district.

The temple town Vishnupur is famous for exquisite craftsmanship of terracotta art work evident on the numerous temples. Susunia Hill and Mukutmanipur Dam are the other attractions in Bankura district.

The undulating terrain woven with the forests and hillocks leading to Ayodhya or Panchakot hills make a happy sojourn to Purulia. Close to Calcutta and on the west bank of the Ganga are numerous attractions including the Ananta Vasudeva and Hanseswari temples, the Bandel Church (reminiscent of the Portuguese settlement), Chandannagar (reminiscent of the French settlement), Srirampore (reminiscent of the Danish settlement), Belur Math and the Botanical Garden at Shibpur.

KOLKATA TOURISM

Kolkata is a city that, in all senses, can be termed as India of past, of present and of future. No other cities, probably in the world show this striking difference between the economic conditions of people living in different parts of the city. On one hand, Kolkata is seen as a city reeling under poverty and human sufferings; and on the other hand, it is considered as the intellectual and cultural capital of India. Drive through Kolkata, and its history zips past you on every corner. Kolkata was the former capital of British India and one can still see the glimpses of that era in the numerous colonial buildings still dominating the surrounding landscape. Situated on the banks of the important Hooghly River, Kolkata was home few of the most eminent and legendary personalities like Noble Laureate Rabindranath Tagore, Philosopher Ramakrishna and well known film director Satyajit Ray. Today, one can visit Kolkata for India's most famous museums like Victoria Memorial, Indian Museum and Science City.

Kolkata is not called the cultural capital of India for no reason. Everyday in Kolkata is as good as a festival, let alone time when a famous festival comes up. No matter where you are, during Durga Puja celebrations, you just can't afford to be anywhere else than Kolkata. Every street, every corner, every house and every heart is drenched in multi colors of festivities. Kolkata is a heaven for food lovers with some of the best known restaurants and street food outlets in India. Don't forget to taste the fabulous 'RasoGulla', a sweet dish. The best time to visit

Shopping In Kolkata

In recent times, the rules of shopping in Kolkata has turned head over heels. What used to be a day long affair in the sweltering heat for Kolkatans; today is a pleasant experience in an air conditioned mall. Blink an eye, and there's a new mall ready to woo customers right in your neighborhood. Style and brand seems to be the mantra for the young generation. Forum Mall at Elgin

Road is the most famous of all malls; to which the credit of changing the tide goes. However, the old timers refuse to let go of their once a month trip into the hustle and bustle of the street markets. For them, it is still a family outing, shopping for their favorite dresses at the cheapest prices, bargaining till both parties exhaust and fix the deal at a mutual price and eating mouth watering spicy snacks at your regular restaurant joints. Some markets in Kolkata have stamped their authority as best place for shopping for a particular item. For Saris, Gariaghat, College Street, Park Street, Vivekananda Road and Rashbehari Avenue are the famous. For Jewelery, College street and Bidhan Sarani are irreplaceable. New market and Lindsay street known for leather items is more of a landmark for Kolkatans. And if you are looking for traditional Indian crafts, visit Central Cottage Industries Emporium at Chowringee. The range of price for which you will get things here is widest you could imagine of. So, throw away disappointment as an option when coming to Kolkata for shopping and expect nothing less than everything.

Accommodations In Kolkata

Hotel Taj Bengal

Being the capital city of West Bengal, Kolkata is home to the some finest luxury hotels in India. Accommodation of all the major hotel chains like Taj, Oberoi and Le Meridien are found here. They cater to the affluent sections of leisure and business travelers. Taj Bengal, Oberoi Grand Hotel and Hyatt Regency Hotel are the prominent amongst the many Deluxe hotels. For people who are more conscious of their spending, there are good budget hotels as well in the city that might not be as luxurious and pampering as the hotels mentioned above, but are lavish enough to make your holidays a memorable one. Peerless Inn, The Senator Hotel, Fort Radisson Resort and Rutt Dean are the best budget hotels in Kolkata.

How To Reach Kolkata

By Air

Kolkata has connection to all important cities of India and almost all countries of the world. Indian Airlines, Air Deccan, Kingfisher Airlines, Jet and Sahara Airways are the flight carriers that connect Kolkata to Indian cities and Air India connects the West Bengal Capital to all parts of the world.

By Rail

Kolkata is not only an important railway station for East India, it is one of the most important in entire India. Trains to and from all major cities like Delhi, Bangalore, Mumbai frequent Kolkata. You can also catch train to other important stations of West Bengal like Durgapur, Kharagpur, and New Jalpaiguri.

By Road

Kolkata is connected to all cities and towns by a networks of national highways. Depending on which destination you wish to depart to, you will get buses from the maidan near Chowringhee Road or from Bus stand at Babu Ghat. There are many more major bus stands in Kolkata but you will find more buses for inside the city.

Local Transport

Taxis are the most convenient way of commuting inside the city. Not only are they comfortable, they are easily available at all times. Buses also play a major role in city transportation. However, it is the metro that is the lifeline of Kolkata citizens. It joins every part of the city to each other.

Darjeeling Tourism

Situated at an altitude of 2134 m above sea level, Darjeeling is one destination for which any number of praising words seems inadequate. The town gets its name from Tibetan words 'dorje' and 'ling' which mean 'thunder' and 'place' respectively which makes Darjeeling 'The Place of Thunder'. The pleasant climate of this place attracted British officers who developed Darjeeling into their summer getaway. There are many places in this sedate town that hold on to the aura and tinge of its colonial past. And with many monasteries, Darjeeling has a touch of religion to it as well. But what glorifies Darjeeling in the world map today are its many varieties of tea. Plucked from different estates and in different seasons, the tea is of varying aroma and tastes.

When visiting Darjeeling, there are none better ways than by taking a ride in the charming toy train which runs on Darjeeling Himalayan Railway, recognized as a world heritage site by UNESCO

Attractions - Religion In Nature's Lap

Nature in itself is an attraction in Darjeeling. Dotted with some fantastic tea gardens, and deep running valleys, Darjeeling is one of the most widely toured destinations in entire East India. The Monasteries, the magical sunrise, the pleasant climate are all a part an non-exhausting list of attractions.

MAJOR ATTRACTIONS OF DARJEELING

Tea Gardens

Darjeeling Tea Gardens are famous not only in India, but in many countries of Europe as well. The entire town is dotted with some of the finest tea gardens known for their different types of tea. Tea from these gardens differ in their aroma, taste, texture and color. Happy valley Tea Estate is the most famous and one of the oldest tea estate in Darjeeling. Some tea plants are as old as 150 years old and you will be surprised to know that the youngest tea plant here is more than 80 years old. Black tea is the most renowned variety, however, Darjeeling oolong and green teas have also made it big in foreign Markets.

OTHER ATTRACTIONS IN DARJEELING

Tiger Hill

There are probably none better place than Tiger Hill in Darjeeling to view a gorgeous sunrise. Watch the sun rise glistening Mt. Kanchenjunga with its rays bathing it in golden hues. Situated at an altitude of nearly 8500 feet, Tiger Hill is the highest place in Darjeeling which can be reached by jeep or by trekking through Chowrasta. If you are lucky, you might just get to view Mt. Everest that peeps through two other peaks. One can also get a glimpse of snow covered peak of Chumal Rhi situated in Tibet. Do not forget to visit Senchel Sanctuary just few kilometers from here which is famous for two artificial lakes. The sanctuary is also the only breeding center of rare snow leopard.

Ghum Monastery

Situated just 8 km from Darjeeling, Ghum Monastery is the popular name of Sampten Choling Monastery in Ghum. Build in the year 1875 by Lama Sherab, the monastery belongs to the yellow sect of Buddhists and is most famous for its 15 feet high statue of Maitreya Buddha. One can see a huge Tibetan influence in the environment and prayer rituals.

Observatory Hill

Observatory Hill is the best spot from where you can get breathtaking views of snow clad Himalayas and Mt. Kanchenjunga. It is situated near Chowrasta Square which is more popularly known as 'The Mall'. This is original location of Bhutia Busty Monastery which today is situated at Chowrasta. This has made the Observatory Hill a revered site by Buddhists. There is a temple as well dedicated to Lord Shiva. The Temple of Mahakala is a sacred place for Hindus who are regular at the temple. Apart from beautiful views of Himalayas, one must visit Observatory Hill for shopping and for pony rides.

Accommodation In Darjeeling

Darjeeling has some of the nicest hill resorts around. Almost every resort provides you with basic facilities and spellbinding scenic views. There are many luxury hill resort that are more strategically placed close to city center. On a clear sky day, you can even get a view of Himalayas from the rooms of these resorts. Darjeeling is not a place where too many people come to work. However, some who wish to do their business amidst the picturesque hills, will find basic business facilities. Hotel Windamere, The Elgin Hotel, Hotel Sinclair are the luxury category accommodations and Dekeling Resort, Hawk's Nest, and Hotel Mohit are slightly cheaper and more affordable.

How To Reach Darjeeling

By Air

Bagdogra has the nearest airport to Darjeeling. It is connected to all the major cities of India like Kolkata, Delhi, Mumbai and Bangalore. Air Deccan, and Indian Airlines are the major flight operators to Bagdogra. It takes around 3 hrs from the airport to reach Darjeeling by road.

By Rail

New Jalpaiguri is the nearest major Railway station to Darjeeling. Although there is a railway station in Darjeeling but it receives only Toy Train from New Jalpaiguri. From NJP (New Jalpaiguri) station, the toy train takes nearly 8 hrs to cover the odd 80 Km journey.

By Road

You can hire a shared taxi or a shared jeep from Bagdogra Airport or New Jalpaiguri Railway station. You can also take a pre paid taxi from both these destinations which is the advised mode of commuting.

Local Transportation

Darjeeling is not a very huge town so you can visit the main destinations by foot itself. However, there are taxis and shared jeeps as well inside Darjeeling. Take note that taxis are not allowed to many parts of the town so it is better to ask before a local guide before you start your journey.

Howrah Tourism

Situated at an altitude of 2134 m above sea level, Darjeeling is one destination for which any number of praising words seems inadequate. The town gets its name from Tibetan words 'dorje' and 'ling' which mean 'thunder' and 'place' respectively which makes Darjeeling 'The Place of Thunder'. The pleasant climate of this place attracted British officers who developed Darjeeling into their summer getaway. There are many places in this sedate town that hold on to the aura and tinge of its colonial past. And with many monasteries, Darjeeling has a touch of religion to it as well. But what glorifies Darjeeling in the world map today are its many varieties of tea. Plucked from different estates and in different seasons, the tea is of varying aroma and tastes.

When visiting Darjeeling, there are none better ways than by taking a ride in the charming toy train which runs on Darjeeling Himalayan Railway, recognized as a world heritage site by UNESCO

Attractions - Making West Bengal Complete

The major attraction of Howrah are all places that hold an important position in the daily life of the people here. Be it the Howrah Railway Station or Howrah bridge. Not only are they a wonders that have stood th test of time and are great to look at, but they also are the lifeline of not only Howrah, but entire West Bengal.

Belur Math

Belur Math is a monastery dedicated to Ramakrishna Order. The monastery was started by the disciples of Sri Ramakrishna after his passing away. Earlier, the math was situated at a place called Baranagar. Then it was called Baranagar Math. After some time, the monastery was moved to Belur in the year 1899, by the great saint, Swami Vivekananda. The math is situated just by the side of Hooghly River and is an important religious center for Hindu Pilgrims. The architecture of this Hindu Monastery is also an attraction of the monastery.

Howrah Bridge

The magnificent Howrah bridge has been dominating the Howrah landscape from even freedom. Opened to Public in 1943, Howrah bridge is a cantilever truss bridge and one of the largest of its kind in the world. Constructed over Hooghly River, Howrah bridge connects the twin cities of Howrah and Kolkata. Earlier Howrah Bridge was a floating pontoon bridge built of timber in the year 1874. It was then replaced by the current bridge which was renamed to Rabindra Setu in 1965. Today, it is used by more than 150000 vehicles and 400000 pedestrians everyday. The best time to view the bridge is during night time when the entire bridge is illuminated. Though traveling on it might not be a very memorable experience as it is often jam packed with vehicles.

The Indian Botanical Garden

A single member of the Indian Botanical Garden has brought fame and glory to entire India. Indian Botanical garden, earlier known as Royal Botanic Gardens, is famous for a Banyan Tree that has made it into the record books for having the largest canopy in the world. Take a look at the tree from a distance, and you will find it to be more of a forest rather than a single tree. More than 250 years old, The Great Banyan Tree is approximately 51 feet in girth and covers an area of 257 feet in diameter. It is not the main trunk that covers such huge area. They are the aerial roots that are scattered all around the tree. There are nearly 350 such roots that have reached the ground each of which seem like a different tree and around 100 aerial roots are still to touch the ground.

Apart from the Great Banyan Tree, the botanical garden which covers an area of 285 acres has many other attractions. There are number of rare species of plants that are not found anywhere else in Asia. Inside the Palm house, one can find the Double coconut plant that produces the largest seeds known in the plant family. This oldest botanical garden in South Asia also has an artificial lake that is home to different species of fishes.

The Howrah Railway Station

Howrah Railway station is considered among the largest railway platforms in the world. The huge crowd, the facilities, and the olden day charm, all add up to make this truly a wonderful destination to visit. Started in the year 1854, the first train that departed from here was to Pandua the very same year. It is the first railway station to have started operating in East India. Today, it caters to all major cities in India. The station is divided into different sections, one is the old terminal from where trains to states further east and south east. The other is the new terminal from where trains to all other parts of India leave. Fro travelers, there is a government run lodge as well inside the station premises that promises to offer good facilities to its guests.

Accommodation In Howrah

There are ample good hotels in Howrah that you can choose for a comfortable stay. Being close to capital city Kolkata, many business travelers choose Howrah for their accommodation. To give them a successful stay, hotels of Howrah have added world class business facilities in their hotel. Hotel Balaji, Centaur Hotel, Hotel Cosy, Hotel Manish and Hotel Meghdoot are the better known hotels in Howrah. Most of these hotels are situated close to the main station in the city.

How To Reach Howrah

By Air

Kolkata is the nearest airport to Howrah which is adjacent to the city. Kolkata airport receives flights from all part of India and all major countries in the world. From the airport, you can either catch a bus or hire a taxi to your hotel in Howrah.

By Rail

Howrah Station is the most important station in West Bengal after the capital city Kolkata. In fact, Howrah is the gateway to Kolkata as all trains to the capital city pass through Howrah. There are trains to and from all major cities of India.

By Road

Howrah is well connected to all parts of the state by transport buses as well privately operated coaches. Howrah borders Kolkata which makes it quite easy to travel to the capital city. The distance between their city center will not be more than 25 Km. One can always go to Kolkata to catch a bus to other cities, but there is a major bus stand in Howrah as well.

Local Transportation

Howrah is one of the major cities in Kolkata that has a good transportation system inside the city. One can easily find buses that connect the entire city and ample number of taxis for a comfortable journey.

Shantiniketan Tourism

Shantiniketan is without a doubt the most serene and laid back town in West Bengal. Famous for the world renowned Vishwa Bharati University, Shantiniketan came into the picture when the father of Noble Laureate Rabindranath Tagore, Maharshi Debendranath Tagore came to this place , then called as Bhubandanga. The peace and tranquility attracted him so much that he built a home for himself and named it Shantiniketan which means Abode of Peace. It was here that Rabindranath Tagore indited many of his literary classics. With time, it became a spiritual center that attracted people from many parts of the world. The tranquil environment made it a suited place for meditation. Today it is one of the biggest attraction of the place. Since then, Shantiniketan has undergone drastic changes. The educational town is today considered to be an upmarket destination. Having a home here is a status symbol, so don't be surprised if you find huge and flashy bungalows belonging to noted personalities lining the streets. Still, there is no dearth of quiet places where you can spend some quality solitary time.

Vishwa Bharati University

Started as a school named Patha Bhavana, the ideas and ideology of Rabindranath Tagore has helped it grow into a university. His principle was that learning in a natural environment can be more enjoyable and fruitful. In 1913, after Rabindranath Tagore was awarded with Noble, the school was expanded further and was renamed Vishwa Bharati Unisversity. The university has given to the world leaders like Indira Gandhi, Satyajit Ray and Amartya Sen. There are many institutes under the university, the most famous of them all being the Kala Bhavana (Institute of Fine Arts). The time of any festival is best to visit Vishwa Bharati University, especially Basant Utsav (Holi). Students dressed in white clothes and drenched in all colors, sing and dance and enjoy without inhibitions.

Other Attractions

The house of Rabindranath Tagore is an important place that cannot be left out. Most of things are still kept the same way and not much alteration are done in the settings of the place. Feel the peace still prevailing inside the house. Another main attraction is the Poush Mela that is held here every year. It starts on the 7th day of Poush Month which generally falls around January. It marks the start of harvesting season. The three day fair attracts vendors from all parts of West Bengal and tourists from every corner of the world. Most of the sellers in the fair are the nearby tribals who bring with them handicrafts that most closely reflects the arts that prevailed decades ago, least influenced by western ways. You can also witness cultural performances as well in the fair.

Shantiniketan Tourist Information

Shantiniketan is situated approximately 211 km by road from the capital city Kolkata. There is regular direct bus service between the two destinations. By train, you can reach till Bolpur from Howrah. From Bolpur, Shantiniketan is just 2 km away. As staying options in Shantiniketan, there are number of tourist guest houses that are run by West Bengal Tourism department and a guest house run by Vishwa Bharati University. You can also opt for many private hotels in Bolpur which are available at reasonable prices.

Siliguri Tourism

Siliguri is one of the most important cities not only for West Bengal, but for many states of North East as well. Situated at a distance of 600 Km from Kolkata, Siliguri is at an altitude of 400 feet above sea level. This not too high and not too low altitude ensures a perfect climate for tourist activities. The second largest city of West Bengal after Kolkata, is the gateway to Darjeeling, the the most important tourist attraction of the state. It is from New Jalpaiguri station that one catches the famous Toy Train to Darjeeling. Siliguri lies at the foot of Eastern Himalayas providing some exceptional views of the snow clad mountains. Apart from visiting pilgrimage attraction like Kali Mandir, Wildlife Attraction like Jaldapara Wildlife Park and nature attraction of Mirik hill station, tourist can indulge themselves in shopping.

Shopping is undoubtedly an attraction in itself as choices and variety for items here is innumerable. Siliguri being at the border of West Bengal and North East, offers best of both cultures. Darjeeling Tea the most shopped for item here, it is closely followed by Tibetan paintings, woolen garments and wooden handicrafts. The best place for shopping in Siliguri is Hill Cart Road and Sevoke Road. Do not forget to take a look at the electronics market here which is famous by the name of Hong Kong market. You will find surprisingly low cost gadgets that will compel you to grab hold of almost everything.

Attractions - Nature At Its Best

Though Siliguri is not as famous as Darjeeling for its tourist attractions but one can not skip Siliguri as few attractions that are there, are simply outstanding. Jaldapara Wildlife Park is the most widely visited attraction of this town.

Kali Mandir

Kali Mandir of Siliguri is an important temple for Hindus which is situated near Sevoke. The temple is said to be the abode of living Goddess Kali. The temple is visited not only by locales but by pilgrims from adjoining areas as well. However, it is most famous among newly weds who come here to attain blessings of Goddess Kali for happy married life.

Jaldapara Wildlife Sanctuary

Spread in an area of nearly 216 sq. Km, Jaldapara Wildlife Park is at a distance of 140 Km from Siliguri and is situated in the Jalpaiguri District. The wildlife park is famous for the endangered one horned rhino. Jaldapara Wildlife park is cut by passing River Torsa making a large part of the park a marshy land, a perfect setting for thriving of one horned rhinoceros. Jaldapara park holds the most number of one horned rhinoceros after Kaziranga National Park in Assam, though the difference between the numbers is mind boggling. Royal Bengal Tiger, leopard, spotted deer, elephants and gaurs are the other main attraction of the park. When visiting the park, do not forget to carry along a binoculars, as Jaldapara is a magnificent spot for bird watching. Famous for Bengal Florican, other birds that can be seen here are paradise flycatcher, crested eagle, fishing eagle, peafowl, racket tailed dongo and many more. The best way to explore the wildlife of the park is by taking an elephant safari deep into the jungle. Jeep safaris are also organized inside the park but not many parts of the park can be covered by jeep because of the marshy nature. During monsoons, that is from June 15 till September 15, the park remains closed to the visitors. On general days, the park is open from 9 AM till 4 PM.

Mirik

Mirik is a perfect option for excursion from Siliguri. Situated around 55 Km from here, it takes nearly an hour and a half to cover the distance. Mirik is a picturesque hill station which has in recent years, become a must visit destination in West Bengal. The main attraction of this quaint hill station is a centrally located natural lake called Sumendu Lake. Tourist can indulge in boating and fishing in the lake which is approximately 1 Km long. While boating, enjoy the views of magnificent green hills that surround the lake from all sides. Mirik is an important pilgrimage destination with revered Hindu Temple of Sangla Devi being present on the western side of the lake. This hill station is dotted with many apple orchards and tea gardens.

Coronation Bridge

Built in 1930, Sevoke Coronation bridge is still considered among the best architectural wonders in the country. The Coronation Bridge was built by Britishers to connect West Bengal to North East India. The Bridge is built over River Teesta and stretches from Salugara till Kalihora. Situated around 20 km from Siliguri, the Coronation Bridge gives us breathtaking views of River Teesta below and high green mountains on both sides.

Accommodation in Siliguri

Siliguri is one of the most important cities in West Bengal as it is virtually the gateway to many tourist places in the state like Darjeeling and Kalimpong. Siliguri is also one of the most developed cities of the state. Therefore it receives both tourist as well as business travelers. To cater to the needs of both categories, Siliguri has good luxury and budget hotels with splendid leisure and business facilities. The appealing feature of Siliguri hotels are that even luxury hotels are quite reasonably priced. Hotel Sinclairs, The Cinderella Hotel and Viramma Resort are the major hotels in the Siliguri.

How To Reach Siliguri

By Air

Siliguri has its own domestic airport which is situated in Bagdogra at a distance of 12 Km from city center. Jet Airways, Indian Airlines and Kingfisher Airlines are the main flight operators to Siliguri. There are flights connecting Siliguri to Delhi, Mumbai, Kolkata and all other major airports in India. There is a regular helicopter service as well to Gangtok.

By Rail

New Jalpaiguri station is the nearest railway head to Siliguri, situated just 16 Km south of Siliguri. Jalpaiguri Station is connected to all major stations in the country like Delhi, Mumbai, Bangalore with regular train service.

By Road

Siliguri is nearly 600 km away from the capital city Kolkata. There is regular bus service to Kolkata and to many other important places in West Bengal like New Jalpaiguri and Kharagpur. Private coaches as well as transport buses are operational between the cities. It is also connected to cities in North East India as well like Gangtok.

Local Transportation

Along with splendid bus facility inside the town, there are numerous jeeps as well that cater to locales and tourists. These jeeps generally run on shared basis.

Hotels and Resorts of West Bengal

Hotels of West Bengal are considered among the best in entire East India. There is no shortage of hotels in the state, neither is there any dearth of the varieties found here. West Bengal has always seen the biggest names form all walks of life visiting the state for reasons as diverse as the state itself. Some come here to explore the many natural wonders that dot the entire length and breadth of the state, some are here just to feel the colonial atmosphere that still holds on strong in many parts of the state. They are the leisure traveler who expect to have some jolly good time. Then there are business travelers who wish to get the best facility to make their trip a successful one. Looking at the requirements of both, West Bengal has hotels that cater to the needs of both groups.

The facilities provided by the 5 star deluxe hotel in the capital city Kolkata and other important cities of the state are at par with the global standards. And when teamed up with gratifying services, the hotels become the key ingredient for a memorable holiday. Another splendid feature of West Bengal hotels that adds up to the list of facilities of the hotel is their location. For a hill resort, a solitary location amidst the beautiful locations, is a rejuvenation facility and a suburban location in a posh locality is a boon for the luxury business hotels. Almost all hotels have rejuvenation facilities like swimming pool, gymnasiums, health centers, amenities for indoor and outdoor games. And for business people, expect huge and spacious conference rooms that can accommodate large number of people at a stretch which are equipped with the most modern communication and multimedia systems. Most of the hotels and resorts in the state are decorated in themes corresponding to the unique and rich culture of West Bengal.

The telling factor that makes the West Bengal hotel stand out apart is the tremendous cuisine of the state. The variety in both veg and non veg dishes is simply breathtaking. And no where else will you find tastier fish curries and the famous Rasgulla, the favorite sweet dish of entire India. In luxury hotels, there are multi cuisine restaurants that give you the best of many worlds.

West Bengal hotels have become a great asset for the state that earns a lot its revenue through tourism. Whether it is a hill resort, a jungle resort, a beach resort or a deluxe luxury hotels, all have provided their guests with facilities that are considered best in the business. Sometimes used a base for entire East India travel, Bengal hotels are in a league of their own.

Staying Options In West Bengal

Taj Bengal Hotel, Kolkata

As is the case with all Taj hotels in India, Taj Bengal in Kolkata too, is way ahead of its competition. This luxury 5 star hotel is the best option not only for leisure travelers, but for business travelers as well. What Taj in all states are known to do are, design their interiors in such a way that reflects the true culture of the state. Taj Bengal too makes all the effort to give the hotel a Bengali touch to it and comes up with the goods. Right from the lobby, to the last corner of your room, the hotel is decorated with the most luxurious setting. It also boosts of few of the best restuarants and bars in the city. Taj Bengal is virtually a heaven for business travelers as it has huge conference halls equipped with the most modern facilities one could ever wish for. The hotel also takes pride in being host to many head of states, international business travelers and dignitaries.

Accommodation

Taj Bengal has 228 rooms and 16 suites, all of which are centrally air conditioned. The rooms are divided into different categories on the basis of facilities provided in them. There are superior rooms, deluxe rooms, luxury rooms, Taj club, executive suites, luxury suites and presidential suites. Facilities like dual line phones, mini bar, personal tea/coffee makers, electronic safes, data port, wireless Internet connection and sound proof windows are basic in all rooms. In luxury rooms and suites have better business facilities like fax machines, telephones with voice mail, one way airport transfer, a bottle of wine on check in, control panels for lights and curtains, and ample of well organized space. In Presidential suites, you get separate bedroom, sitting place, dining room and an additional private terrace. Leaving the coziness of these magnificent rooms, come out to find far more pampering awaiting you. You can avail the facilities of bookshops, fitness center, live band performance, nightclub, swimming pool, jacuzzi, steam sauna and much more.

There is a different section for kids as well so you need not worry of them getting bored. For sports buffs, there is facilities for golf, squash and tennis.

Business center in Taj Bengal is considered among the best in East India. There are 6 banquet halls that can accommodate up to 800 people in different seating styles. They are equipped with the hi-tech and latest broadband Internet connectivity, multi media computers, laptops, copier and secretarial service that promise you a successful stay here.

Dining

In Taj Bengal, you have access to some of the best restaurants and bars in Kolkata. Chambers restaurants which is strictly for its members and hotel residents, serves delicious Continental and European cuisine, Chinoiserie offers great Oriental foods and to taste specialty Indian cuisine, you can visit Sonargaon. You can enjoy different flavors of tea and coffee along with watching the displayed art works in Tea Lounge named By The Way. Junction Bar designed in a railway junction theme, serves rare whiskeys, exotic vodkas and martinis. Enjoy these special drinks while enjoying a live band performance. The Hub is the main restaurants that has been awarded the best restaurant in Kolkata. Though it serves all cuisines, it specializes in Italian.

Tourist Information

Hotel Taj Bengal is located on Belvedere Road, opposite to Kolkata Zoo. It is situated around 25 Km from International airport, 15 Km from the railway station and only 10 min from the city center. The hotel falls in the path of many bus routes, so you can reach the hotel form any corner of the city.

So if you are traveling to any part of East India, then you don't have to think twice for choosing a place for comfortable stay. Just pack your bags and come to Taj Bengal. They have served dignitaries from all fields, now it is your chance to get the same special attention and pampering.

HOTEL WINDAMERE, DARJEELING

Referred to as a jewel of Raj, Windamere Hotel, Darjeeling is one of the most well known hotels among foreign travelers. Started as lodging for English and Scottish tea planters in 19th century, it was converted into a hotel only during the time of Second world war. Withstanding the test of time, Windamere hotel has not only remained functional, it has retained its olden day charm and elegance, and has become a dream destination for travelers to Darjeeling. The intimidating views of the snow clad mountains of the great Himalayas is what keeps tourists attracted to this heritage hotel. Everyday that is spend in Windamere, the morning starts by witnessing the sun rising on the horizon, coloring the giants with their golden rays. Every room is decorated in a way to give the guests the feel of yesteryears. During the first ever national award ceremony for hotels, the Windamere hotel was awarded for its excellent achievements as a heritage hotel. Windamere sees most rush coming in during its Christmas celebration which starts from 18th December till 1st January. Every year, performers from famous West End Theater of London come here to entertain the guests. Not only Indians, it is famous among the foreign travelers as well.

Accommodation

Accommodation in Windamere Hotel is unlike in any other hotels or resorts. The hotel accommodation is divided into two wings, Windamere and Little Windamere. The division here is not based on the luxuries that are provided, but on the the solitude of the cottage. The Windamere wing is preferred by people who like not to be disturbed by anyone during their stay or by people who wish to relive the ages gone by. The rooms are decorated to give an ambiance of the Darjeeling during the British era. There are no TVs or telephones in the main house called Ada Villa. Telephone facility can be provided on request, but that too in the Annexe. Then there is other group of people who like to have even more privacy, not for the above reason though. The newly wed couples most of the times book for Tinker Belle's cottage which is also called as Honeymoon cottage. These cottages are at a slight distance away, located above the Ada Villa. The Little Windamere wing however has all such modern facilities and have telephones and televisions. Although the setting of the room keeps you in touch with past and royalty.

Windamere hotel has its own set of performing artists who bring alive the evenings which are sometimes chilly. They perform 'The Songs and Dances of Hills' or put forth a stunning and soothing Ghazal performances. They are generally performed in the open area of the hotel called Bearpark Parlour. There is a library as well for the members that stocks books related to travel and facility for slide and video viewing. The Itati Institute which is a centre for well being of mind and body offers space for rejuventaion.

For business traveler, if they could help themselves from not not getting distracted by the enchanting beauty of Darjeeling, there is no better place to hold meetings and conferences. Windamere hotel provides splendid business facilities. There are 5 conference halls, The Centre's Fred Pinn Room, The Henry Carpenter Room, The Pinnell Board Room, The Director's Lounge, and the Hill Charm meeting room seating 40, 20 , 10, 16 and 60 people respectively. All these rooms have hi tech projection equipment and Internet facility.

Dining

In Windamere Hotel you get the best starts to a day that you could wish for. Sipping on a glass of freshly picked tea, and that too Darjeeling Tea, is not something that happens everyday, though you would wish it was so. The restaurants in the hotel serve food that have a distinct western aroma to them.

Tourist Information

Windamere Hotel is situated on the Observatory Hill, overlooking Chowrasta. Bagdogra is the nearest airport from where a 3 hr drive is needed to reach the hotel. From New Jalpaiguri, one can catch the famous toy train, a world heritage site to Darjeeling.

Darjeeling Railway station is just half a kilometer away from the hotel.

West Bengal Tour Packages

The hardest part of traveling in West Bengal is to choose which places to visit. So much is on offer in West Bengal that picking the best becomes a bit hard. This is a state rich in history, culture and natural beauty. Nestling on the foot of Eastern Himalayas, West Bengal proudly presents its many hill stations as its best kept treasures. Darjeeling being the most important of them all. Apart from the views of mighty Himalayas, the state shows off its history as another major tourism aspect. Kolkata, the present capital of West Bengal, was the former capital of British India. It still has many architectural wonders which were built during British Rule. The past seems to come alive in West Bengal.

To relieve you of your tensions, there are some well thought out tour packages that will ensure that you don't miss out on the best, while exploring the great. You name it, you get it, seems to be the mantra of West Bengal. If you are looking for adventurous holiday, take up an adventure tour; if you are a nature lover, tour packages taking you to many national parks will serve you the best; and if you are short on time but still like to get the taste of the everything, you will find specially designed packages just to your liking. Not only do they take you to all the important destinaions of West Bengal, the main feature of these tour packages is that their duration can be altered if tourists wish for it. Most of the time, the tour gets longer and covers more. Even when there are tour packages that cater to wildlife parks of West Bengal; there are special packages that take you only to Sunderbans National Park. Exploring the largest national park of India, truly is an experience that can't be skipped.

All these tour packages deliver everything that they claim they do, but these tour packages are also filled with small moments that make the entire trip even more sweeter. Like starting your day with a hot cup of freshly picked Darjeeling tea, or getting the views of sun rising on Mt. Kanchenjunga, might not be mentioned any where, but are very much the part of the these tour packages. Uncomplicated and uncompromising, the tour packages are the unparalleled way of exploring the mystical state of West Bengal.

Chapter 9

Heritage Tourism Categories

Pilgrimage Tourism

The multi hued country, India is probably the ultimate destination of all kinds of pilgrims following any faith around the world. The great religions like Hinduism, Buddhism, Jainism, Islam, Christianity and Sikhism are the integral part of Indian culture and heritage whose values and faiths are mingled with the air, soil and the sky of India. You can feel the blissful serenity of the Indian atmosphere where Lord Buddha, Mahabir Jain, Shri Sathya Sai Baba and Guru Nanak once walked turning the Indian soil pious and blessed at the different circle of time wheel. There are numerous destinations in India which are considered sacred by people following different faith because of their religious importance. A visit to the Kedarnath or Badrinath will take you to the Himalayas which is believed to be the abode of 330 million gods and goddesses and you can feel the immense divinity in the air itself. It is widely believed that after breathing in the holy atmosphere of Varanasi or Haridwar or taking a dip into the sacred Pushkar Lake or river Ganges washes away the sins and helps one to attain nirvana (salvation). The divine Buddha pilgrimages, Bodhgaya and Sarnath are the destinations of thousands of Buddhist pilgrims every year coming from each and every corner of the earth.

A pilgrimage tour in the divine land of India will surely bring all the faces of Indian devotions and you will be moved by seeing the unconditional faiths and beliefs of the Indians foı the God, who may have any name or identity. Your spirituality and devotion is sure to attain a new height after a pilgrimage tour in India and who knows, you may return home with an enlightenment which you have searched for all your life.

Ajmer Tourism

Ensconced in the famous Aravalli ranges, Ajmer exudes bustling life with its engaged market places and moving (and obstructed) traffic. One specific street sells just silver items!

A religious place with a famous dargah of a pious Muslim saint, Ajmer is known to fulfil the wishes of many a disheartened soul. The qawwalis at the dargah on Thursday and Friday nights (and also during Urs festival) inspires the spirit of devotees and tourists like never before. The history of city reveals changing of ruling dynasties, from Chauhan Rajputs to Ghoris, Mughals and finally British.

The city has numerous other attractions in store for tourists. The famous Mayo college established by British had the Maharaja of Alwar as its first student. The Maharaja arrived in a true royal style, seated on an elephant and followed by a whole fleet of servants, trumpeteers and not to forget camels and horses! One remarkable example of the countless eccentricities of the Maharajas and Nawabs of India.

Ajmer also provides a good base for a day visit to Pushkar. Infact, the city provides shelter (whatever little facility it has) to considerable number guests during the highly famous Pushkar festival.

Pushkar Tourism

Myths and legends float throughout India and Pushkar is no exception. The holy lake here is believed to have appeared miraculously when a lotus flower fell off from the hands of

Brahma. The name itself draws from the flower that fell off - Puspa meaning flower and kar meaning hand. But legends do not end here. The story also has inputs from Goddess Savitri, wife of Brahma. After all, it was she who made Pushkar the land of Brahma, the only place where he was to be worshipped by future generations.

Pushkar today is an esteemed religious destination for Hindus and Brahma highly venerated god here. Around 400 temples and 52 bathing ghats make other attractions of the city appear dwarfish. The nights do not have just stars to sparkle up the atmosphere, rather there are deep rooted faith in the hearts of devotees that makes this place radiate with unparalled charm.

The Pushkar fair is a riot of colours, especially red and yellow. Turbans, lehangas and dupattas seem to fill the entire atmosphere with bright enthusiasm. The atmosphere is charged up as if the accumulated enthusiasm of the people throughout the year has finally found expression. It is a time when tribals, general tourists and filmakers from all over the world make a beeline for Pushkar. Giving them company are thousands of camels, horses, goats and sheep. And behold! they come completely decked up and walk with a panache that eludes even the most confident person around. No wonder, they are the celebrities of this fair.

Explore Pushkar, a small place on foot or on a bicycle. Some really good experience lay hidden in this mystical town.

Haridwar Tourism

Haridwar - the land that signifies god. It is one of the twelve most holiest places revered by Hindus and also believed to be one amongst the seven cities touched by god. Numerous legends are associated with every holy spot in Haridwar and that is what makes every bit all the more captivating. An ancient city, it finds mention in most old scriptures like in the writings of first millennium Chinese traveller, Hyuen Tsang.

At no time of the year you will find it devoid of any devotees. Reasons are many. For one, Haridwar is the place where Ganga first enters the plains. It is one of the four venues of Kumbh Mela

(Nasik, Prayag and Ujjain being the other three) which is held once at each of these locations in twelve years. It is also the location of some of the ancient schools of tradition, the original kind of gurukuls, where ayurveda is taught. The entire landscape is dotted with Siddhapeeths and Shaktipeeths as well as old and new temples.

Getting There

By Air—The nearest airport from Haridwar is Jolly Grant Airport near Dehradun, 35 kms from here.

By Rail—Haridwar is connected with all the major cities via train. Haridwar railway station is halt of some major trains coming from Ujjain, Delhi, Mumbai, Varanasi, Calcutta, Allahabad, Gorakhpur and Sri Ganganagar. The trains from and to all these cities are till Dehradun and halt at Haridwar.

By Road—Haridwar is amongst the most easily accessible cities. It is located on National highway number 45. There are state run buses from some major cities, or one can also arrange his own conveyance. Distance from some major cities is Delhi - 214, Agra - 386, Ambala - 168, Badrinath - 325, Dehradun - 52, Kedarnath - 250, Saharanpur - 81 and Nainital - 386.

Badrinath Tourism

Protected by two mountain ranges 'Nar' and 'Narayan' on either sides is the holiest of pilgrimage place of Hindus, Badrinath. With Neelkanth peak forming a beautiful backdrop, Badrinath, the abode of Lord Vishnu is in the itinerary of every devout Hindu. It is one of the four pilgrimage places called Chardham which every Hindu must undertake to attain salvation. The place is called Badrinath because of the wild berries found here ('badri' means berries). The Badrinath temple here is the main complex where devotees seek blessings. Every year thousands and thousands of pilgrims pay a visit to this place in summers, since due to snowfalls, the temple remains closed during winters. At an altitude of 3,133 metres, it is a difficult journey to this place yet faith defies every hurdle on the journey to salvation. The temple stands facing River Alaknanda on its banks. Facing the temple near the river is Tapt Kund, a thermal spring where people refresh before going to the temple.

The Legend

The legend behind the famous temple is that Lord Vishnu after being reprimanded by Narad for indulging in worldly pleasures came here at Badri van to meditate for penance. The place at that time used to be covered with wild berries and was called Badri Van. The main deity worshiped here is a meditating Vishnu. Also according to the mythology, when goddess Ganga was requested to descend on earth, her flow was so strong that earth could not with stand it and hence to reduce the flow it passed through the locks of Lord Shiva and was divided into many streams, River Alaknanda is one of the streams on the banks of which later Lord Vishnu came to meditate.

Badrinath Attractions

The Temple

The main temple where people seek blessings is dedicated to Lord Vishnu. The temple is considered to be here since Vedic times. However according to the history, Adi Shankaracharya established it here in 8th century. The present structure of the temple was built three centuries ago by Garhwal kings. It is a five metre high complex built like a cone with a small cupola of gilt bull and spire.

The temple has three sections to it, a Garbha Griha or the sanctum sanctorium where the main deity rests, a Darshan Mandap for puja and a Sabha Mandap for devotees to assemble. In all there are 15 idols in the complex, all in black stone. These consist of idols of Lakshmi, Vishnu's wife, Garud, his mount and Lord Shiva, his wife Parvati and and son Ganesha. The idol of Lord

Vishnu is sitting with crossed legs in a meditative posture, his hands folded.. Its often argued that it is an idol of Buddha, though Buddha is considered to be the ninth incarnation of Vishnu himself.

The temple remains closed in winters when the entrire area gets under snow cover and opens only in summers (sometime in April-May). The temple has been damaged many times due to avlanches and has been rennovated time and again. Presently its facade is quite modern and colourful, a Singh Dwar (main gate) adorns its entrance.

Panch Badri

The main temple of Badrinath along with four other temples or Badris forms Panch Badri , Panch meaning five. The temples of these other badris are located within few kilometres of the temple of Badrinath. Yog Dhyan Badri is located 24 kms from here at Padukashwar(1920 mts). Pandavas handed over their empire to King Parikshit here before retiring.

The second Badri is Bhavishtya Badri at Subain near Tapovan. Bhavishya Badri means future badri. It is beleived that a time will come in history when the present route to Badrinath will become inaccessible and then Bhavishya Badri will be worshipped instead. Adi Badri is the remains of 16 temples, it can be reached from Karnprayag. And lastly Vriddha Badri, situated 7 kms from Joshimath, is believed to be here several years before the existence of Adi Shankarcharya, idol of Badrinath was enshrined and worshipped here.

Other Attractions

Tapt Kund

These are the natural thermal springs on the bank of Alaknanda River where pilgrims refresh before visiting the temple. Believed to be infused with medicinal properties, Tapt Kund is also considered to be holy expereince.

Brahma Kapal

This is a flat platform on the bank of river Ganga where devotees perform rites of their deceased ancestors.

Sheshnetra

Sheshnaga is a legendary character in the Hindu myhtological epics and tales of Lord Krishna. The palce has a boulder on which an impression is believed to be of the eye of this mighty serpent, netra in Hindi means eye.

Charanpaduka

It is a beautiful meadow on which footprints of Lord Vishnu are visible.

Neelkanth

These are the pyramid shaped snow capped peaks which form the beautiful background to the temple of Badrinath.

Getting There

By Air—The nearest airport to Badrinath is Jolly Grant in Dehradun which is 317 kms from here.

By Rail—The nearest railheads from Badrinath are at Rishikesh(297 km) and Kotdwar(327 Km).

By Road—Regular buses are available for Badrinath from Rishikesh, Haridwar, Dehradun and other important Kumaon regions.

Historical Tourism

Indian deep rooted heritage and culture have been finding their place in the pages of history books for centuries. Indian civilization is one of the oldest of all the civilizations of the world and it requires ages go through the entire history in short time. Let's have a glimpse on the major Indian historical eras.

Pre-Historic Era

The historians still differ in their opinions while quoting about pre-historic era of India. The remains of the Harappa civilization which is still a big question mark to the world, carries the flag of ancient Indian civilization. This is the time when the biggest two epics Ramayana and Mahabharata were played in the real soil of India, where myth, legend and history seem to collide with each other. The composition of Upanishads are another gift to the generations to come.

Medieval Era

A new light of enlightenment and philosophy touched people as Lord Buddha arrived into the world and attained his salvation. The invasion of Alexander, rise of Mauryas and Ashoka dynasty are some of the other historical milestones which keep historians craving for more about medieval India. India reached a new height at this time while walking on the path pioneered by the Lord Buddha, Lord Mahavira and Shankaracharya. You will still find the heritage and culture of medieval era is still well preserved in the ancient temples and monuments.

Mughal Era

This is the time of successive dynasty and political disorder and commotion. The beginning of Mughal reign is the time when the country went through a huge social and cultural change. A new kind of architecture that revolutionized Indian traditions are still fascinating the world in the form of majestic Taj Mahal, Red Fort and Jama Masjid. The Rajput architecture in Rajasthan and Maratha forts in Maharashtra are the other attractions of this era.

Modern India

Modern India got a chance to interact with the western culture for the first time. Indian thinkers were not far behind to come up with their paintings, novels and poetry and the world acknowledged them with open hearts. After a long fight for independence, India attained sovereignty holding the hands of Mahatma Gandhi, one of the most prominent world leaders of all time. With the advent of British Rulers, India saw a new light of revolutions which is depicted in the rich colonial architecture fringed in every corner of the country. Now, India is a modern country with a globally open market, high-tech cities, excellent communication and ancient heritage.

Goa Heritage Houses

For a state that was under the domain of Portuguese for 450 years, its difficult to root out the influence. Portuguese left Goa in 1961 but wherever you set your eyes here, you can see their mark on everything. From a considerable Christian population to Portuguese architecture, everywhere you see deep rooted influence. Goa has been a holiday destination for decades but it's not just the trance parties or miles of virgin beach territories that Goa offers. The landscape of Goa is dotted with heritage houses, villas, mansions that are reminiscent of the Portuguese era. There are also some unique examples of clever blend of the Indian and Portuguese styles. At places glimpses of European and Italian styles are also available. These architectural heritages also attract a number of tourists.

Some Famous Mansions of Goa

Salvador Da Costa mansion

Situated in Loutolim, a south Goa village, this mansion was built in nineteenth century. This house is an example of how practicality and functionality took priority over grandeur. Single storeyed, this mansion built by Padre Pedrinho and Padre Laurence is inspired from so many styles that its architecture is quite difficult to define with a single term. It would be appropriate to say that the mansion carries the best of both worlds: what was and what is now. It has a low pitched tile roof and a wide veranda (typical of Indian style) and designs include Gothic style windows, and columns clustered. This mixed architecture has come to be referred as the Goan eclectic style.

Solar Dos Colacos Mansion

Situated on the left bank of river Mandovi, this is probably the only Goan mansion facing the river. The facade of the mansion is baroque in style. The mansion offers a spectacular view of the islands of Chorao and Divar and churches of old Goa. The construction of this mansion began in 1730 by Joao Colaco. As years passed by, and the house passed from one generation to another features were added to it ambivalent to that time. Nazario Colaco, who inhabited the house after 1890 was an artist and craftsman. Evidence of his creativity are visible all around the house. For example the floor of entire ballroom being built in wood of 16 different types. The mansion has other interesting features such as the intricately carved Goan furniture, chandeliers, mirrors, the dining hall has scenes from Ramayana. On the other hand the private chapel has Roman Catholic influence with an altar being dedicated to Our Lady of Rosary. A visit to this house will liven up different prevailing trends of different times.

Menezes Braganza, Braganza Pereirera Mansion

Situated in Chandor, this mansion is considered to be one of the grandest mansions in the state. The sheer magnificence of the mansion from outside as well as inside is beyond comprehension. Italian patterned flooring (tiles and marble mosaic), stained glass windows, china ware and vases, the mansion will itself narrate stories of its magnificent past. The windows when the house was made earlier were made out of the mother of pearl shells. Antique furniture, Italian chandelier, Goa's first private library all these and much more add to the beauty of this mansion.

Mascarenhas Mansion

This mansion lies in close proximity of Goa's most happening beach Anjuna.Mascarenhas Mansion has rich and classic 'balcoes' (balconies). An L shaped seat along the porch is carved out of expensive wood. There are also some fine stained glass floral etchings.

Dr Pinto De Rosario Mansion

Dr. Pinto De Rosario Mansion lying between Panjim and Mapusa is in Porvorim. The mansion is filled with Indo-Portuguese furniture, European and Chinese wares. There are rare pieces of cut glass, blue china and ivory. All these things piled up in sideboards and cupboards are yet to be categorized and dated. However what surprises one is the quality and quantity in which these items are present. There is an exquisite Italian flooring in the parlour and the love chair in the mansion is supposed to be 200 years old. The tapestry placed above the intricately carved sofa carriers the replica of Rembrandt's Night Watch.

Other Mansions

For a landscape that is dotted with architectural examples, every other house is an example in itself. In Loutolim is a Figueredo mansion raised on a high plinth and its balcao (porch) is interesting to see as it shows evolving of convenience architecture. Miranda mansion (1710) in the same area is a typical country mansion with a separate chapel for worship, internal verandas etc. Another country mansion in Margao, Sat Burnzam Ghor (1790) is a replica of Portuguese style with a grand double storeyed facade. This mansion has the first private chapel that was allowed in Goa. Dr. Alvaro Loyola Furtado Mansion in Chinchinim displays richness unrivaled at the time it was built (1833). If you have an eye for architecture then just set on foot and you will discover numerous examples yourself.

Shivaji Heritage

The land of Maharashtra is adorned with the rich heritage of great Maratha warrior Shivaji Maharaj. Chhatrapati Shivaji, who started the Maratha Empire, was the man who stood out as a great fright to the mighty Mughal dynasty in the Deccan Plateau. The stories and folklores associated with the famous battles he fought and tricks he applied from time to time have now turned into legends. For the people of India, Shivaji is the epitome of extra ordinary courage and perspicaciousness, who is still remembered with due honour and dignity.

History Behind The Legend

Born in the Bhosale clan of the Maratha caste, Shivaji's father was a chief of the kingdom of Bijapur. Shivaji was brought up in Pune city and in the early days of his youth, he inspired the local peasant youth to follow his ideas, which can be claimed as the origination of guerrilla warfare in India. Soon he took control of various forts of Bijapur and eventually arose as a big threat to Ali Adil Shah, who sent his general Afzal Khan with a troop to catch Shivaji. The most celebrated act of Shivaji's life is his killing of Afzal Khan, when Shivaji killed him with a small dagger and a tiger's claw. Shivaji's next encounter was even bigger and it was with the Mughal Emperor Aurangzeb. His escape from Agra hiding in the sweet-box is a well cherished story of Indian history.

The tiny kingdom set up by Chhatarpati Shivaji known as Hindavi Swaraja (Sovereign Hindu State) flourished hugely in Shivaji's reign, eventually becoming the strongest power in India. After the death of Shivaji Maharaj, his son Sambhaji took the control but it is the Peshwas who later ruled the Deccan Plateau.

Shivaji Heritage Spread in Maharashtra Forts

Sky kissing forts along the coastline of Maharashtra still narrate the immense grandeur of Chhatrapati Shivaji Maharaj that had shaken the Indian soil at that era. Standing proudly on the coastline and crumbling the huge sea waves, the forts of Maharashtra are synonymous with the brave and courageous heritage of Shivaji. Whether it is Pratapgarh, immortalized by his encounter with Afzal Khan or Raigad, where he was coronated or even Sindhudurg, which still houses the hand and foot prints of Shivaji, the forts in Maharashtra flaunt the true flavour of Shivaji. The fact that Shivaji actually used to take part in the fort construction himself makes these even more precious.

Chapter 10

World Heritage Sites in India

MAMALLAPURAM TOURISM

Situated some 60 km south of Chennai, Mamallapuram has become famous for its monuments and stone carvings. Mamallapuram once served as a port city to the great Pallava kings, the history of this city dates back to more than 2000 years. Many temples were built in that era and most of them were fashioned out of rocks, are considered among the oldest in south India and showcase the Dravidian style of architecture to perfection. The most famous of all is the Shore temple situated at a picturesque location just by the side of Bay of Bengal. The temple is at its imperious best to look at under the moonlit skies. The temple was battered by waves and winds of 13 centuries and too was a victim of people's inattention, but now, after Mamallapuram being tagged as a World heritage site by UNESCO, it gets all the deserved attention and accolades. There are other tourist places worth a visit in Mamallapuram like the Panch Rathas, Arjuna's Penance and many well carved caves like the Mahishasurmardini Cave.

Mamallapuram Trivia

Being adjacent to a sea, the climate here is pleasant throughout the year and can be visited at any time in the 12-month period.

The people in the city of Mamallapuram are very warm and hospitable. Majority of the population here understands English, which makes moving around in the city easier for the international tourists. Travelers who love to explore new and fascinating things are in for a treat in this resplendent city. Every monument is completely different from the other and is a marvel in itself. Nature has also been very generous to the city, beaches are quite pleasing and tempting, so bring along your swimming suit and enjoy the refreshing waters. Shopholics too will not leave Mamallapuram empty handed, there are ample of items to choose from like locally made handy crafts, artifacts and many homemade delicacies. Come aboard for an experience so rare and precious that you would like not to forget even a single moment of it.

Attractions - World Heritage Sites

Mamallapuram is a city that has monuments as grand and as majestic that you will not find a competition anywhere in whole of India. The monuments here have everything that make a site memorable, tradition, history, piety, and magnetism that attracts hordes of tourist to Mamallapuram. The city contains nearly forty structures of different kind like temples and bas- relief, of which, one is the biggest in the world.

Arjuna's Penance

Arjuna's Penance, a sculpted rock situated opposite to Talasayana Perumal Temple is the world's largest bas-relief. The rock has carvings of Arjuna in deep meditation and many other sculptures of Gods, elephants, monkeys, and other creatures looking on. A naturally built cleft down the rock is said to be a representation of the Ganges, which seems to be life like during the rainy season when water flows into a tank below. Just a few meters away, to the left of Arjuna's Penance, is Krishna Mandapam, another bas-relief, carved in the mid-7th century, definitely able to catch your attention, watch carefully the carvings of Lord Krishna indulging into his day to day activities, you will be stun by such a fineness of details. Near Arjuna's Penance, to the north, is the huge spherical boulder known as Krishna's Butter Ball, balanced on a hillside, a sight worth a watch.

Mahishasurnardini Cave

Mahishasuramardini cave, remarkable for the two impressive friezes at each end of its long hallway. On the panel to the right, Durga, the mother of the universe, is shown seated on her lion,. She is shown in the process of killing the buffalo-headed demon, Mahisha. At the opposite end of the veranda, there is a sculpture in which Lord Vishnu is depicted sleeping peacefully on his serpent bed. On top of the hill, there is another section that portrays sculpted figures and mythical scenes, including one large panel of Lord Vishnu as a gigantic boar.

Shore Temple

Sitting pretty on a sandy beach on the Bay of Bengal, early-8th-century Shore Temple is considered to be one of the oldest temples in South India. Its two towers started a trend that was copied by temples throughout the southern region and to other Asian shores. A sculpture of reclining Lord Vishnu is found inside one shrine, whereas the other two shrines are dedicated to Lord Shiva. The temple is a classic example of Dravidian style architecture. Make your travel worthwhile by paying a visit to the presiding deities.

Panch Pandava Rathas

Placed in a sandy land, the five chariots (Panch Rathas) are named after the five Pandava brothers. Although they are not completed, but even these incomplete structures provide you with a mesmerizing view into the past. The five chariots are so well crafted that it seems as if they are trying to show off their architectural brilliance. All five structures are carved out of a single pieces of rock that underlines the fact that, even without super technology, the people in that era were highly skilled and crafty. These shrines are an epitome of perfect and precise planning. The dome-shaped tower found on some of the temples here, became an inspiration and example for other South Indian temples.

Accommodation

Accommodation is not a problem in Mamallapuram as the options to choose from are plenty. There are various star rated hotels along with government approved hotels. For a pleasant stay, count on Golden Sun Hotel & beach Resort, GRT Temple Bay and K.G Emerald Beach Hotel.

Getting There

By Air

The nearest airport is Chennai around 50 km away. It takes around 1 hr by road to reach Mamallapuram. Transportation is easily available from airport to Mamallapuram.

By Rail

Nearest railhead is Chennai which is well connected to all parts of India. Pondicherry station is also close by and can be used as an alternative.

By Road

The national highway that runs through Mamallapuram connects the city to all major parts of Tamil Nadu. Buses and Taxis from nearby areas ferry people in and out of the city.

Local Transport

Apart from an impressive bus service, Taxis, auto rickshaws, and mopeds are also available for hire in good numbers.

TAJ MAHAL

aj Mahal, where poet's words find an ultimate direction to articulate their emotion. It is a place where the artistry embraces the eternity and love attains divine salvation. The marble edifice situated on the bank of river Yamuna has suffered many ravages of time and with each sunrise and sunset, it has become immortal with its grandeur of heritage and legend. Taj Mahal was built by Mughal Emperor Shah Jahan to enshrine the remains of his beloved empress Begum Mumtaz Mahal which manifested the immortal love between the two.

A Monument that Redefines Artistry

Designed by the Persian architect Ustad Isa, Taj Mahal is renowned for its architectural magnificence and aesthetic beauty. Resting on 313 square feet marble platform, Taj Mahal is guarded by four marble minarets that are embellished with intricate marble inlay work. The main dome is offset by four smaller domes; in fact, from whichever angle you look at it, the Taj presents a graceful configuration of lines, curves, colour and perspective. The graves of Emperor and Empress lie in the basement where no one is allowed to enter and a false grave structure is made for visitors which is enclosed by a screen of exquisitely wrought white marble, fine as lace. The jewel-inlaid cenotaph of the king and queen have the verses of the holy Quran inscribed on them. Intricately proportioned filigree work and scooping tiny excavations in the marble wall are nothing but masterpiece in itself. Touch the small holes in the wall which used to contain precious stones in the Mughal era and now holding the reminiscence of the past. Moreover, Pietra dura – the superb craftsmanship of inlaying semi-precious stones into the beautiful patterns are something that give Taj Mahal a unique look.

Taj Fascinates All Day Long

The Taj, which is nothing but a tender elegy in marble, blossoms with its marvelous beauty uniquely at different hours of the day. As the sun spreads its vermilion in the East, Taj blooms like a fine pink rose and its marble architecture seem to spread fragrance, but it takes no time to change its view to a sparkling diamond as the sun reaches the mid sky. In the evening, when the sun completes its journey for the day, and moon comes to heal the world, Taj becomes a mystery in itself. You may even forget to breathe or blink wondering it to be real or some illusion.

Myriad Colours of Taj Mahotsav

A non-stop ten days long carnival, Taj Mahotsav, held at Shilpgram near Taj Mahal in the month of February re-invents the great Mughal heritage of the city in large manner. An extravagant procession of beautifully caparisoned elephants and camels along with drum beaters, dancers and folk artists through the quiet roads of Agra takes it to re-live the royal memory of the Mughals. The festival brings a golden opportunity for the legendary artisans and master craftsman in order to display their exquisite work of art. With folk music , shayari (poetry recitation) and classical dance performance, Taj Mahotsav celebrates finest crafts and cultural nuances of India with Taj Mahal creating the majestic backdrop. Get engulfed in the multiple hues of Indian culture and craft and plan your Taj Mahal trip at the time of Taj Festival as nothing can be more exciting.

Tourist information

Taj Mahal is open for public viewing from sunrise to 19 hours. The best time to make your plan in the year is from November to February. Being the one of the most renowned world heritage sites, you have to go through security checking and we suggest you co-operate with the guards. Any kind of food or baggage is not allowed inside and if you have any, you have deposit it to the counter. On payment of some charges you can use your camera inside the premises. Video cameras are restricted to the first platform inside the Taj entrance, 600 m away from the monument itself. Photography at the graves inside is forbidden. While entering in the mausoleum you will have to take off your shoes; you might also hire shoes that are put on rent or just go ahead bare footed.

Access

Agra is well connected to Delhi by Indian Airlines and other private airways operating flights on regular basis. One can also opt for train journey by the Shatabdi Express and the Taj Express running daily from Delhi Nizamuddin Station. Agra is only 204 km from Delhi and the excellent national highway caters smooth and luxurious journey by air-conditioned and deluxe coaches to Agra.

You must park at a short distance from the Taj premises and you may take the battery operated buses or horse carts to the entrance. Alternatively, you can walk the 2 km route also.

Where to Stay

Agra has a wide range of hotels and rest houses. The 5 star deluxe hotels provide luxurious accommodation in the city . UPSTDC`s tourist complex, Taj Khema near the Taj Mahal offers accommodation in tents and deluxe rooms. There is a UPSTDC Tourist Bungalow as well. Hotels and restaurants offer both Indian, Continental and Chinese cuisine with Mughlai cuisine, which is Agra's specialty.

AJANTA ELLORA CAVES

The world heritage sites Ajanta- Ellora caves are wonders to the world with their pre-historic sculptures and exquisite stone carvings. People from various parts of the world make their visit to this place just to have a glimpse of those excellent sculpture that have seen many ravages of time. UNESCO did not hesitate to declare the caves as world heritage sites in 1983.

Splendours that Define Ajanta Caves

Situated at 112 km from Aurangabad, the journey to Ajanta cave through ancient hills and windy road is also an extraordinary experience which will make a preface for you before unveiling the immense treasure hidden in the layers of time. As you enter in the cave, along with the intricate rock work, the calmness catches your senses; that has been prevailing here for centuries and millennia. There are 30 caves at Ajanta chiselled out of hard rock by Buddhist monks between 200 BC and 650 AD as Chasityas (chapels) and viharas (monasteries), that exhibit intricate stone-work and frescoes. As you take a view from the Ajanta caves ticket office, the beautiful ensemble of green and gray make visual treat for your eyes. A tour to the caves of Ajanta is nothing but an unparalleled experience to savour.

Ellora Caves Sheen with Pride

The primeval caves of Ellora are the epitome of art, spirituality and religious harmony. The Ellora caves represent 34 Buddhist, Hindu and Jain cave temples carved out of the rock between 350 AD and 700 AD. The temples exhibit the extreme artistry of the human hands creating magic on the rocks as if making them alive and speak. The most famous amongst them is the Kailasa Temple, the world's largest monolithic sculpture, covered with a variety of finely carved panels. You can give a special look at the elephant standing outside the Kailasa temple, his trunk being lost in the mystery of time. Scenes from the great epics Mahabharata and Ramayana intricately carved on the walls of Kailasa temple narrating the minutest details of the epics is something jewel on the earth.

Getting There

By Air

The nearest airport to the Ajnata and Ellora caves is Chiklthana airport in Aurangabad at a distance of 112 km and 27 km respectively. Indian Airlines daily operate flight from Aurangabad to Delhi via Mumbai. Jet Airways and Air Deccan have also started their flight service from Auranagabad to Mumbai and Delhi. The nearest international airports to Ajanta-Ellora caves are Mumbai and Pune.

By Train

The nearest railhead to both Ajanta and Ellora caves is situated at Aurangabad. Direct train link between Aurangabad and Mumbai is available as Devgiri Express and Tapovan Express run on daily basis. Direct train connection to Hyderabad is also available from the city. Sachkand Express ply in a regular basis from New Delhi and Aurangabad.

By Road

Regular tourist bus services are available to the Ajanta-Ellora caves from Aurangabad. The air conditioned deluxe buses ply on a regular basis. Ajanta and Ellora is connected with Mumbai, Pune, Ahmednagar, Jalgaon, Shirdi, Nasik, Dhule, Ahmedabad, Hyderabad, Indore, Bijapur, and Aurangabad by excellent road network in Maharashtra and neighbouring states.

Agra Fort

Agra Fort, built by the successive contribution of three Mughal generations – Akbar, Jehangir and Shah Jehan – still fascinates the entire world with its majestic glory. The fort stared its journey in the days of Akbar under the supervision of Mohammed Quasim Khan, his commander-in-chief. Originally planned to build an invincible military structure by Akbar, the Agra Fort gained its elegance, lavishness and royalty of a palace at the time of Emperor Shah Jehan.

Splendrous Mughal Architecture

The remarkable architecture and the majestic fort complex stores the innumerable essence of the Mughal Emperors and you may fee like riding in the time machine. More like a city inside, the fort was built to fulfill the military purpose which spreads on the banks of Yamuna enclosing a humongous area of 3 km radius. Surrounded by a 70 foot high wall the fort houses the beautiful Pearl Mosque and numerous palaces including the Jahangiri Mahal, Diwan-i-Khas, Diwan-i-Am and Moti Masjid. The fort has four gates and is enclosed by a double barricaded wall of red sand stone. Many buildings were constructed within the fort of which very few remain till date. One of the most significant ones is the multi-storeyed Jahangiri Mahal built by Akbar for his wife Jodha Bai. The Mahal is reached through an impressive gateway and its inner courtyard consists of beautiful halls, profusse carvings on stone, exquisitely carved heavy brackets, piers and cross beams. Most of the panels in the eastern hall are decorated with the Persian styled stucco paintings in gold and blue.

It is believed that a century later, most of the structures were dismantled by Shahjahan and were replaced with white marble pavilions covered with intricate inlay work. Of which the most prominent ones are - the Diwan- i-khas, the Mausam Burj and the Shaha Burj. Away from the waterfront he built the Moti Masjid and the Diwan-i-Aam. If you check carefully you can find the dimples on the walls that were embellished with precious stones which could not survive in the ravages of time. Touch them and you will have a spine chilling experience. This is the place where Emperor Shah Jehan spent last days of his life after he had been imprisoned by his son Aurangzeb, seeing Taj Mahal, a symbol of eternal love where the heart-broken Shahjahan was subsequently buried and re-united finally with his beloved Mumtaz.

Tourist Information

Open on all weekdays from sunrise to sunset, the fort offers free visit on Fridays. Ample space of parking available just outside the fort makes it easily accessible by both cars and heavy vehicles. The best time to visit the fort is from November to February. The Son-et-lumiere show is performed at 7.30 pm in English and at 8.30 pm in Hindi on every weekday evenings.

Access

Agra is well connected to Delhi by Indian Airlines and other private airways operating flights on regular basis. One can also opt for train journey by the Shatabdi Express and the Taj Express running daily from Delhi Nizamuddin Station. Agra is only 204 km from Delhi and the excellent national highway caters smooth and luxurious journey by air-conditioned and deluxe coaches to Agra.

Where to Stay

Agra has a wide range of hotels and rest houses. UPSTDC`s tourist complex, Taj Khema near the Taj Mahal offers excellent sojourn in the deluxe rooms. There is a UPSTDC Tourist Bungalow as well. A number of 5 star deluxe hotels make accommodation facility in Agra comfortable.

Darjeeling Toy Train

Remember Bollywood superstar of yesteryears, Rajesh Khanna, in a jeep, singing the superhit number mere sapno ki rani as Sharmila Tagore watches on from a train in the 1969 blockbuster Aradhana? Now, try recalling the more recent song kasto maja from Saif Ali Khan &Vidya Balan starrer Parineeta which was yet again on a train. What is common between the two songs or rather two trains is that they were toy trains and that also Darjeeling Toy Trains.

For those who have seen the songs, it is easy to understand why a trip aboard the Darjeeling toy train should not be missed. However, for those who have not seen them and are looking for a genuine reason for taking up a journey on this route, well here it is. The beautiful atmosphere of the hilly terrain through which the train traverses is extremely refreshing and relaxing. Infact, it was the bewitching beauty of the place that inspired Mr Franklin Prestage (a representative of East Bengal Railway Company) to lay down a train line between Darjeeling and Siliguri back in the mid 19th century.

So, if you are yearning to slow down the pace of your life and enjoy life at its most relaxed self, then a trip in the Darjeeling Toy train is your solution. The toy train, twisting its way up from Siliguri to Darjeeling in the east Indian state of West Bengal, is meant exactly for souls like you who do not hurry to finish off their journey. Rather what they want and do is to enjoy the journey itself.

The Splendid Route

A marvellous journey awaits you in the Darjeeling Toy Train which runs on a 2 feet gauge for a distance of 86 km. The entire journey is covered in around 71/2 hours with a maximum of 15 kmph.

The scenery that greets you range from the dense jungles to tea plantations. Sukna, the first station after the commencement of the journey, has trees of sal and teak along with purple bougainvillea, red poinsettia and moderate purple orchids creating a riot of colours for you. From Sukna, the actual climb begins. Steep gradients and curves marks the route all through.

After crossing Chunabhati, Tung Chutlinkpur and Jorebunglow, you reach Ghoom. At a height of 2257.65m, you are now at the second highest railway station in the world that is accessed by a steam locomotive. A 6 km downhill journey from here brings you to your final destination, Darjeeling.

A unique feature about this route is that wherever there is a lack of clearcut path due to steep gradient, the climb is proceeded through reverses and loops. Infact, there are as many as six reverses and 3 loops in the entire journey. Moreover, there are also 5 important and 498 less important bridges along with 177 unmanned level crossing enroute through which the train traverses.

What will also strike you throughout your journey from Siliguri to Darjeeling is that the track runs almost on the same alignment as the Hill Cart road. Infact, they also cross each other a number of times, 150 times to be a bit more precise. This gives you an opportunity to enjoy the movement on the road while sitting in the train. It gives you a feeling as if the whole world is hurrying to complete their job while you are at leisure to be with yourself and your family and enjoy the beauty of life.

The Toy Train

The train that first ran on the track was way too different from what you will see today. It was a mini four wheeled trolley with canvas and two wooden benches. Moreover, at that point of time it was also an important source to transport both people and cargo. It was only with the development of more convenient way to reach Darjeeling that the load on this toy train lessened and it became. As of today, this toy train whistles past its way through scenic beauty with a grace that is adorable. Take a trip in this train to enjoy the beautiful pleasures it has to offer.

SUNDERBANS WILDLIFE TOURISM

Situated on the largest delta in the world, is the largest national park in India, the name of which means 'The Beautiful Jungle'. And the world knows it by the name 'Sunderbans'. This magnificent destination in West Bengal has many such distinctions in its possessions. The delta on which the park is situated is formed by River Ganges, River Brahmaputra and River Meghna. Covering an area of 4264 sq. Km. in India itself, Sunderbans National Park is the largest protected area and tiger reserve in India. A large part of the forest today is a part of Bangladesh which is considered as a different park. Sunderbans National Park has been recognized as a UNESCO World Heritage Site in the year 1997. The park is not only famous for its wildlife inhabitants, but equally for its lush green forest cover, especially Mangrove trees. Sunderbans also claims to be the largest Mangrove forest in the world. The entire park is cut through by the many tributaries that serve as the path to the interiors of the park.

Flora And Fauna Attractions

Sunderbans National Park is famous as the home for the magnificent Royal Bengal Tigers. There are more than 250 tigers found in Sunderbans. Though a larger part of the tiger reserve is in the Bangladesh occupied park. The recent census show that the number of Royal Bengal tigers in Sunderbans is among the highest in India. The best chances of watching the majestic beast is when he comes out of the jungle to drink water on the banks of tributaries. Chital deer and rhesus monkey are the animals that are most commonly seen in the park. Other attraction of the park include reptiles like lizards, pythons, king cobras and chequered killback. Sunderbans park has been specially appreciated for preserving the rare Ridley Sea Turtle whose number has been dwindling quite quickly. The wildlife park is a hot spot for bird watching as well. Inside the park, there is a bird sanctuary named Sajnekhali. One can sight plovers, lap wings, seven different varieties of Kingfisher, sea eagle, whimbrels, and pelicans. Always keep your cameras ready, as you never know when you will come across a mud bay on the banks covered with lethargic crocodiles. The aqua fauna includes different fishes like saw fish, butterfish, starfish, red fiddler crabs and hermit crabs. If lucky, you might just spot a dolphin as well.

Sunderbans is as diverse in flora attractions as is in fauna. Around 245 genera and 334 species of plants are found in the park. Though Sunderbans is the largest mangrove forest in the world, the main tree is the Sundari tree. In fact, the park earns its name from this tree.

Riding Into The Jungle

Safaris in the wild lands is an experience that cannot be forgotten very quickly. You can take a jeep safari as well as an elephant safari into the deep jungles of Bandhavgarh. If possible, don't miss even a single safari tour as sighting a tiger is not at all guaranteed. Most of the safaris are organized in early mornings or in the afternoons. The best thing about roaming inside the park is that you can take your own four wheeler but only in company of an authorized guide. You can also take up a tiger show tour on an elephant, that is a stage managed encounter with the tiger. The position of the tiger is kept track of, and you are taken to the place where the tiger might be resting.

Staying Options

The only way of exploring the large Sunderbans National Park is by taking a a boat ride through the many tributaries that criss cross through the park. Sajnekhali is the main base from where these safaris start. The steamers that are used for the safaris are quite big and comfortable. If you wish you can also opt to stay overnight in the boat and look out for animals at night. In fact, it is during night that the probability of sighting a tiger is the most when they come to the banks to drink water. Almost all boats have a kitchen and all basic facilities for a one day stay.

Tourist Information on Sunderbans National Park.

The Best time to visit Sunderbans is between September and March . It is during winters that one gets to see the most number of migratory birds. Though no permit is required for a ride in the outer region of the park, one needs to acquire permission for visiting project tiger areas and Sajnekhali Bird sanctuary. The permit can be acquired from the office of the field director. Sunderbans National Park is situated nearly 131 Km from the capital city Kolkata. There are regular bus services between the two destinations.

For Accommodation inside the park, Sajnekhali is the only place where you will get resorts for overnight stay. The tourist lodge is not very luxurious, however, the thrill and excitement of staying amidst the tigers easily compensates for the lack. There are numerous tourist resorts outside the park at Piyali and Bakkhali.

Badami Caves Tourism

Situated in the once mighty capital of Chalukya Empire, Badami; the caves are the most stupendously carved caves in South India. Carved on top of a hill, there are four major caves. These are not just plain caves; they are temples dedicated to different religions. They generally are temples dedicated to Hindu and Jain temples. All the four caves are carved out of Deccan sandstone. They were built by the Chalukya Empire around 6th century. The architecture of these caves shows a mixture of North Indian Nagara style and South Indian Nagara. Apart from the caves, there are many temples on the banks of an artificial lake, on which Badami town is located. The lake is named 'Agasthya Tirtha'. Some of these temples were built at the same time along with caves and date back to 7th century. The temples are dedicated to Lord Vishnu, Lord Shiva and Lord Mahavir Swamy. There is an archaeological museum maintained by ASI, which shows many sculptures of the Chalukyan era. However the main attraction without a doubt are the four magnificent caves.

Cave 1

Carved in 578 AD, this is probably the oldest of the four caves. As you climb 40 odd steps, you come across a hall full of pillars and a square shaped sanctum. From top to bottom, the cave is filled with splendid carvings and paintings that will mesmerize you, the moment you get a glimpse of them. Apart from the walls, even the ceilings have some exceptional art work. The ceiling has painting of Lord Shiva and Goddess Parvati. Verandah has a painting of Lord Shiva as Nataraja. The Lord is shown with 18 hands and in 81 dance poses.

Cave 2

Cave 2 is situated just above cave 1 and is a cave temple is dedicated to Lord Vishnu. You will find different forms of Lord Vishnu portrayed here. Lord Vishnu is shown as Trivikrama. The image is shown with one foot conquering the earth and the other covering the sky. There is another image of Lord Vishnu in incarnation as Varaha, 'a boar'. Then there is one that is in form of Lord Krishna, riding a Garnda and the lotus encircled by 16 fishes.

Cave 3

Few more steps above Cave 2, is the biggest and most attractive caves of the four caves. Dating back to 578 AD, the cave has paintings and sculptures of both Lord Shiva and Lord Vishnu. You also get to see some inscriptions that tell us that the cave was built by Mangalesha. The front of the cave is nearly 70 feet wide with some exquisite carvings. Inside, there are images of Trivikrama, Narasimha, Shankaranarayana, Bhuvaraha, Anantasayana, Harihara and many carvings of Ganas.

Cave 4

This is the only Jain Temple among the four Badami Caves. It is situated to the east of other three caves and its construction was completed nearly 100 years after the other three were completed. There is a magnificent image of Lord Mahavira inside the sanctum. There is an image of Lord Parsvanath with a serpent at his feet. Images of Padmavathi and tirthankaras can also be seen inside the cave. Near the cave, are the steps that lead to Badami Fort, another interesting attraction of the town.

Badami as a town has become a great tourist spot in Karnataka. Apart from the magnificent caves, there are many other attractions inside the town like temples, forts and the artificial lake; all deserving your attention and accolades.

Bhimbetka Cave Tourism

Bhimbetka Caves, in a very short span of time have become the most visited attraction in Madhya Pradesh and have earned a place in the list of one of the best in India. Situated just 46 km from Bhopal, these exquisite caves are surrounded by the northern limits of Vindhya mountain Range. As the legend goes, these hills got their name after Bhima, one of the five Pandava brothers. The name 'Bhim-bet-ka' means 'where Bhim sat down'. There are more than 600 caves that have the collection of oldest Prehistoric paintings in India. These caves were found by Dr. V.S Wakankar, the famous Indian archaeologists in the year 1958. It took around 16 years to excavate the entire area covered by these caves. Although there are more than 600 caves , only 12 are open for tourists at the moment, but they show you the best paintings that are there in all other caves. And out of the 24 world heritage sites that have been recognized by UNESCO in India, Bhimbetka caves are the oldest one.

Attractions of Bhimbetka Caves

These caves had been used as a shelter by people from the earliest of periods. Thus you will find paintings of all periods starting from Paleolithic era to Medieval era. The paintings turn out to be a mirror showing evolution of humanity through time. The style of the paintings of separate periods are so different that you can easily differentiate between them. The paintings of Paleolithic age are huge linear figures of animals like tigers, bears and rhinoceroses. As the time passed, the paintings became smaller, shapely and more precise. The paintings now depicted the daily chores of people like hunting and dancing. Slowly the artistry from raw art turned into religious images showing the change in the mindset. Oldest painting is said to be around 12000 years old whereas the most recent is around 1000 years old. The colors used by the cave dwellers, were prepared by combining manganese, hematite, soft red stone and wooden coal. The paintings over the years have stayed unharmed by nature due to the reaction between the chemicals present in rocks and the color. Even animal fat and plant leaves were also used in the mixture.

When and How to Reach

You can visit the cave any time of the year although July and March is the best time to enjoy the charm of the caves. There are not many staying options around the caves, but Bhopal is just 46 km away and you will find world class accommodation there. Reaching to Bhimbetka caves is not very difficult due to its proximity to Bhopal. The city is well connected by flights as well as rail line from all parts of the country. From Bhopal, there are many buses that run to and fro between the caves and the city. You can also hire a taxi to the caves.

The walls of these caves are literally the unspoken story of our ancestors who once walked on this land. Just few miles from Bhopal, Bhimbetka caves are an ideal day long excursion from the capital city. Come and lose yourself in the many fascinating caves that are a dream world in themselves.

NANDA DEVI NATIONAL PARK

Three hundred kilometres north east of Delhi is Nanda Devi National Park. It lies in the vicinity of Nanda Devi Peak which is the second highest peak in India and very tough to climb. Nanda Devi National Park lies in the Upper Himalayas in the Chamoli district in the Garhwal division of Uttaranchal.

Best time To Visit

Nanda Devi is at a very high altitude and for a major part of the year is under the cover of snow. The best time to be here is from April to October. In the months of June to August, there is heavy rainfall in the area.

About Nanda Devi National Park

You have to enter the park from Lata Village which is 23 kms from Joshimath. The park is surrounded by peaks from three sides and on the fourth side there is a gorge (this route is virtually inaccessible). Spreading over an area of 630 kilometres, Nanda Devi was established in 1980 and declared a National park in 1982 to protect from excessive human interference.

The park has a long history. Because of its tough route it laid protected and untouched by humans for long. W.W. Garden was the first person to be here in 1883. However, the place caught people's fancy only after 1936 when Tilamen and N.E. Odell made a trip here. After that, organised trips began to be conducted here and people started frequenting this place a lot. Then to protect and preserve the place, Nanda Devi National Park was set up here in 1982 and later on was given this special status of Biosphere Reserve. It is this richness of biosphere that makes the park extremely special. Nanda Devi also offers some of the most picturesque views you will get in the world and that's what makes it a world heritage site preserved by UNESCO.

ATTRACTIONS OF NANDA DEVI NATIONAL PARK

Flora

Nanda Devi has remained inaccessible for mankind and that's the reason why it has been so well preserved for last so many years. However vegetation is very thin in the inner regions of sanctuary and almost none around the glacier. Whatever little vegetation is there is limited to Rishi gorge. All one sees here are some trees of fir, birch, rhododendron and juniper. Gradually moving towards Ramani, there is a change in vegetation as well. Alpines and Juniper scrubs are found largely and then slowly grasses, prone mosses and lichens start appearing. Nanda Devi has one of the richest preserves of flora in the world. There are some 312 floral species here of which 17 are rare ones.

Animals

The park has some 14 species of mammals according to a survey conducted by UNEP of which 6 are nationally endangered. Blue Sheep is very common and so are Musk Deer, Serow and Himalayan Tahr. One might not be able to spot White Leopards here that easily but the park has fairly large numbers of them. Other animals here are black and brown Bear and Yellow Leopards.

Birds

The survey by UNEP says that there are some 114 species of birds here. Number of birds increases here around May to June (may be because of the pleasant weather). Some of those present in large numbers are crested Black Tit, yellow-bellied Fantail Flycatcher, orange-flanked Bush Robin, blue fronted Redstart, Indian Tree Pipit, Vinaceous Breasted Pipit , Common Rosefinch and Nutcracker. Because of the presence of large numbers of flowers, butterflies are also here in large numbers. There are some 28 varieties of butterflies here.

Things to do

Trekking

Trekking is a great experience in Nanda valley largely due to the pleasant weather here. Summers are pleasant but winters are tough. If you have the stamina then there are better chances of spotting wildlife in winters.

KHAJURAHO TEMPLE TOURISM

A cluster of temples in the small town of Khajuraho has become the greatest attribute of tourism in Madhya Pradesh. They are the unparalleled masters when it comes to alluring tourist from all regions of the world. The temples were built by the rulers of Chandela dynasty in a short span of hundred years between 950 AD to 1050 AD. It is said that there were around 85 temples in all, but after thousands of years, only 22 odd still stand. After being lost in flow of time, they were rediscovered by British officer T.S Burt in the year 1838. Since then, millions have visited these temples just to be left speechless and hooked to the beauty, charm and probably detailing of these one of a kind temples. The town by the virtue of the temples has been recognized as a world heritage site by UNESCO. What brings hordes of tourist to explore Khajuraho temples are the erotic sculptures that cover the walls of many temples here. The erotic crafts only make up a small section of what these temples have to offer. The major share of the carvings is of Gods, deities and depiction of day to day activities of people in that era. The temples have been divided into three sections according to their location in the town. The western Group, The Southern Group and the Eastern Group.

The Western Group

This group is centrally located and has the most splendid and magnificent set of temples. The main temple is Kandriya Mahadeo which is dedicated to Lord Shiva. Reaching to a height of 31 m, it is the largest temple in Khajuraho. The temple has exquisite carvings of deities and celestial lovers on the main shrine. Lakshmana Temple is another temple that is in the group and is probably the oldest temple in the town. It is famous for the exquisite three headed statue of Lord Vishnu' incarnations. The other main temples are Devi Jagadambi and Vishwanatha Temple.

The Eastern Group

This group contains few of the best and most important Jain Temples along with Hindu Temples. The carvings and structures in this group are nothing less than what you will find in western group temples. Parsvanath temple is the biggest Jain Temple. The sculptures on the outer walls depicts of people engaged in their daily chores. The statue of Parsvanath, inside the sanctum sanctorum was only installed in the year 1860. Adinatha and Ghantai Temple are the other main Jain Temples in the group. The three Hindu temples in the group are Brahma Temple, Vamana Temple and Javari Temple. The walls of these temples have the major share of erotic sculptures.

The Southern Group

Chaturbhuj Temple and Duladeo Temple make up the Southern group. The temples fall deep into the village and are farthest from the road. The Chaturbhuj Temple is dedicated to Lord Vishnu and has an admirable statue of his in the Sanctum.

Few similar temples have also been found some kilometers away in other villages but they are not counted in any of the groups. However you should visit these temples as well as they too are equally appealing. You can visit the temples at any time of the year but the best time is just after the rains when the dust in the atmosphere would have subsided. Cleaned by the rain, the beauty of the temples increases two folds. Prefer September to March period.

Hampi Tourism

Hampi can very well be compared to a phoenix. Hampi was the capital of last great Hindu Kingdom of Vijayanagara before it was attacked by Muslims rulers. Suddenly, one of the marvels of medieval era faded away. It remained very many unknowns to the outside world till UNESCO recognized it as a World Heritage

Site. Hampi started getting the attention and accolades that it deserved. And now it is one of the most visited and admired places in India. Situated around 300 Km from Bangalore, Hampi is the second largest world heritage site in the World. The govt. recently has been actively taking measures to preserve this marvel of time. The ruins of the once great kingdom, scattered in an area of 26 sq. km is slowly positioning itself for the title of 'Pride of Karnataka'

Attractions - Built For Gods

Every part of Hampi is an attraction in itself Step into the city and you are greeted by magnificently carved Dravidian style temples and forts. The place had been a tourist attraction even in the 15th and 16th century.

Vithala Temple

Vithala Temple is one reason why Hampi is so famous all over the world. This is the most splendidly carved building you will ever see. The temple is dedicated to Lord Vishnu. The temple was completed in the year 1565, almost five decades after the Krishnadevaraya started it. The main attraction in the temple is Stone Chariot standing in the courtyard and a 56-pillared hall. It is said that the pillars produce musical sounds when they are stroked. The temple is situated to the east side of main market of Hampi.

Virupaksha Temple

This is the most sacred temple as well as the biggest structure of the city. The temple is also known as Pampapathi Temple. The temple has shrines dedicated to Lord Shiva, Goddess Pampa and Goddess Bhuvaneshwari. This is the only temple in Hampi where still regular pujas and prayers are held. The main temple has a Sanctum, a mukha mandapa, an open pillared hall and three chambers. The Ranga Mandapa is the most splendid of all.

Hazara Rama Temple

Hazara Rama Temple is one of the most splendid works that you will find in Hampi. You will find carvings on the outer walls of the temple are not very common in structures of Hampi. The carvings are generally depicting different scenes from Ramayana. That is how the temple got its name as 'Hazara Rama Temple'. The temple now lay deserted but is believed to be the private place for royal family to worship.

Ugra Narasimha

According to the inscriptions found on the statue of Lakshmi Narasimha called the Ugra Narasimha, it was build in the year 1528 during the rule of Krishnadevaraya. Ugra Narasimha is a gigantic statue that rises to a height of 6.7 meters. The huge statue of Lord Narasimha sits atop a coiled snake Adishesha. The artistry of the statue is simply unbelievable. The statue is completely build of granite which is a very hard substance. It is said that the artist could not manage delicate carvings on granite. So they made the statue huge so that the carvings can be done accordingly. There was a small figure of Lakshmi sitting on the lap of statue which came loose. The figure of Goddess Lakshmi is now kept in Kamalapura Museum.

Accommodation in Hampi

When Visiting Hampi, you have the option of either staying in Hampi or keep your base in Hospet which is at a distance of 13 Km. Though both of the places have same quality of hotels. There are more lodges and tourist homes in both the towns. The best places to stay are Lokare Lodge, Hotel Mayura Vijayanagar in Hospet and Mayura Lodge.

Getting There

By Air

Nearest airport is at Bellary which is at a distance of 77 Km. Bellary receives regular flights from Bangalore and Goa. Air

Deccan is the major flight operator to Bellary. There is road transportation available in form of buses and taxis. It will take around 2 hrs to cover the distance.

By Rail

Hospet is the nearest railway station which is at a distance of 13 km from Hampi. You can take a bus or hire a taxi from the railway station to Hampi. More than 10 trains pass through Hospet everyday. There are trains coming in from Bangalore.

By Road

Hampi is connected to all the nearby areas and all the major cities of Karnataka. Buses into the city from these destinations are regular. KSRTC buses from Hospet are the most frequent. Htis ensures good connectivity with other cities as well.

Local Transportation

Taxis and auto rickshaws are the main mode of transport in India. To explore the famous ruins of Hampi, you can alos hire a bicycle. By far the best option for people with good endurance as you can roam around at your own pace.

Manas Wildlife Tourism

Manas National Park is yet another gem in the already star studded list of Assam Wildlife Parks. The wildlife park nestles on the foot of Eastern Himalayas with a large part of the park extending in to Bhutan territory. The park got its name from Manas River that flows right though the park which itself is named after God Manasa. Covering an area of around 391 sq km, Manas National Park was declared a wildlife sanctuary on October 1st 1928. Since then it has been endowed with many more titles and responsibilities. In 1985, it was recognized as a World Heritage Site by UNESCO. Manas park is also an elephant reserve, and a biosphere reserve. It is also the only national park in entire Assam to be included under Project Tiger.

What To See

Manas National Park is completely covered with thick dense forest which is a great feature for becoming an great wildlife park. More than 55 species of mammals have been found in the park along with 50 species of reptiles, 3 species of amphibians and around 380 species of birds. Many species in above list are included in the list of endangered and many of them are rare animals. Tigers, elephants, rhinoceros and wild buffaloes are the main attraction of the park. Other animals in the park are leopards, swamp deer, capped langurs, hoolock gibbons, Sambar and many more. Manas National Park is also home to animals like Assam Roofed Turtle, Hispid Hare and Golden Langur which are found only in Assam.

Out of the 380 species of birds recorded here, most important is the endangered Bengal Florican as its population is the highest here. Jungle Fowls, bulbuls, Brahminy Ducks, Gray hornbills are few other birds that are commonly sighted in Manas national Park.

A Ride In The Jungle

The best way to explore the magnificent wildlife of Manas National Park is by taking a boat ride in River Manas. Most animals, mainly wild buffaloes come to the river bank which is the best time to sight them. Make sure you keep your cameras ready to capture some splendid snaps. The boat ride starts at Mathanguri and ends 35 km away. The other option you can choose is an elephant safari that takes you through to the jungle interiors. There are well laid out roads as well which are quite helpful if you are traveling inside the park using a jeep.

Tourist Information

For a stay right in the heart of the jungle, there are two bungalows in Mathanguri. It is advised that you make early bookings for these bungalows as they are a favorite staying option for many tourists. There is no catering service in the bungalow and you will have make arrangements for yourself. There are many more places to stay on the outskirts of Manas National Park on

Barpeta Road. The park is nearly 140 km from Guwahati which takes around 3 hrs to cover by road. There is rail connection as well from Guwahati to Barpeta Road which is 40 km from Manas national park.

Amazement and awe are the feeling that never stop flowing in your heart, when you are exploring the wildlife splendors of Manas National Park. Along with wildlife attractions, you come across some enthralling views of Himalayan beauty. Just pack your bags and start your trip to Manas National Park, disappointment word will be a history in your dictionary.

Kaziranga Wildlife Tourism

Kaziranga is an important national park in Golaghat District of Assam that covers an area of around 430 sq Km. The park was considered a forest reserve in the year 1908, and in 1916 it was recognized as a game reserve. Till 1968 it remained a wildlife sanctuary after which it was designated as a National Park by Assam Government. The Park is most famous for the one horned Rhino. The population of one horned rhino in the park forms two-third of their total population in the whole world. Not only are the rhino its prized possession, Kaziranga also boasts of the highest density of tigers among the protected areas in the world. This led to Kaziranga being declared as a Tiger Reserve in the year 2006. Kaziranga National Park is now also recognized as a UNESCO World Heritage Site. Rhinos and tigers are definitely the biggest attractions of the park, but there is more to Kaziranga than these two majestic animals.

Wild Attractions

Kaziranga National Park is now synonymous with one horned rhino and is known to have largest number of them in the world. But what many people don't know is that the park also has the largest density of tigers in a protected area in the whole world. In total there are around 35 mammalian species in the park out of which 15 are seen as endangered. Kaziranga also has the largest population of Wild Asiatic water buffalo and eastern swamp deer. The park is the best place to sight different large cats of the wild. Other than tigers, you can also see Jungle Cats, fishing cats, and leopards. Smaller mammals include Indian grey mongoose, large Indian civet, Bengal Fox, Hog Badger, sloth bear and many more. 9 species of primates are also found here like Assamese Macaque and the most important Hoolock Gibbon. Kaziranga is also home to two of the world's largest snakes Reticulated Python, Rock Python and the world's largest venomous snake King Cobra.

There are probably none better places than Kaziranga National park to go for an interesting bird watching spree. For the number of local and migratory birds found here, Bird International has identified Kaziranga as an Important Bird area. The park is brimming with different species of birds like spot billed pelican, dalmatian pelican, black bellied tern, Blyth's kingfisher and black necked stork. The birds of prey found here are eastern imperial, greater spotted, Pallas's fish eagle.

Jungle Safaris

Best way to experience the wildlife in Kaziranga National Park is by taking an elephant safari in the park. The park is so full of animals that it is almost sure that you will get to see the rare animals in their natural habitat. Most of the safaris are arranged early in the morning or in the late afternoon when it is most probable of sighting a tiger or a rhino. The mahouts are all very trained and know every part of the park and also serve as a tour guide. So a trip with them really turns out to be quite rewarding. There are Jeep rides also deep into the jungle. On all your safaris, make sure you carry your binoculars along , as bird watching in the park is truly an unforgettable experience.

Tourist Information

For your stay, there are number of jungle resorts situated on the outskirts of the park. Located right in the lap of nature, a stay in the well equipped resorts is also a highlight of your trip in

Kaziranga National Park. Some resorts also show visuals educating tourists about the do's and don't s in the park. Best time to visit the park is between October and May. It is situated at a distance of 217 Km from Guwahati and the closest railway station is at Furkating at a distance of 75 Km The main gate to the park is situated on the NH 37 at Kohora.

Nothing comes close to the excitement and thrill that you get while on an elephant safari in Kaziranga National Park. One gets to see the untamed nature at its best and its wildest creation right in their backyard. Visit Kaziranga National Park to explore the many of nature's wonders.

Fatehpur Sikri

Fatehpur Sikri, which was once abandoned by Akbar has not lost its charm even a bit after so many years. The majestic marble and red stone structures of the city still narrate the formidable past of this ancient city. The hustle-bustle may not be echoed from the abandoned lanes of the city any more, but the exquisite architectural splendour of Fatehpur Sikri has left a permanent impression in the legacy of Indian architecture.

Turning the Pages of History

Once a small village, Fatehpur Sikri holds a fascinating tale behind its being the capital of Mughal Emperor Akbar. As the legend goes, Akbar, who had no son, decided to seek the blessings ofShaikh Salim Chisti who used to live in the village, Sikri. The saint prophesied that Akbar would have three sons and soon the saint's foretelling came true and Akbar saw the face of his first son Salim, whom he named after the saint. Akbar was so glad that he decided to build his new capital near Sikri and he renamed it Fatehabad (later it became Fatehpur) meaning 'city of victory'.

But the brief glory of Fatehpur Sikri came to an end when Akbar left Sikri and shifted to Lahore to escape the water scarcity in Fatehpur. The abandoned city then slowly started to see the signs of negligence and never regained its lost glory again. But history never forgot the city and now it is one of the most visited tourist destination and is now one of the World Heritage Site in India.

The Attractions That Fascinate

The number of architectural treasures that ornate the city with the colours of red and pink are the finest treasures of the Mughal artistry and royalty. As you take a walk inside the barren palaces and halls, the great majesty and excellence of the Mughals slowly unfolds in front of you.

Buland Darwaza (Gate of Victory)

Designed with precious stone and marble, Buland Darwaza claims to be the largest gateway in the world. Its semi-octagonal shape and dome like roof exhibit typical Muslim architecture. The main gateway is crowned by a row of thirteen domed small kiosks representing a true grandeur of the Mughals.

Diwan-E-Am (Hall of Public Audience)

Diwan-E-Am is a spacious quadrangular hall used for celebrations and public prayers. The pavillion situated in the west holds the Emperor's throne and its intricate artistry beautifies the hall even more. This was the supreme criminal court, which dealt with the cases of treason and armed revolt. According to the traditions, an elephant was tied at the north-eastern corner of the hall. You can see the stone ring even today in that particular corner.

Daulat Khana or Khas Mahal (Hall of Private Audience)

It is the imperial palace that consisted 'Kwabgah' or Emperor Akbar's private apartments. The palace stands apart from other Mughal architectures due to its Indian style of execution and the absence of Persian grandeur can be felt. The richly carved bell shaped pedestals and elephant head columns of the palace are the features that give it an immense grandeur of royalty.

Jodha Bai's Palace

Built by Akbar for his Rajput wife, Jodha Bai, the palace flaunts the spirit of Hinduism in every bit of its corner. The sacred 'Tulsi' plant situated in the midst of the large courtyard, square doors in place of archways and jutting balconies over doors, all flaunt the Hindu architecture that blends beautifully with the Mughal style with domed turrets and excellent interior ornamentation.

Shaikh Salim Chisti's tomb

Chisti's tomb is built on an inlaid marble platform a metre high from ground level and the cenotaph inside the mausoleum is enclosed by white marble screens adorned with exquisite lattice work. The walls of the verandah are filled with holy inscriptions from the Koran. This mausoleum is venerated especially by childless couples, who come on pilgrimage to invoke the blessing of the saint.

Jami Masjid

Built by Akbar in 1571 at a cost of 5 lakh rupees, Jami Masjid is one of the largest mosques in India. The walls of the mosque are decorated with excellent marble tracery and exquisite paintings that demand your attention.

Getting There

By Air

Nearest airport is in Agra at a distance of 40 km. Indian Airlines and private alliance airways connect Agra to Delhi, Khajuraho and Varanasi with regular flights. The airport in Kheria is about 6 km from the town and a good service of tourist taxi and auto-rickshaws are available at the airport.

By Rail

Agra Cantt railway station is the nearest railhead of Fatehpur Sikri. Agra is an important railway station of Indian Central

Railways and is served by Delhi-Mumbai. Delhi-Chennai and Delhi-Kolkata trunk lines. The two fastest connections from Delhi are the super-fast Shatabdi Express taking 2 hours and Taj Express taking 2.5 hours to reach Agra. Both the trains return to Delhi giving you a chance of day long excursion to Agra. Pre-paid taxis and auto rickshaws service are available outside the station.

By Road

Fatehpur Sikri is connected to Agra and neighbouring centres by regular bus services of UPSRTC. Some of the major road distances are: Agra – 40 km, Bharatpur – 25 km and Jaipur – 225 km.

Konark Sun Temple

Sun Temple, located in Konark, is probably the best known attraction that is there in Orissa. The temple was build by King Narasimhadeo in the 13th century. Sun Temple is also referred to as 'Black Pagoda' as it is build of black granite. The temple dedicated to Sun God was build as a chariot to him with wheels on all sides of the temple. It is one of the earliest places where Sun God was worshiped. Although few sections of the temple are now in ruins, but still the aura and the elegance of the temple is retained. Konark was once a busy port and many ships came and went. To Europeans, it served as a landmark who started calling the temple Black Pagoda. Sun Temple is considered a marvel among other temples and has been the inspiration for many writers and poets. Numerous books and articles related to its history and architecture have been written. Looking at the temple. Rabindranath Tagore, once said, "Here the language of stone surpasses the language of man".

History of Sun Temple

It is said that Sun Temple is built on the place where Samba, the son of Lord Krishna worshiped Sun God for liberation from a curse put upon him by his father. Legend has it that Samba was arrogant about his beauty and once made fun of a great sage Narada. Sage Narada planned to take revenge. He once lured Samba to the side of the lake where his step mothers were taking bath. Lord Krishna came to know of this unacceptable act by his son. Infuriated, he cursed his son with Leprosy. When Lord Krishna realized that his son was tricked by Sage Narada, he asked Samba to worship Sun God, who is the healer of all diseases. Samba Worshiped Lord Surya on the sea coast. He spent 12 years of penance worshiping Sun God. After long, Surya God appeared and asked Samba to take a holy dip in Konark. As soon as he was relieved of Leprosy, he planned to built a temple dedicated to Sun God at the very same place where he appeared.

Architecture of Sun Temple

Few sections of the temple are now in ruins, but still major portions are still intact. The temple is an unparalleled example of medieval temple architecture. Sun Temple is a form of Vahana (vehicle) style as it is in the shape of a chariot. There are many such temples in India, however none come close to the magnificence of Sun Temple. The main temple structure stands on a platform. There are 12 wheels carved on the two sides of the platform. Each wheels is more than 10 feet in height. The spokes of the wheels work as sundials predicting the exact time of the day. Just stand under one of the wheels and feel the grandness of them. To complete the chariot, there are structures of 7 galloping horses at the entrance of the temple. These seven life size horses are a major attraction of the temple. Once you are close to the walls of the temple, notice the intricate carvings that have been done on the walls. There are images of God and Goddesses, men, women, warriors and scenes from day to day life. It is said that the temple was not build how it was envisioned. But some say that it was build exactly the way it was planned. The magnetic dome was removed from the top as it was causing many ships to crash around the shores. It is kept in the ASI (Archaeological Survey of India) museum for display.

Other Information

Sun Temple in Konark is close to both Bhubaneswar (64 Km) and Puri (35 Km). So it makes a easy reach to the temple by any mode of transportation. Closest airport is at Bhubaneswar whereas nearest railhead is in Puri. And if you are visiting Konark around December, do not forget to be a spectator at the electrifying Konark Dance Festival which showcases all Indian classical dances like Bharatnatyam, Odissi, Kuchipudi and many more. They are performed by dancers who have earned great appreciation for their work from around the world. You can visit Konark any time of the year, as it has a favorable climate throughout the 12 month period.

Sun Temple is one of the most celebrated temples in India. It has been the pride of Orissa since the day it was constructed. Considered as a marvel in temple architecture, Sun Temple is the most stunning structure on the shores of Orissa.

Chapter 11

Heritage Railways

La Trochita

La Trochita, (El Viejo Expreso Patagónico), in English known as the Old Patagonian Express, is a 750 mm narrow gauge railway in Patagonia, Argentina using steam locomotives. The nickname La Trochita means literally "The Little Narrow Gauge" in Spanish. It is 402 km in length and runs through the foothills of the Andes between Esquel and El Maiten in Chubut Province and Ingeniero Jacobacci in Río Negro Province, originally it was part of Ferrocarriles Patagónicos, a network of railways in southern Argentina. Nowadays, with its original character largely unchanged, it operates as a heritage railway and was made internationally famous by the 1978 Paul Theroux book The Old Patagonian Express, which described it as the railway almost at the end of the world.

In 1908, the Government of Argentina planned a network of railways across Patagonia. Two main lines would join San Carlos de Bariloche in the central Andes with the sea ports of San Antonio Oeste on the Atlantic coast to the east, and Puerto Deseado on the coast to the south east. Branches were to be built to connect the mainline with Buenos Aires Lake (connecting at Las Heras) and Comodoro Rivadavia (connecting at Sarmiento). Colonia 16 de Octubre - the Esquel and Trevelin area - would be connected via a branch line to Ingeniero Jacobacci. The whole network would connect to Buenos Aires via San Antonio Oeste.

The project ran out of steam following ministerial changes and the start of World War I which affected the economy of Argentina and the input of technology and investment required from Europe. The northern main line from the coast reached Ingeniero Jacobacci in 1916. 282 km of the southern main line from Deseado to Las Heras, and the 197 km branch line from Comodoro Rivadavia to Sarmiento were laid, but never connected with each other or the northern network. After 1916, the only further work was the completion of the link from Jacobacci to Bariloche, finished in 1934.

Southern Fuegian Railway

The Southern Fuegian Railway or the End of the World Train (Spanish: Ferrocarril Austral Fueguino (FCAF) or El Tren del Fin del Mundo) is a 500 mm (1 ft 7 3?4 in) (narrow-gauge) steam railway in Tierra del Fuego Province, Argentina. It was originally built as a freight line to serve the prison of Ushuaia, specifically to transport timber. It now operates as a heritage railway into the Tierra del Fuego National Park and is considered the southernmost functioning railway in the world.

In the late 19th century, Ushuaia on Isla Grande de Tierra del Fuego developed as a penal colony, with the first prisoners arriving in 1884. In 1902 work began on a proper set of buildings for the prison by inmates, and a railway on wooden rails was constructed to assist the transport of materials, mainly local rock, sand and timber. Oxen pulled wagons along the narrow gauge of less than 1,000 mm (3 ft 3 3?8 in) (metre gauge). In 1909, the prison governor informed the government of the need to upgrade the line and Decauville tracks at a 500 mm gauge were laid in 1909 and 1910 for use with a steam locomotive. They connected the prison camp with the forestry camp and passed along the shoreline in front of the growing town of Ushuaia. It was known as the 'Train of the Prisoners' (Tren de los Presos) and brought wood for heating and cooking as well as building.

The railway was gradually extended further into the forest into more remote areas as wood was exhausted. It followed the valley of the Pipo River into the higher terrain. Constant building allowed expansion of the prison and of the town, with prisoners providing many services and goods.

In 1947 the Prison was closed and replaced with a naval base. Two years later the 1949 Tierra del Fuego earthquake blocked much of the line. Nevertheless the government made efforts to clear the line and put the train back in service despite the absence of the prisoners. However the service was not viable and closed in 1952.

In 1994, the railway was refurbished and began services again, although now in luxury relative to its origin as a prison train, with champagne and dinner services. A new 2-6-2T steam locomotive (Camila) was brought from England in 1995 with another made in Argentina and three diesel locomotives also serving on the line.

Services leave from the 'End of the World' station 8 km west of Ushuaia. The route takes passengers along the Pico Valley in the Toro gorge and to Cascada de la Macarena station where visitors are able to learn about the Yámana people and climb to a viewpoint at a 15-minute stop. The train then enters the national park and the forest, travelling through the valley below the mountains, reaching El Parque station where tourists can return by coach or train.

There is a plan to extend the line to a new station closer to Ushuaia and connect the station to the city with a tram.

Tren a las Nubes

The Tren a las nubes or Tren de las Nubes (Train to/of the Clouds) is a train service in Salta Province of Argentina, that connects the Argentine Northwest with the border with Chile in the Andes mountain range, over 4,220 m (13,845 ft) above mean sea level, the third highest railway in the world. Originally built for economic and social reasons, it is now of primarily touristic value as a heritage railway.

The train leaves from General Belgrano station in the city of Salta for the 15 hour, 434 kilometre round trip to the viaduct La Polvorilla, located 4,220 m (13,845 ft) above sea level. The curved viaduct is 224 metres long and 70 metres high. From Salta, the train enters first the Valle de Lerma and then the Quebrada del Toro before reaching the Puna. It is known as the Train of the Clouds because clouds can be often be seen around and under the bridges and slopes of the landscape through which the railway passes .

The railway line has 29 bridges, 21 tunnels, 13 viaducts, 2 spirals and 2 zigzags. Because of the design decision of not using a rack-and-pinion for traction, the route had to be designed to avoid steep grades. The zigzags allow the train to climb up driving back and forth parallel to the slope of the mountain.

The 10-car train can carry 640 passengers at an average speed of 35 km/h (21.7 mph). The C-C diesel-electric General Electric (GE) locomotive with 2,475 hp (1,846 kW) has two triple-sets of powered axles for traction, weights of over 100 t (98 LT; 110 ST), and consumes around 6 L (1.59 US gal; 1.32 imp gal) of fuel for every 1 kilometre (0.62 mi). The train, which stops in each station for tourists to get off, see the town and buy local handicrafts, has a restaurant, folkloric events, and an on-board medic. The construction of the railway started in 1921, to connect the North of Argentina with Chile across the Andes, and to serve the borax mines of the area. The La Polvorilla viaduct, the highest of the line, was finished on November 7, 1932. The complete railway was inaugurated on February 20, 1948, but it was not until the late 1970s that it started being visited by tourists. The route was designed by US engineer Richard Fontaine Maury., after whom one of the stations has been named.

THE TREN A LAS NUBES TODAY

After several years of refurbishing, the train was again open to the public on 6 August, 2008, it is operated by a private company, Ecotren.

An average of 30,000 tourists visit the train each year, which is also the only public transport for some of the small towns on its path, and is thus used by their local inhabitants.The train runs from April to November and departs from Salta every Wednesday, Friday, and Sunday at 07:05, returning to Salta around 23:48. The train services include dining car, medical practice, audio, video, and bilingual guides. During the summer, from December to March, the Tren al Sol (Train to the Sun) travels from Salta to the Diego de Almagro station, at an altitude of 3,500 metres.

DORRIGO STEAM RAILWAY AND MUSEUM

The Dorrigo Steam Railway and Museum in Dorrigo, New South Wales, Australia has the largest privately owned collection of preserved railway vehicles and equipment from the railways of New South Wales. Covering both Government and private railways its exhibits range from 1855 to the present day. The museum was opened very briefly in 1986, but has been described as "not yet open to the public" ever since.

The museum's origins stem from the creation of Dorrigo Steam Railway and Museum Ltd. in 1973 which formed following the closure of the Glenreagh - Dorrigo branch line the previous year to preserve and restore the 69 kilometres as a tourist railway.

GLENREAGH MOUNTAIN RAILWAY

Glenreagh Mountain Railway, known as the GMR, was established in 1989 as a heritage tourist railway at Glenreagh, near Coffs Harbour, New South Wales, Australia. GMR's objective is to restore and operate a heritage tourist railway on the Glenreagh to Ulong section of the Glenreagh to Dorrigo railway line.

GMR is a non-profit, community-based organisation run entirely by volunteers, and has an authority to raise funds under the Charitable Collections Act.

The GMR acquired the 35-kilometre section to Ulong in 1999 from the then State Rail Authority of New South Wales, and is currently restoring this section of line as well as rolling stock, to enable the heritage tourist railway to operate.

GMR's current rolling stock includes steam locomotive Z19 class 1919, 4-wheel watergin L568, TAM sleeping car, 2 heritage end-platform cars, S trucks, ex-Sydney interurban cars ("U-boats") and numerous trikes and track maintenance vehicles.

As of December 2005, GMR has completed trackwork to safe working standards for train operation from Glenreagh West Depot 3.5 km west to Talawajah Creek. Steam train operations were scheduled one weekend a month subject to fire bans. Recently, operations have ceased while GMR works to fulfil its obligations under the Rail Safety Act.

Lachlan Valley Railway

The Lachlan Valley Railway Society Cooperative Limited is a non-profit rail preservation society based in the NSW Central Western town of Cowra, New South Wales, Australia. The museum's ex-NSWGR Fleet ranges from their operational steam and diesel locomotives, to the fleet of heritage passenger railway carriages, and the "Tin Hare" CPH railmotors in its collection. The society is based in the former NSWGR Locomotive Depot in Cowra, and operates both short and long distance trips from this depot to destinations within NSW.

New South Wales Rail Transport Museum

The New South Wales Rail Transport Museum (NSWRTM) located in Thirlmere, New South Wales south-west of Sydney, is a museum dedicated to displaying former locomotives, carriages and goods wagons from the New South Wales Government Railways as well as private operations in NSW. The collection features steam, diesel and electric locomotives and other rolling stock. A large proportion of the collection is owned by RailCorp NSW.

The Blue Mountains division of the museum is located at the Valley Heights Locomotive Depot Heritage Museum.

The museum operates steam heritage trains on the Picton Loop railway line between Thirlmere, Picton and Buxton. It also hosts the Thirlmere Festival of Steam, in March each year. In addition to this, the museum operates mainline tours under the name Heritage Express. These can consist of day or extended tours, usually over a weekend. NSWRTM/Heritage Express has an office on the Main Concourse at Sydney Central Station.

Established at the Sydney suburb of Enfield in 1962, the museum was forced to move in the mid 1970s due to a proposed redevelopment of the Enfield site by the railways, who selected Thirlmere as an alternative due to the disused "loop line" which could be used for train rides. The new museum opened in 1975.

In 1984 the Museum became a foundation, management member of 3801 Limited - an organisation created to oversee the operation of the locomotive 3801.

The famous British railway locomotive 4472 Flying Scotsman visited Thirlmere in 1988 as part of its tour around Australia.

Classes of locomotives preserved at the museum include steam: J&A Brown 4 & 5, Z12, Z13 Z27, C30 tank and 30T Tender, C36, C38, D50, D55, D59, AD60. Diesel include: 442, 45, 43, 42, 40, 79, 49, 44. Electric locomotives preserved at the museum include 4638 and 8646.

The museum played a major role in the 2005 celebrations marking 150 years of the NSW railways, restoring locomotive 3526 in 2004, for the occasion. They provided much of the rolling stock for a 150 years display at Sydney's Central Station in September

2005. 3526 joined other non-museum locomotives in shuttles to the suburb of Hurstville during the weekend.

The RTM was removed as a board member of 3801 Limited and the loco subsequently returned to the RTM in November 2006 after 3801 Limited's 20-year operating contract expired. Before 3801 Limited's lease expired there was an unsuccessful campaign to renew it, despite the fact that the organisation had funding and a long-term plan in place for the locomotive's overhaul and boiler replacement. Unfortunately there is much scuttlebutt and innuendo placed on the internet regarding the situation by ignorant individuals who have muddied the truth of the situation.

In 2008 steam locomotive 3642 was returned to service having been a static exhibit for 12 years, with the replacement of its previous boiler with an already steamable spare and some minor mechanical work, not a full restoration as expressed by some.

The RTM is now a regular provider of services at the Hunter Valley Steamfest, however in the most recent years a staged reduction of services offered and a refusal to bring passengers from Sydney has put a cloud on said involvement.

Richmond Vale Railway Line, New South Wales

The Richmond Vale Railway was a colliery railway line in the Hunter Region of New South Wales, Australia, servicing coal mines at Minmi, Stockrington, Pelaw Main and Richmond Main. It was over sixteen miles long and passed through three tunnels, and was the last privately-owned, non-tourist, railway in Australia to use steam locomotives.

The line was privately owned, by J. & A. Brown and Abermain Seaham Collieries Limited and then its successor company, Coal and Allied Industries. It was constructed in sections, the earliest section being from Hexham to Minmi, built by John Eales in 1856 to service his colliery at Minmi (later bought out by J. & A. Brown). At the Hexham Exchange Sidings trains either joined the New South Wales Government Railways main north coast line or instead continued across it to J. & A. Brown's coal-loader at Hexham Wharf, on the Hunter River. (The last ship to load coal there was the '60-miler' collier Stephen Brown on 1 November 1967 after which the wharf ceased its operations).

The New South Wales Legislative Assembly passed the Richmond Vale Coal-mine Railway Act in 1900 and a major branch was then constructed from the Minmi line (Minmi Junction) to serve the mines at Stockrington, and from there onwards to Richmond Main Colliery, the line being largely built upon land owned by John Scholey, the founder (c.1890) of Richmond Main.

The Richmond Vale railway had two connections to the privately owned South Maitland Railway lines at Pelaw Main, where another large colliery of the same name was situated with locomotive repair facility sheds, and Weston. From 1918 coal from Kurri Kurri's Stanford Merthyr Colliery was taken by rail to the Pelaw Main Colliery (both opened in 1901), and from there transported over the Richmond Vale Railway to either the exchange sidings or the shipping staiths at Hexham. In addition a limited amount of gas coal, from Brown's Stanford Main No.2 Colliery at Paxton, near Cessnock, also destined for the shipping staiths at Hexham, was also shipped over the line.

The Richmond Vale railway provided a separate route and connection to the Main north line at Hexham and was occasionally used as an alternate route when the South Maitland lines were flooded. However during the great flood of 1955 the Richmond Vale Railway crossing the Hexham Swamps also gave way on 26 February. It took a week to restore just single-line working from J. & A. Brown's collieries along it, as well as for those served by the wrecked South Maitland Railways. It was not until 8 April 1955 that the latter was returned to service.

The fastest recorded journey on the line was a late passenger train from Minmi to Hexham at 60 mph (97 km/h).

Sydney Tramway Museum

The Sydney Tramway Museum is an operating tramway museum, located in Loftus in the southern suburbs of Sydney,

Australia. Sydney Tramway Museum is the trading name of the South Pacific Electric Railway (SPER).

The museum was officially opened at its original site at the edge of the Royal National Park by NSW Deputy Premier Pat Hills in 1965. It was subsequently relocated to its new, larger site which opened on March 19, 1988. Besides an extensive collection of trams from Sydney and other Australian and world cities, the tramway museum includes two running lines radiating from the museum. One line runs 1.5 km north almost to Sutherland railway station, paralleling a suburban highway in a way typical of Sydney's previous tram system.

The second utilises a former railway branch off CityRail's Illawarra railway line to penetrate 2 km into the Royal National Park that flanks Sydney's southern boundary. A number of Sydney's suburban electric train services used to terminate at Royal National Park, but the line closed in 1991, and Waterfall is now the southern terminus for suburban electric train services on the Illawarra line.

Zig Zag Railway

The Zig Zag Railway is a heritage railway at Lithgow in New South Wales, Australia on the site of the famous Great or Lithgow Zig Zag which operated between 1869 and 1910. As built, the line formed part of the Main West line from Sydney across the Blue Mountains and served to lower the line from its summit into the Lithgow valley on the western flank of the mountains. The Zig Zag railway run steam and diesel hauled trains over the Zig Zag for tourists. They are unique in NSW as being the only heritage operator to run everyday except Christmas day.

In 1975 it was decided to restore the Lithgow Zig Zag as a heritage railway, albeit on a different gauge (3 ft 6 in (1,067 mm) instead of the original 4 ft 8 1?2 in (1,435 mm)). Rolling stock for the museum thus comes from states other than New South Wales – Queensland and South Australia in particular. This was due to the difficult nature of obtaining standard gauge rolling stock from the NSW Government of the time. Thus the Zig Zag Railway cooperative was born.

As of 2005 the railway is operated as the Zig Zag Steam and Diesel Tourist Railway.

The railway currently has 3 operational steam locomotives, DD17 1049, BB18 1/4 1072 City of Lithgow, and AC16 218 (There is no "A" in the loco number). C17 934 is currently withdrawn from service. The Railway also has 4 non-operational steam engines, DD17 1046, DD17 1047, C17 966 and South Australian garratt 402. 1046 was the first loco run by the cooperative in 1975 and was operational until the 1980s. 1047 operated between the early 80s and mid 90s. The railway has a large collection of other rollingstock including Queensland Railways 2000 class rail motors, Queensland Railways Evans carriages, South Australian end platform carriages and several older carriages. Former Emu Bay 10 class loco 1004 provides diesel motive power and there are also a couple of small mine locos to compliment. The railway also own 10 class loco 1003 but it is currently withdrawn because the transmission is non-operational.

The Zig Zag Railway runs every day of the year except Christmas day. On Mondays, Tuesdays, Thursdays, Fridays, and Sundays railmotors are operated. Every Wednesday, Saturday, and Sunday a steam loco with train will operate. Sunday has a two train timetable. Special events include a Day Out with Thomas and a Wizards express event held a couple of times per year.

Bellarine Peninsula Railway

The Bellarine Railway is a volunteer-operated steam-driven tourist railway located in Victoria, Australia. It operates on a 16 km section of a formerly disused branch line on the Bellarine Peninsula between the coastal town of Queenscliff and Drysdale, near Geelong.

The original line was commissioned in September 1878, and opened on 21 May 1879. It connected Queenscliff with South Geelong station, the terminus of the Geelong line, and junction of the Warrnambool line. It was acknowledged at the time that although passenger traffic alone might not justify a railway line, military traffic from both the port and Fort Queenscliff - a key defence installation - would warrant its construction. It initially carried passenger, goods and military traffic, and continued to do so for several decades.

In the first months of operation, the carried only one service per day, but at its peak, in January 1885, four trains per day ran in each direction, enabling the line to be used by commuters. However, this was decreased to three not long after, and was cut back to two trains a day in 1910. Traffic on the line continued to fall over the next twenty years, and in 1931, passenger services were dropped completely - apart from the occasional Sunday excursion train. Goods services continued to run, although they were cut to back at first to twice-weekly, and then weekly operation.

The line saw a revival during World War II, carrying mines from the Swan Island military base, but returned to pre-war levels afterwards. After the war, services became less frequent, with passenger services dropped altogether, apart from occasional special trains, and with goods services cut back to one a fortnight. The line was closed on 6 November 1976.

Daylesford Spa Country Railway

The Daylesford Spa Country Railway (which is operated by the Central Highlands Tourist Railway) is a volunteer-operated 1,600 mm (5 ft 3 in) broad gauge tourist railway located in Victoria, Australia. It operates on a section of the formerly disused and dismantled Daylesford line. It presently operates between Daylesford and the hamlet of Bullarto.

The original line was opened in two stages—from the mainline junction at Carlsruhe to the town of Trentham, on February 16,

1880. The remainder of the line was opened a month later on March 17. The line initially had significant goods and passenger traffic, with 50,000 passengers travelling the line in 1884 alone. However, over the next seventy years, both traffic and the quality of line gradually degraded, until the last passenger service was replaced with a road coach in 1978.

The Central Highlands Tourist Railway was founded two years later, and set about restoring the railway to operating condition. After several years of restoration, trolley services commenced to a temporary terminus located in the Wombat Forest in the latter half of the 1980s. On September 15, 1990, rail services commenced between Daylesford and the nearby hamlet of Musk. Another section of line was opened on March 17, 1997, allowing services to operate as far as Bullarto. As the station had been demolished, this required building a new platform and installing a portable station building, which remains as of 2004. In 2002, the organisation changed its trading name from the Central Highlands Tourist Railway to the Daylesford Spa Country Railway.

Mornington Railway

Today the Mornington Railway is a heritage railway near Mornington, a town on the Mornington Peninsula, near Melbourne, Victoria. The line is managed by the Mornington Railway Preservation Society and operates on part of the former Victorian Railways branch line which ran from Baxter to Mornington.

Puffing Billy Railway

The Puffing Billy Railway is a narrow gauge 2 ft 6 in (762 mm) gauge heritage railway in the Dandenong Ranges near Melbourne, Australia. The primary starting point, operations and administration centre, main refreshment room (also selling souvenirs) and ticket purchasing are located at Belgrave station.

Journeys may also be commenced at out-stations of which some have limited facilities for the purchase of tickets, refreshments and souvenirs.

The railway was originally one of four narrow gauge lines of the Victorian Railways opened around the beginning of the 20th century. It runs through the southern foothills of the Dandenong Ranges to Gembrook. Being close to the city of Melbourne and with a post-preservation history spanning over 50 years, the line is one of the most popular steam heritage railways in the world, and attracts tourists from all over Australia and overseas.

The Puffing Billy Railway is kept in operation through the efforts of volunteers of the Puffing Billy Preservation Society, although intensive year-round operations necessitate a small band of paid employees to keep things going behind the scenes.

The railway aims to preserve the line as near as possible to how it was in the first three decades of its existence, but with particular emphasis on the early 1920s.

South Gippsland Railway

The South Gippsland Railway is a tourist railway located in south Gippsland, Victoria, Australia. It controls a section of the former South Gippsland line between Nyora and Leongatha, operating services from Leongatha to Lang Lang via Korumburra taking around 65 minutes, trains operate on Sundays, Public Holidays (except Good Friday and Christmas Day) and Wednesdays during Victorian school holidays. The line passes through the rolling Strzelecki Ranges and lush dairy farmland.

The South Gippsland line was opened from Dandenong to Cranbourne in 1888 and extended to Koo Wee Rup, Nyora and Loch in 1890, Korumburra and Leongatha in 1891. The section from Lang Lang to Leongatha was transferred to the South Gippsland Railway in 1994. Freight trains continued to use the line from Dandenong as far as Koala Siding near Nyora until 1998.

VICTORIAN GOLDFIELDS RAILWAY

The Victorian Goldfields Railway is a 1,600 mm (5 ft 3 in) broad gauge tourist railway in Victoria, Australia. It operates along a formerly disused branch line between the towns of Maldon and Castlemaine.

The original line was opened on June 16, 1884, opening up rail access from the established station at Castlemaine to the towns of Muckleford and Maldon. The area was prosperous, as Castlemaine and Maldon had both experienced gold rushes in the preceding years, and local residents had been petitioning the state government for a railway since 1874. On August 2, 1884, a contract was let for an extension to Laanecoorie, however further construction was suspended after the line reached the small town of Shelbourne in 1891.

The line was served by twice-daily trains for the first forty years of its life, which was increased to four-times-daily trains in 1924. However, these were cut back at the end of the 1920s due to a decrease in the local population, and passenger services were eliminated altogether during World War II. This meant that the line was only used by a weekly goods train which went through to Shelbourne. When bushfire damage caused the closure of the Shelbourne extension in 1970, the remainder of the line was rendered largely useless, and it was officially closed in December 1976.

The response to the closure from the local community was swift, and the Castlemaine and Maldon Railway Preservation Society was founded in the same month, with the intention of reopening the line as a tourist railway. While Maldon station was intact, and was able to used as a base for their operations, they were faced with numerous problems: a line that needed substantial repairs, a lack of rolling stock, and rebuilding the demolished station at Muckleford.

WALHALLA GOLDFIELDS RAILWAY

The Walhalla Goldfields Railway is a 2 ft 6 in (762 mm) gauge (narrow gauge) tourist railway located in the Thomson River and Stringers Creek valleys in Gippsland, Victoria, Australia, near the former gold-mining town and popular tourist destination of Walhalla.

The Walhalla line was the last of four experimental narrow gauge lines of the Victorian Railways, the Moe-Walhalla railway commenced in 1904, but was not completed until 1910. The railway was expected to be a boon for Walhalla, which was in a state of decline with gold mining operations becoming uneconomical. The largest gold mining company closed in 1914.

After the closure of the Walhalla mines, substantial timber traffic was carried from sawmills around Erica until the late 1940s. Freight and passenger traffic declined, with the railway closed in sections from 1944 with the final section from Moe to Victoria closed on June 25, 1954. The tracks and buildings were removed by 1960, leaving only the roadbed and a number of bridges.

The former station building at Walhalla was re-located to the Melbourne suburban station of Hartwell. The centre span of the National Estate listed Thomson River Railway Bridge was formerly part of a road bridge over the Murray River at Tocumwal (NSW). The website of the Australian Heritage Commission confirms this fact.

AUSTRALIAN SOCIETY OF SECTION CAR OPERATORS, INC.

The Australian Society of Section Car Operators, Inc. (ASSCO), is an accredited railway operator that seeks access to railways for its members. It is a non-profit organisation, registered under the Associations Incorporations Act (SA).

Ballyhooley Steam Railway

The Bally Hooley Steam Railway is a heritage railway operating in Port Douglas, Queensland, Australia. It operates on approximately 4 km of 2 ft (610 mm) gauge line from the Marina Mirage to Saint Crispin's Station. The railway is operated by a group of volunteers and runs services on Sundays.

Brisbane Tramway Museum

Brisbane Tramway Museum is a transport museum which preserves and displays trams and trolley-buses, most of which operated in Brisbane, Queensland, Australia. The museum also has a collection of vehicles and other equipment used in maintaining Brisbane's electric street transport system which operated from 1897 to 1969. The Museum is located at Ferny Grove, a north-west suburb of Brisbane.

The museum is operated by the Brisbane Tramway Museum Society, a not-for-profit public company. It is run entirely by volunteers. The society was established in 1968, when it became apparent that the Brisbane City Council was preparing to close Brisbane's tram system.

Kuranda Scenic Railway

The Kuranda Scenic Railway is a name for the railway line that runs from Cairns, Queensland, Australia to the nearby town of Kuranda. The tourist railway snakes its way up the Macalister Range and is no longer used for regular commuter services. It passes through the suburbs of Stratford, Freshwater (stopping at Freshwater Station) and Redlynch before reaching Kuranda. The line is used for some freight services and other passenger services, such as the savannahlander.

The tropical gardens Kuranda rail station are a well-known attaction in the area. Downhill the line cuts through the Barron

Gorge National Park. The tourist train stops at a lookout, with a sweeping view of Barron Falls. A number of smaller waterfalls are passed, including Stoney Creek Falls, just metres from the train. As the train travels up and down, a detailed commentary of the railway's construction is provided.

The railway was completed as far as Kuranda in 1891. Many lives were lost as numerous tunnels and bridges were built. The first operation of a tourist train from Cairns to Kuranda was in 1936, using four longitudinal seating carriages. In 1995 major repairs had to be carried out after a severe rockfall damaged the track.

Mary Valley Heritage Railway

The Mary Valley Heritage Railway conduct steam train trips and tours from Gympie through the Mary Valley in the Cooloola Region of Queensland, Australia.

"Ride The Rattler" scenic tours are operated by The Mary Valley Heritage Railway (MVHR) every Saturday, Sunday and Wednesday from the historic Gympie Railway Station. This historic 40 km journey commences at Gympie, and after crossing the Mary River, negotiates an abundance of curves, gradients and bridges to pass through the small country villages of Dagun, Amamoor and Kandanga to Imbil.

The steam train, a fully restored C17 class locomotive from the early 1920s, departs Gympie station at 10 am. The Gympie Station itself dates back to pre-1880. As the train travels south, it passes through the southern end of the city of Gympie.

After crossing the Mary River, the railway line enters the Mary Valley. The line wanders away from the river to negotiate the valleys of some of its main tributaries, including the Yabba, Kandanga and Amamoor Creeks. In this area there are a number of curves, gradients and bridges as you head towards the station of Kandanga.

The country village of Kandanga was established in 1910 to service patrons travelling on the proposed Mary Valley line which became operational as far as Kandanga in 1914. The original station, now restored to its former glory, contains an interesting pictorial record of the history of the Mary Valley line.

Travelling through to Imbil, the lines traverses an interesting gorge section through mainly timbered country, before reaching a short tunnel that pierces a ridge of coastal ranges. The track then descends quickly to the line's largest town, Imbil.

LIMESTONE COAST RAILWAY

The Limestone Coast Railway was a former tourist railway that operated around Mount Gambier in South Australia's Limestone Coast region. Due to problems with public liability insurance, it was forced to suspend operations in about the year 2000. It resumed a limited service to Tantanoola and Naracoorte but again suspended its operations as of 1 July 2006. All rail operations have ceased as of December 2006.

PICHI RICHI RAILWAY PRESERVATION SOCIETY

The Pichi Richi Railway Preservation Society (PRRPS) is a non-profit railway preservation society and operating museum formed in 1973. The society, managed and staffed by volunteers, operates heritage steam and diesel trains on the restored 39 km section of track between Quorn and Port Augusta in South Australia. This railway line, constructed in 1878 as part of the South Australian Railways Port Augusta and Government Gums Railway, once formed a part of the former Central Australia Railway and east-west Transcontinental line, and is the oldest remaining section of track of the former narrow gauge Ghan.

PRRPS bases its operations in Quorn and runs through the Pichi Richi Pass to Woolshed Flat and Port Augusta, and also operates out of Port Augusta to Quorn. The volunteer organisation has fully restored a fleet of South Australian Railways (SAR), Commonwealth Railways (CR) and Western Australian

Government Railways (WAGR) steam and diesel locomotives, passenger and freight rolling stock. The society has progressively restored the railway to Summit (1974), Pichi Richi (1974), Woolshed Flat (1979) and Stirling North (1999) on the original alignment, and to Port Augusta (2001) on a new alignment between Stirling North and Port Augusta.

Pichi Richi is the name of the pass through which the railway travels, and is also the name of the former township located in the pass, after which the society is named. The name Pichi Richi is believed to come from the Australian native plant pituri, which was traditionally chewed by Australian Aborigines.

SteamRanger

SteamRanger is a historic train society in South Australia running trains on the Victor Harbor railway line. They are the only group regularly running broad gauge steam locomotives in South Australia. It is run by volunteers of the South Australian Division of the Australian Railway Historical Society.

Prior to 1995 when the Adelaide to Melbourne line was converted to standard gauge, SteamRanger was based at Dry Creek, an industrial suburb in the northern suburbs of Adelaide, and home to the main road-rail freight depots in Adelaide. The Southern Encounter operated from Adelaide instead of Mount Barker, including six tunnels through the Mount Lofty Ranges. Special services were also operated to other places on the South Australian broad gauge network including Burra (near the Clare Valley), Nuriootpa in the Barossa Valley and shorter services on the metropolitan network.

Steamtown Heritage Rail Centre

The Steamtown Heritage Rail Centre is a static railway museum based in the former railway workshops located in Peterborough, South Australia.

Peterborough was the administrative and service centre for the Peterborough Division of the South Australian Railways, employing up to 1,500 people in the workshops during its heyday. The railway workshops covered an extensive area mainly to the west of the township, and it is in these original buildings that the exhibits are displayed.

The turntable and roundhouse are the main features of the exhibit. The turntable is unusual in that it accommodates three rail gauges: Narrow Gauge (1067 mm), Standard Gauge (1435 mm) and Broad Gauge (1600 mm). In Australia there were only two similar turntables (located at Port Pirie and Gladstone); all three were on the same line, with that at Peterborough the only one remaining. This unique situation arose from the standardisation project of the late 1960s. At this time the Broad Gauge line was extended from Terowie to Peterborough and the Port Pirie to Broken Hill section (passing through Peterborough) was replaced by Standard Gauge line. The Peterborough to Quorn section remained Narrow Gauge.

Prior to the cessation of railway operations by Steamtown, Peterborough Railway Preservation Society Inc in June 2002, a steering committee, made up of the Federation of North East Councils, the Northern Regional Development Board, and the Flinders Ranges Area Consultative Committee, as well as Society representatives, was established. This led to the establishment of a project to formalise development of the workshops precinct, which in turn led to the development of the Steamtown Heritage Rail Centre.

National Railway Museum

The National Railway Museum, Port Adelaide, South Australia, is the current site of the Port Dock Station Railway Museum's vast Australian Railway Collection.

The museum was founded in 1963, by a group of rail preservationists who managed to convince the South Australian

Railways Commissioner to allocate land on the site of the former Mile End Roundhouse to house a small collection of withdrawn steam locomotives. The original site, on Railway Terrace Mile End, had only a small number of exhibits under cover. Most items had to be housed on the site in the open air. The effects of weather took their toll on the exhibits, so an alternative undercover venue was sought.

In 1988 the Museum was fortunate enough, with the involvement of the History Trust of SA, to obtain a $2m Australia's bicentennial Commemorative Grant to relocate to its current site and to provide covered accommodation for the exhibits. On 2 January 1988 the gates at the Mile End Railway Museum closed for the last time and on 10 December 1988, after almost a year of frantic activity, the Port Dock Station Railway Museum Port Adelaide was officially opened by the Premier of South Australia, The Hon John Bannon.

In 1999, special funding was received as part of Australia's Centenary of Federation to construct the Commonwealth Railway Museum within the museum's precinct. This new facility, which was opened on 21 October 2001, houses a representative sample of exhibits from the "Commonwealth Railways" and "Australian National". Included is the original Tea and Sugar train, as well as a number of vehicles that were used on the Ghan and Trans-Australian passenger trains.

At the opening of the Commonwealth Railway Museum the Port Dock Station Railway Museum was renamed the National Railway Museum. The name change is a response to the Commonwealth Railways operations being integrated into a National Transport Network that spans the whole of the Australian continent.

he museum currently houses their large static collection in two pavilions and the historical goods shed at the site of the original Port Dock railway station. On the site, all three gauges of Australia are represented, these being Narrow (3' 6" or 1067mm), Standard (4' 8½" or 1435mm) and Broad Gauge (5' 3" or 1600mm).

Operational locomotives and railcars on these gauges respectively are Steam locomotive Peronne (1918 Andrew Barclay 0-6-0 Tank Locomotive), DE 507 (South Australian Railways) and 801 (SAR), Redhen Railcars 400, 321 and trailer 863. The museum also operates a number of 18" gauge (457mm) equipment, mainly steam locomotives Bub (0-4-2T) and Bill (2-4-0 with 4 wheel tender).

In 2008 the museum received the 1949 Overland roomette sleeping car Allambi, donated by the Victorian Government after being stored after the ned of the Vinelander service.

Bennett Brook Railway

The Bennett Brook Railway is a tourist oriented railway operated by the West Australian Light Railway Preservation Association and is located within the boundaries of Whiteman Park, nineteen kilometres from Perth. In 2009, the Bennett Brook Railway celebrated its 25th year of operation.

The West Australian Light Railway Preservation Association (WALRPA) was formed on 26 April 1976 by a group of rail enthusiasts. The railway started from small beginnings in a members backyard located in the Perth Hills to the present day fully fledged railway operation based in Whiteman Park.

Hotham Valley Railway

Hotham Valley Tourist Railway (WA) Inc., which operates a heritage railway in Western Australia, has its origins in a small group of enthusiasts who met together in 1974 with the object of preserving steam locomotives and the railway line from Pinjarra to Dwellingup.

Today, Hotham Valley's operations are based around their facilities at Pinjarra, and the Hotham Valley Railway between Alumina Junction and Etmilyn. In past years, the organisation ran a number of trains across the Westrail narrow gauge network, which is now leased to WestNet Rail. This included tour trains to such destinations as Albany, Bridgetown, Northam, Geraldton or York. Steam trains run during non-summer months including regular services from Pinjarra to Dwellingup. As with many other tourist railways, escalating insurance costs, and human resourcing issues, contributed to a curtailment of its operations from the broader network to the Hotham Valley Line.

From the Dwellingup station, Hotham Valley runs the Etmilyn Forest Tramway, which runs 8km east to Etmilyn. This service includes the perennially popular Etmilyn Forest Diner.

Hotham Valley locomotives have also recently been contracted for infrastructure trains, for example running rail trains to Geraldton. An interesting working occurred in June 2003 when light diesel locomotive Z1152 was transported by road to the new Nowergup railcar depot to assist with the placement of the overhead wiring.

Pemberton Tramway Company

Pemberton Tramway Company operates a tourist railway from Lyall to Pemberton in Western Australia. Trams run from the old WAGR railway station at Pemberton to Northcliffe. A steam hauled passenger train operates between Lyall and Pemberton.

Spirit of the West

The Spirit of the West is a restaurant train that operates out of Perth, Western Australia. The train consists of carriages restored by the Australian Railway Historical Society, some of which are over ninety years old and in themselves are unique sole remaining examples of carriages no longer seen in service in Australia.

The train operates under the old Midland Railway Company name, an offshoot of South Spur Rail Services. The train runs regular Sunday lunch and Saturday dinner trips from East Perth Terminal into the Avon Valley, running to West Toodyay and return.

Evening services to Leighton and return via Fremantle were halted due to vandalism on the Forrestfield to Cockburn section of the railway line. The first revenue service was on Friday, 18th of October 2002. The service has been nominated for Tourism awards for its unique rolling stock and service.

Bush Mill Railway

The Bush Mill Railway was a 1 ft 3 in (381 mm) gauge miniature railway, situated 2 km (1.2 mi) from Port Arthur, in Tasmania. It opened in 1986. The Bush Mill Railway climbed steeply through a series of loops and zig zags up a hillside, then across a spectacular Serpentine Bridge. A half-size replica of the world's first Beyer-Garratt locomotive, North-East Dundas Tramway, Tasmania's K1, was constructed to operate on the line in 1990.

A replica settlement was established which featured a 19th century sawmill and a number of items which were directly related to the logging tramways which once dotted much of Tasmania.

Derwent Valley Railway

The Derwent Valley Railway is a heritage railway in Tasmania, Australia. It operates from New Norfolk. It is 3' 6" narrow gauge. Tasmanian Government Railways opened the Derwent Valley Line in 1886. Initially, it ran from the junction at Bridgewater along the main north-south Hobart to Devonport line to New Norfolk, a distance of 18 kilometres. It was extended another 29 km to Plenty in 1887, and then a further 41 km to Glenora in 1888. It closely follows the course of the River Derwent for the first 39 km as far as Coniston, and crosses the river at three different points.

The following years saw a number of plans to extend the line further up the Derwent Valley or to connect it to the West Coast. Finally, twenty one years later, in 1909, it was extended along the Tyenna River, another 49 km to what is now Westerway. In 1917 another extension was added to extend the railway to Fitzgerald (66 km), and a final extension was opened in 1936 to Kallista (74 km), making it a total of 249 km in length from New Norfolk to Kallista. The last extension replaced an earlier wooden tramway on the same alignment. The primary usage of the line was to provide a service to the rural areas and the logging areas around Kallista. In 1940 there was a significant increase in log traffic along most of the line with the opening of a paper mill at Boyer, 14 km from Bridgewater. This increased traffic resulted in the construction of two deviations and additional facilities at a number of stations.

Sometime later, parts of the railway began to close. Firstly, the logging branches around Kallista, and then the section from Kallista to Florentine were closed. In 1995, TasRail completely closed the line beyond New Norfolk after floods and heavy rain substantially damaged the track.

Don River Railway

The Don River Railway is a vintage railway in Don, a suburb of Devonport, Tasmania. They run a short train ride from Don to Coles beach, about ten minutes away. They are presently trying to restore an M class steam locomotive. They have a few running diesel locomotives and a railcar for use until they get their steamer running. The running diesels are; V-2, 866, X-4 and Y-6. They use them on holidays and the railcar on normal days.

West Coast Wilderness Railway

The West Coast Wilderness Railway, Tasmania is a reconstruction of the Mount Lyell Mining and Railway Company railway between Queenstown and Regatta Point.

The Mount Lyell Mining Co (reformed on 29 March 1893 as the Mount Lyell Mining and Railway Company) began on November 1892. The railway officially opened in 1897, and again on 1 November 1899 when the line was extend from Teepookana to Regatta Point and Strahan.

The railway was the only way to get the copper from the mine at Queenstown, Tasmania to markets. Until 1932 when a Hobart road link was completed, it was the only access through to Queenstown. The motto of Kelly and Orr was, Labor Omnia Vincit, shows the achievement of this railway because it ran, even though multiple surveyors said it was not possible, the weather was extreme, the trains had to climb 1m in 16m (6.25%), and the train had to carry many tonnes of copper and the rail line had to survive natural disasters (including 1906 floods).

The railway utilised the Abt rack system of cog railway for steep sections. Because of the gradients, tonnages were always limited on the railway. The gauge is 3 ft 6 in (1,067 mm).

The railway ceased operation on 10 August 1963 due to its financial costs and the alternative road option. The last train run was performed by the same engine that ran the first run (ABT 1 in 1896 was the first engine to steam into Queenstown). The line and most removable constructions were lifted, however some of the bridges were left intact.

The formation and some of the bridges remained intact for decades after closure, however most required replacement when reconstruction occurred in the late 1990s.

The original line continued into the Mount Lyell mining operations area in Queenstown, and at Regatta Point the line linked around the foreshore of Strahan to link with the Government Line to Zeehan.

Following the closure of the railway - rolling stock was dispersed - carriages to the Puffing Billy Railway in Victoria - and the Abt locomotives were put on static displays or in museums.

Dendermonde–Puurs Steam Railway

The Dendermonde-Puurs Steam Railway (Stoomspoorlijn Dendermonde-Puurs) is a heritage railway situated in the Belgian provinces of East Flanders (Oost-Vlaanderen) and Antwerp (Antwerpen).

It runs from the town of Dendermonde to the town of Puurs over about 14 km of 1,435 mm (4 ft 8 1?2 in) (standard gauge) track. The railway is maintained by BVS, a non-profit historical railway society. BVS, which stands for Belgische Vrienden van de Stoomlocomotief, or Belgian Friends of the Steam Locomotive, has a depot at the railway station in Baasrode-Noord. The trains are pulled by both steam and diesel locomotives.

The railway has been used occasionally by various film and television production companies to shoot movie scenes that are too elaborate to be filmed on the Belgian national railway network because of the potential disruption to traffic. The best known example of a movie that includes several scenes shot on the railway is Toto le Héros.

Corcovado Rack Railway

The Corcovado Train (Portuguese: Trem do Corcovado) is a mountain railway in Rio de Janeiro in Brazil, from Cosme Velho to the summit of the Corcovado Mountain at an altitude of 710 m (2,329 ft). The summit is known for its statue of Christ the Redeemer and its views over the city and beaches of Rio.

The line is 3.8 km (2.4 mi) long. It is a 1,000 mm (3 ft 3 3?8 in) gauge rack railway using the Riggenbach rack system. The line was opened by Emperor Dom Pedro II on the 9th October 1884. Initially steam hauled, the line was the first railway to be electrified in Brazil in 1910, and was re-equipped in 1980 with trains built by SLM of Winterthur in Switzerland.

It is one of the few remaining railways using three-phase electric power with two overhead wires, at 800 V 60 Hz. There are four trains, each of two cars. The trip takes approximately 20 minutes and departs every half hour, giving a capacity of 360 passengers per hour. Due to this limited capacity the wait at the entry station can be several hours. The line operates from 08:30 to 18:30. The line has been ridden by many famous people, including Pope Pius XII, Pope John Paul II, Alberto Santos-Dumont, Albert Einstein and Diana, Princess of Wales.

ESTRADA DE FERRO OESTE DE MINAS

The Estrada de Ferro Oeste de Minas was a 2 ft 6 in (762 mm) narrow gauge railway located in the southeastern Brazilian state of Minas Gerais. At its peak the railway's route totalled 775 km (482 mi). A portion of the railway still operates as a heritage railway, and one of the major stations is now Brazil's largest railway museum.

Alberta Railway Museum

The Alberta Railway Museum (ARM) located in Edmonton, Alberta the Alberta Railway Museum houses a collection of railway equipment and buildings. It has locomotives from both the Canadian National Railways (CNR) and Northern Alberta Railways (NAR).

Alberta Prairie Railway Excursions

Alberta Prairie Railway Excursions is a heritage railway originating in Stettler, Alberta. The destination for all excursions is Big Valley - trips last five to six hours, with stopover (all excursions include a buffet meal). Many trains (see the schedule) are pulled by the No. 41 1920 Baldwin 2-8-0 steam locomotive.

Galt Historic Railway Park

The Galt Historic Railway Park has many displays of life and travel in the 1880s that are set up in the restored 1890 North West Territories International Train Station from Coutts, Alberta, Canada and Sweetgrass, Montana, USA. The station was moved to the current location near Stirling, Alberta in 2000.

Heritage Park Historical Village

Heritage Park Historical Village is a historical park located in Calgary, Alberta. The park is located on 127 acres (0.51 km2) of parkland on the banks of the Glenmore Reservoir, along the city's southwestern edge. As Canada's largest living history museum by number of exhibits, it is one of the city's most visited tourist attractions. The park is branded as a living history museum since it features a village that was recreated to appear as it might have in late 19th and early 20th century Alberta. Many of the buildings are historical and were transported to the park to be placed on display. Others are re-creations of actual buildings. Most of the structures are furnished and decorated with genuine artifacts. Staff dress in historic costume, and antique automobiles and horse-drawn vehicles service the site. Calgary Transit provides regular shuttle service from Heritage C-Train station.

Rocky Mountain Rail Society

he Rocky Mountain Rail Society operates a heritage steam locomotive in Stettler, Alberta. The RMRS is dedicated to the preservation of Canadian National Railway Mountain steam locomotive #6060, known as The Spirit of Alberta. Excursions are operated on a regular schedule using #6060 as well as Alberta Prairie Railway Excursions locomotive #41.

Royal Canadian Pacific

The Royal Canadian Pacific is a luxury excursion passenger train operated by the Canadian Pacific Railway (CPR), inaugurated on June 7, 2000, after the CPR received the royal designation for the service from Elizabeth II, Queen of Canada.

The train operates seasonally from June to September, on CPR trackage through the Rocky Mountains in Alberta and British Columbia. All trains are based out of Calgary, Alberta, at the former VIA Rail station near CPR's corporate headquarters. A typical excursion would be a 1,050 km (650 mi) route from Calgary through the Columbia River Valley and Crowsnest Pass, before returning to Calgary. Such a trip would take six days and five nights with no operating at night in order to preserve the sight-seeing of mountain scenery during the daylight hours. The train consists of up to eight luxury passenger cars built between 1916 and 1931, and is powered by restored first-generation diesel locomotives.

Alberni Pacific Railway

The Alberni Pacific Railway is a heritage railway originating in Port Alberni, British Columbia. The railway is powered by a 1929 Baldwin steam locomotive departing from the 1912 CPR Station. It uses rebuilt cabooses as passenger cars. The 35 minute excursions go to the McLean Mill National Historic Site.

BC Forest Discovery Centre

The BC Forest Discovery Centre, located in Duncan, chronicles the history of logging in British Columbia, Canada. Its mission is to be British Columbia's foremost interpreter and presenter of the forest community – past, present and future.

Fort Steele, British Columbia

Fort Steele is a heritage town in the East Kootenay region of British Columbia, Canada. It is located north of the Crowsnest Highway along Highways 93 and 95, 10 miles (16 km) northeast of Cranbrook.

Kamloops Heritage Railway

The Kamloops Heritage Railway is a heritage railway in Kamloops, British Columbia. The railway operates throughout the year, running trains within Kamloops and to Armstrong. The train is pulled by restored steam locomotive Canadian National Railway 2141, the "Spirit of Kamloops". 2141 was built in 1912 by the Canadian Locomotive Company, in Kingston, ON - built for the Canadian Northern Railway, prior to it being absorbed into the Canadian National Railway. She is a 2-8-0, 'Consolidated' class of steam locomotive built for branch line railways. Originally a coal burner, she was converted to burn oil in 1954, and retired from active duty in 1958. 2141 was sold to the City of Kamloops in 1961, and placed on display in Riverside Park until restoration work began in 1995. The restoration was completed in 2001, and 2141 has been working for KHR from May until December each year since.

Kettle Valley Steam Railway

The Kettle Valley Steam Railway is a heritage railway near Summerland, British Columbia. The KVSR operates excursion trains over the only remaining section of the Kettle Valley Railway through beautiful vistas, orchards, vineyards, and over the 238' tall Trout Creek Trestle. Trains depart at 10:30 and 1:30 Sat-Mon during the spring and fall and Thurs-Mon through July and August. Check the schedule for special events such as the Great Train Robbery and the Christmas Express. Trains are pulled by ex-Canadian Pacific 2-8-0 steam locomotive #3716 (N-2-B class), built in 1912. The railway also has a 2-truck shay locomotive, Mayo Lumber #3.

Vancouver Downtown Historic Railway

The Vancouver Downtown Historic Railway is a heritage streetcar line that ran between Granville Island and the Cambie Station (north of 6th Ave just east of Ash Street) in Vancouver, British Columbia, Canada. It operated only on weekends and holidays, from May to mid-October, and was aimed primarily at tourists. Two restored interurban streetcars were used on the line, which used a former freight railway right-of-way. The VDHR has not been operated in 2010; its web site states an "anticipated reopening" in late August 2010. The line and cars are owned by the City of Vancouver, and they are restored, maintained and operated by volunteers from the Transit Museum Society.

Service was inaugurated on July 29, 1998 and was considered to be a demonstration project for a modern downtown streetcar system that the city plans to develop. It has continued to operate almost every summer since then, as an excursion-oriented historic streetcar line. Currently, the line runs from Granville Island to a stop near Science World and Main Street-Science World SkyTrain station. The proposal for a modern line would extend the existing line through Chinatown and Gastown to Waterfront Station, and eventually to Stanley Park. There would be a separate line into Yaletown with longer term potential for a number of other lines.

West Coast Railway Association

The West Coast Railway Association is a heritage railway and museum located on Government Road in Squamish, British Columbia, near Vancouver, whose purpose is to collect, preserve and restore railway cars and artifacts and operate a licensed railway.

To this end, the Association acquired the Royal Hudson #2860 steam locomotive from the cash strapped BC Rail and in 2006 restored it to operation. The Association has the largest collection of railway rolling stock and artifacts in Canada outside of the Canadian Railway Museum.

Prairie Dog Central Railway

The Prairie Dog Central Railway is a heritage railway in Winnipeg, Manitoba. Regular trips are every Saturday, Sunday and Holiday Monday from May through September, and last almost four hours with two stops totalling just over two hours. Special dinner excursions occur in July and September, as well as Howlin' Halloween and Santa Trains in October, November and December. Details of the operations can be found by reviewing the Schedules and Charters are also available.

Salem and Hillsborough Railroad

The Salem and Hillsborough Railroad (S&H), now the New Brunswick Railway Museum, was a Canadian tourism railroad and museum located in Hillsborough, New Brunswick. The S&H was created in 1982 by a group of volunteer railroad enthusiasts and retired railroad employees. They took possession of a section of former CN Rail branch line trackage which ran from CN's Moncton-Saint John mainline at Salisbury east to just beyond the village of Hillsborough, approximately 20 miles away. CN had operated this subdivision to service a gypsum quarry until the late 1970s when the quarry was closed, resulting in the company applying for abandonment.

The S&H initially operated several historic CN and CPR steam locomotives which had been used in New Brunswick until the early 1960s when both railways completely dieselized. The S&H operated regular coach and dinner tourist trains between Hillsborough and a location halfway between Hillsborough and Salisbury, named Salem, from 1982 until 2004.

In 1994, a disastrous fire occurred as a result of an arson attack on the railway's engine shop in Hillsborough, destroying or damaging several locomotives and historic freight and passenger cars. The rebuilding effort took many years, during which time the volunteer base began to dwindle.

Following the 9/11 terrorist attacks, the S&H saw its liability insurance increase dramatically. In addition, ongoing repairs to two bridges over Weldon Creek, a small tributary of the Petitcodiac River near Hillsborough, were proving to be extremely expensive for an organization which did not receive much support from the provincial or federal governments.

It was decided in 2005 to not operate any passenger excursion trains and to maintain the equipment for static displays only, in addition to a museum which was recently established on the station and shop grounds in Hillsborough.

Excursion trains did not operate in 2006, 2007, nor 2008 due to lack of funding and volunteers and train operations are now indefin:tely canceled.

Formerly operating rail equipment and numerous railway artifacts are now available to view at the New Brunswick Railway Museum, formally the Salem and Hillsborough Railroad.

HALTON COUNTY RADIAL RAILWAY

The Halton County Radial Railway is a working museum of electric streetcars, other railway vehicles, trolleybusses and buses. It is operated by the Ontario Electric Railway Historical Association. It is focused primarily on the history of the Toronto Transit Commission, with a collection including PCC, and Peter Witt cars, earlier streetcars and Gloucester series and Montreal-built subway cars.

The museum is open to the public, with rides on many of its vehicles. It is located between the villages of Rockwood and Campbellville in Milton, Ontario, Canada, along part of the Toronto Suburban Railway's former right-of-way. The tracks conform to TTC's gauge of 1,495 mm (4 ft 10 7?8 in), 60 mm (2.36 in) wider than 1,435 mm (4 ft 8 1?2 in) Standard gauge. Vehicles from other systems must be altered to accommodate the tracks, and cars intended for third-rail power must be reconfigured for use with overhead wire. In 1889, electric railway service on routes radiating from Toronto, Ontario began. An Ontario Historical Plaque was erected at the Halton County Radial Railway Museum by the province to commemorate the Radial Railways' role in Ontario's heritage. Museum Peter Witt streetcars can be seen in the 2005 film Cinderella Man on the streets of Toronto to give it a 1930's New York City appearance.

PORT STANLEY TERMINAL RAIL

The Port Stanley Terminal Rail is a heritage railway that passes over the historic tracks of The London and Port Stanley Railway (L&PS) between Port Stanley and St. Thomas. The tourist trains began operating in 1983, after volunteers started maintaining the abandoned L&PS train corridor.

Port Elgin and North Shore RailroadThe Port Elgin and North Shore Railway is a narrow-gauge heritage railway in Port Elgin, Ontario.

The railway operates excursion trains along the beach on a 1 mile (1.6 km) route in downtown Port Elgin. The round trip takes approximately 20 minutes.

Trains on the PE & NS are scheduled on weekends in June from 11 a.m. to 8 p.m. with cooperative weather (meaning no rain or winds), and from June 20th until September 7 days a week from 10 a.m. to 10 p.m. September has the same schedule as June. In the summer, trains run as frequently as five times per day except for Mondays.

South Simcoe Railway

The South Simcoe Railway is a steam heritage railway in Tottenham, Ontario, north of Toronto. Operating excursions since 1993, it is the oldest operating steam heritage railway in Ontario and features the oldest operating steam locomotive in Canada.

Excursions last about 50 minutes over 4 miles of track from Tottenham through the scenic Beeton Creek valley to Beeton and back. Although the trains stop in Beeton, passengers cannot disembark, as there is not a station there. The railway has plans to add a Beeton station, but as is common with many heritage railways, this sort of project is highly dependent on fundraising.

The railway has two ex-Canadian Pacific steam locomotives, the best known being an 1883 4-4-0 A2m #136 (which many Canadians have seen, as it was used in the 1970s CBC Television series The National Dream). #136 helped build the transcontinental railroad, the Canadian Pacific, across Canada in the 1880s. The railway also owns a 1912 4-6-0 D10h, ex-CPR #1057, and two road-capable diesel locomotives, (ex-Canadian Pacific D-T-C #22 and ex-Norfolk Southern GE 70-ton diesel-electric #703). Rounding out the collection is a diesel-electric yard switcher, Ruston-Hornsby 165DE #10.

The excursion train is made up of restored 1920s era coaches, previously owned by the Canadian Pacific Railway, Canadian National Railway, Toronto, Hamilton and Buffalo Railway and the Louisville & Nashville Railroad. The railway's equipment collection also includes rolling stock not used on the excursions, including a former Ontario Northland Railway business car #200, a combination passenger/baggage coach used as a museum, two wooden cabooses, one steel wide-vision ex-CPR caboose, a ballast car, various boxcars, flat cars, and steam generator cars.

Regular excursions operate from the May long weekend through to the weekend after Thanksgiving. Excursions feature the Conductor's friendly commentary on the scenery, the history of the line, and the historical place of the railways in Canadian history. Special events during the year include the Easter Express, Hallowe'en Adventure and the Santa Claus Express at Christmastime, which have a holiday focus. The PBS series Shining Time Station was shot here and at Union Station.

Waterloo Central Railway

The Waterloo Central Railway (WCR) is a non-profit organization that is owned and operated by the Southern Ontario Locomotive Restoration Society (SOLRS). In May 2007, SOLRS received approval from the City of Waterloo to run trains from Waterloo to St Jacobs. From April to October the train runs three times a day on Tuesdays, Thursdays and Saturday from June until December.

York–Durham Heritage Railway

The York–Durham Heritage Railway is a heritage railway in Uxbridge, Ontario, just north of Toronto.

The railway operates excursion trains over a 20 km route between the historic towns of Stouffville, Goodwood and Uxbridge. The round trip takes approximately 2 hours and 30 minutes.

Trains are scheduled June through mid-October, and are pulled by an Alco RS-11 diesel locomotive, #3612, which was built for the Duluth, Winnipeg & Pacific Railway in 1956. Coaches include both vintage heavyweights built in the 1910s and 1920s, and lightweight cars from 1954.

Canadian Railway Museum

he Canadian Railway Museum (Exporail) (French: (Le) Musée Ferrovaire Canadien) is a rail transport museum in Delson/ Saint-Constant, Quebec. Operated by the Canadian Railroad Historical Association and using the brand name ExpoRail, the museum maintains the largest collection of railway equipment in Canada with over 140 pieces of rolling stock. There are also over 250,000 objects and documents from Canada's railway history in the collection which is maintained in an archives on the property.

The museum operates a heritage streetcar line around the grounds as well as a heritage railway which pulls a small passenger train on a former freight spur to Montée des Bouleaux. The streetcar operates daily during the spring, summer and fall while the railway operates every Sunday during the same period. The museum underwent a significant expansion during the 2000s when the Angus Exhibit Pavilion opened. Some of the most valuable items were placed in the new pavilion, which became the main exhibition building. One of the most notable artifacts is former Canadian Pacific Royal Hudson 2850, which in 1939 pulled the royal train across Canada. Because of this 2850 is known as "The" royal hudson.

Hull–Chelsea–Wakefield Railway

The Hull–Chelsea–Wakefield Railway is a 33 km (20.5 mi) heritage railway in Quebec, Canada, running tourist trains through the scenic Gatineau Hills and beside the Gatineau River between Hull (part of the city of Gatineau) and the tourist town of

Wakefield (part of La Pêche municipality) from May to October, using a 1907 Swedish steam locomotive and 1940s-built Swedish passenger cars. On average, the railway attracts about 50 000 tourists and generates revenues of about $8 million for the region.

In 2007, a disagreement erupted between the owner of the steam train line and the municipality of Chelsea and city of Gatineau over the railway safety and maintenance. In July, a rain storm caused damage to some parts of the railway. The owner mentioned that without funding from the cities, he would have ceased the operations of the line and sell the steam train. In November, an agreement was made when the province of Quebec and the municipalities involved provided fundings for studies for future improvements to the railway. There were also plans for refurbishing the wagons as well as adding a station at the Casino du Lac-Leamy about 2 kilometers south of its current southern terminus at Quebec Autoroute 5 and Boulevard Saint-Joseph

However, following a landslide in Chelsea during the spring of 2008, the railway was halted after two weekends of activity. The owner decided to sell the train and ceased activities for good. The railway will not run for the summer of 2008.

From the official website it would appear that the train has not been sold and that it will be running in the summer of 2009 . The train is currently in service July 2010.

White Pass and Yukon Route

The White Pass and Yukon Route (WP&Y, WP&YR) (reporting mark WPY) is a Canadian and U.S. Class II narrow gauge railroad linking the port of Skagway, Alaska with Whitehorse, the capital of Yukon, Canada. An isolated system, it has no direct connection to any other railroad. Equipment, freight and passengers are ferried by ship through the Port of Skagway, and via road through a few of the stops along its route. The railroad is a subsidiary of Clublink Enterprises Limited, which is traded on the Toronto Stock Exchange (TSX:TWH) and operated by the

Pacific and Arctic Railway and Navigation Company (in Alaska), the British Columbia Yukon Railway Company (in British Columbia) and the British Yukon Railway Company, originally known as the British Yukon Mining, Trading and Transportation Company (in Yukon), which use the trade name White Pass and Yukon Route.

WHITEHORSE TROLLEY

The Whitehorse trolley is a heritage railway in Whitehorse, Yukon, Canada. It uses a single reconditioned trolley which carries tourists along Whitehorse's waterfront along the Yukon River. It runs from the Rotary Peace Park, located on the south end of the city centre, up to the north end of the city centre at Spook Creek Station. The trolley originally served in Lisbon, Portugal, from 1925 to 1978. In 1978 it was sold to a railway museum in Duluth. It was sold to Whitehorse in 2000.

The trolley is a narrow gauge vehicle, and runs on the track built for the White Pass and Yukon Route. It has a capacity of 25 passengers. When the trolley was first put into commission in 2000 its electric motors were not powered by overhead wires, rather it was powered by diesel generators towed in a trailer.

HONG KONG TRAMWAYS

Hong Kong Tramways is a tram system in Hong Kong and one of the earliest forms of public transport in Hong Kong. Owned and operated by Veolia Transport – RATP Asia, the tramway runs on Hong Kong Island in Hong Kong between Shau Kei Wan and Kennedy Town, with a branch circulating Happy Valley. Each day 240,000 residents commute by tram. Trams in Hong Kong have not only been a form of transport for over 100 years, but also a major tourist attraction and one of the most environmentally friendly mass transit systems. It is the solely exclusively double-decker operated tram system in the world.

Peak Tram

The Peak Tramway is a funicular railway in Hong Kong, which carries both tourists and residents to the upper levels of Hong Kong Island. Running from Central district to Victoria Peak via the Mid-Levels, it provides the most direct route and offers good views over the harbour and skyscrapers of Hong Kong.

The Peak Tram is owned and operated by the Hongkong and Shanghai Hotels group (HSH), the owner of Hong Kong's famous Peninsula Hotel along with many other properties. The line, along with HSH's Peak Tower leisure complex at the line's summit, is promoted using the brand The Peak.

Tren Turistico de la Sabana

The Tren Turistico de la Sabana or Turistren runs heritage trains in Bogota, Colombia. The company runs steam trains from Bogota (Sabana railway station) to Parque and Zipaquira.

The idea of tourist trains with steam locomotives in Bogota was born 1982. When the National Railways in Colombia stopped running trains in 1990, people with knowledge of the railway, started to renovate a steam locomotive and carriages for a tourist railway. In 1992, the private company "Turistren Ltda" was founded by four friends, and a contract with the National Railways was made to use the tracks for running tourist trains. In 1993, railway tours started with steam locomotives under the name "Tren Turistico de la Sabana".

Nordsjællands Veterantog

Nordsjællands Veterantog (NSJV) was founded as Helsingør Jernbaneklub in 1958 as a model railway club in Helsingør, Denmark. The club had its ups and downs in the early years, but the big turning point was when it was decided to try and work with scale 1:1. In 1968, the first service was operated and soon the club had turned into a heritage railway rather than a model railway club.

Acitivies soon grew and kept doing so steadily over the years. In 1992 it was decided to reorganise activities, essentially creating a foundation to take care of "business" issues. This foundation is the proper hold of the name Veterantog, which translations into Heritage Railway of North Zealand. The club was responsible for the maintenance and operations, and this was renamed in 1995 to Nordsjællands Jernbaneklub (Railway Club of North Zealand) in order to match the name of the foundation.

NSJV has never owned their own tracks. Instead, services are operated on regular railway tracks used by operators such as DSB and Lokalbanen. Services run mostly in Northern Zealand, with scheduled services running on weekends and Wednesdays throughout the summer. Activities are based around two locations: The old station in Græsted is the home of the foundation and the club and also houses maintenance for carriages and diesel locomotives, whereas Rungsted depot is the home of the steam locomotives. Operational locomotives include three steam locomotives, two diesel locomotives, and various shunting and service vehicles. Both depots are now onwed by NSJV.

In 2009, restored steam locomotive DSB K-582 entered service after a long project to bring it back to life. It has been restored to the class K look with the new, larger boiler and round dome. While it is still air-braked and thus has a Knorr pump on the side, most components of the air braking system (including the tanks) have been hidden from view to get as close as possible to the vacuum-braked look. The Rungsted depot is now being prepared for the next major project, the restoration of DSB S-740, which was featured in the James Bond movie Octopussy. Work still continues in the Græsted depot on the GDS 11 locomotive.

Jokioinen Museum Railway

The Jokioinen Museum Railway is located in Jokioinen, Finland. It is based on the last narrow gauge railway in Finland, the 750 mm (2 ft 5 1?2 in) gauge Jokioinen Railway. The museum was born on February 2, 1978, 4 years after the discontinued operation of the actual railway, when the specifically established Joint stock company Jokioinen Museum Railway Ltd. (Jokioisten Museorautatie Oy) have bought the Minkiö-Jokioinen Railway line with its land and buildings. Museum steam train began running the same year. In 1994 the line was extended with a 8 km stretch between Minkiö and Humppila. The museum railway station at Humppila is beside the station of the Turku-Toijala VR line, providing a convenient access to the museum. The Minkiö station has a narrow gauge museum with a collection of carriages and locomotives. There are a number other attractions in the vicinity of the railway.

Froissy Dompierre Light Railway

The Froissy Dompierre Light Railway (CFCD) is a narrow-gauge light railway near the village of Cappy, in the Somme department, France. It is run as a heritage railway by APPEVA (Association Picarde pour la Préservation et l'Entretien des Véhicules Anciens). It is the last survivor of the 600 mm (1 ft 11 5/8 in) gauge lines of the World War I battlefields.

Tarn Light Railway

The Tarn Light Railway (CFTT) is a narrow-gauge light railway near the village of Saint-Lieux-lès-Lavaur, in the vicinity of Saint-Sulpice in the department of Tarn, France. It is run as a heritage railway by a French association, the ACOVA (Association pour la Conservation Occitane de Véhicules Anciens) incorporated in 1975 and based in Toulouse. It operates on a 500 mm (1 ft 7 3?4 in) gauge and the line was reconstructed from 1974 over a length of 3.5 kilometers (2 mi) on the platform of the former line from La Ramière to Saint-Sulpice which operated only from 11 April 1925, to 20 June 1931. The line starts from the Saint Lieux-lès-Lavaur terminus at the former station ex-TVT and follows the streets of Saint-Lieux till a 132-metre (433 ft) long viaduct over the river Agout. Then it runs in the Tarn countryside and woods before arriving at the present terminus at les Martels.

Chemin de Fer de la Baie de Somme

The Chemin de Fer de la Baie de Somme (Somme Bay Railway), is a preserved railway in northern France. The line is one of the closest French heritage lines to the UK, Noyelles is 73 kilometres (45 mi) from Boulogne-sur-Mer and 105 kilometres (65 mi) from Calais. A part of the line has dual gauge track, and although forming part of a group of five lines, at least a part of it has always been open to traffic.

Ulm Railway Society

The Ulm Railway Society (Ulmer Eisenbahnfreunde or UEF) is a German society for encouraging the preservation of historically valuable railway stock. It is based in the vicinity of Ulm, a city in the state of Baden-Württemberg in southern Germany. The society was founded in 1969, has about 600 members and around 12 steam locomotives as well as numerous historical wagons.

Calcutta Tramways Company

The Calcutta Tramways Company Limited (CTC) is a West Bengal state government undertaken company that runs trams in Kolkata and buses in and around Kolkata. The Kolkata tram is the oldest operating electric tram of Asia, running since 1902.

Darjeeling Himalayan Railway

The Darjeeling Himalayan Railway, nicknamed the "Toy Train", is a 2 ft (610 mm) narrow-gauge railway from Siliguri to Darjeeling in West Bengal, run by the Indian Railways.

It was built between 1879 and 1881 and is about 86 kilometres (53 mi) long. The elevation level is from about 100 m (328 ft) at Siliguri to about 2,200 metres (7,218 ft) at Darjeeling. It is still powered by steam locomotives. Modern diesel engines are used for Darjeeling's mail train.

Since 1999 the train has been a World Heritage Site as listed by UNESCO. In 2005, UNESCO added the Nilgiri Mountain Railway as an extension to the original designation.

Nilgiri Mountain Railway

The Nilgiri Mountain Railway (NMR) connects the town of Mettupalayam with the hill station of Udagamandalam (Ootacamund or Ooty), in the Nilgiri Hills of southern India. Both towns are in the state of Tamil Nadu. It is the only rack railway in India and uses the Abt system.

Matheran Hill Railway

Matheran Hill Railway is a heritage railway in Maharashtra, India. It was built between 1901 and 1907 by Abdul Hussein Adamjee Peerbhoy, financed by his father, Sir Adamjee Peerbhoy of the Adamjee Group at the cost of Rs.16,00,000. Sir Adamjee Peerbhoy visited Matheran often and wanted to build a railway to make it easier to get there.

Kalka-Shimla Railway

The Kalka-Shimla Railway is a 2 ft 6 in (762 mm) narrow gauge railway in North-West India travelling along a mostly mountainous route from Kalka to Shimla. It is known for breathtaking views of the hills and surrounding villages.

Bernina Railway

The Bernina Railway is a single track metre gauge railway line forming part of the Rhaetian Railway (RhB). It links the spa resort of St. Moritz, in the Canton of Graubünden, Switzerland, with the town of Tirano, in the Province of Sondrio, Italy, via the Bernina Pass. It also ranks as the highest adhesion railway in the Alps, and - with inclines of up to 7% - as one of the steepest adhesion railways in the world. On 7 July 2008, the Bernina Railway and the Albula Railway, which also forms part of the RhB, were recorded in the list of UNESCO World Heritage Sites, under the name Rhaetian Railway in the Albula / Bernina Landscapes. The whole site is regarded as a cross border joint Swiss-Italian heritage area. The most famous trains operating on the Bernina Railway are known as the Bernina Express.

Sagano Scenic Railway

The Sagano Scenic Railway or Sagano Sightseeing Railway is a wholly owned subsidiary of West Japan Railway Company (JR West) that operates the Sagano Scenic Line or Sagano Sightseeing Line in Kyoto. The line uses once-abandoned tracks of the Sagano Line (officially a portion of the San'in Main Line) of JR West, from Torokko Sagano in Arashiyama, and passes a gorge offering a scenic view along the Hozu River, then enters and terminates in the basin of Kameoka. It is closed on Wednesdays and in the winter. The tram line is locally known as "Torokko in Hozu gorge." Torokko is a Japanese word derived from the English "truck" once used for mining cars hauling ore, but presently means rail carriages for scenic view with rough accommodations.

Interoceanic Railway of Mexico

The Interoceanic Railway of Mexico (Ferrocarril Interoceánico de México) was one of the primary pre-nationalization railways of Mexico. Incorporated in Great Britain in 1888 to complete an unfinished project and compete with the Mexican Railway, it completed a narrow gauge main line from Mexico City to Veracruz in 1891. Branches included Mexico City to Puente de Ixtla (the constructed part of an incomplete line to Acapulco), Puebla to Cuautla, Atencingo to Tlancualpicán, and a cutoff between Oriental and Santa Clara (bypassing Puebla). Through subsidiary Mexican Eastern Railway, the Interoceanic acquired a branch from San Marcos to Teziutlán in 1902, and in January 1910 it began operating the Mexican Southern Railway from Puebla to Oaxaca under lease. The Mexican government acquired control of the Interoceanic in 1903, and subsequently sold it to the National Railroad of Mexico in exchange for ownership of that company.

Although the National Railroad became part of the Ferrocarriles Nacionales de México (National Railways of Mexico) in January 1909, the Interoceanic and its two subsidiaries remained separate companies until a later time. The company operated some of the last steam locomotives in regular revenue service in North America. Following privatization in the 1990s, Transportación Ferroviaria Mexicana (now Kansas City Southern de México) acquired most of the main line of the former Interoceanic, while several branches, including the old line to Puebla and the Mexican Southern, were assigned to Ferromex. A portion of the former Interoceanic and a station have been preserved as a heritage railway and museum in Cuautla.

Steamtrain Hoorn Medemblik

The Museumstoomtram Hoorn Medemblik is a heritage railway in the Netherlands. It runs from Hoorn to Medemblik, a distance of about 20km. The original connection was run by

Locaalspoorwegmaatschappij Hollands Noorderkwartier (1884 - 1935). The line was opened on November 3, 1887. The connection follows a curving path, to reduce the amount of land that had to be confiscated. The train used steam traction, with diesel traction being introduced in 1929. The line was closed for passenger service from January 1, 1936 until May 29, 1940. On January 5, 1941 the line was permanently closed for passenger service, just as the railway station in Medemblik.

Old Voss Line

The Old Voss Line (Norwegian: Gamle Vossebanen) is a heritage railway between Garnes and Midttun near Bergen, Norway. Originally constructed as a narrow gauge line, it formed part of the Bergen to Voss railway opened in 1883. Following the decision to complete the railway to Oslo in standard gauge, the line was upgraded in 1904. Electrified in 1954, it continued to serve as part of the Bergen to Oslo main line until the 7.5-km Ulriken Tunnel, which opened in 1964, resulted in the closure of the line.

Today, the museum railway is operated by the Norwegian Railway Association (Norsk Jernbaneklubb) and runs on Sundays between June and September over a distance of 18 km between Garnes and Midttun, taking just under one hour. The Midttun terminus is located near Nesttun, and there are further intermediate stops at Arna, Espeland and Haukeland. The service operates with a type 18 steam locomotive, no. 255, built in 1913, decommissioned in 1969 and restored by volunteers between 1981 and 1993. It pulls a series of teak carriages built between 1921 and 1938. The locomotive is stored at the restored Garnes station that features a museum, engine shed, yard and turntable.

Narrow Gauge Railway Museum in Wenecja

Narrow Gauge Railway Museum in Wenecja (Polish Venice) near Z.nin (Poland) is an open air museum collecting and exhibiting steam locomotives, passenger and freight cars, trolleys, railwaymen's tools, signalling equipment, contents of an old waiting room, old maps. The 600 mm Narrow Gauge Railway Museum in Wenecja is a department of the Muzeum Ziemi Pa?uckiej (the Z.nin's Museum of Pa?uki Land) and was established in 1972 at a suggestion of enthusiasts of the Pa?uki region, of which Z.nin is considered the capital. The Museum has collected numerous steam locomotives. One of the oldest is the German one made by Orenstein & Koppel in Berlin in 1900. The Tx-1116 locomotive made by Henschel & Son (Kassel, 1918) and the Tx4-564 locomotive made by Hanomag (Hannover, 1923) are also very interesting. A real rarity is the Belgian locomotive made by Les Ateliers Metallurgiques Nivelles with the unique wheel arrangement 2-3-1 ("Pacific"), and the only one which has steam brakes. There are also steam locomotives made in the first Polish plant in Chrzanów. The Narrow Gauge Railway Museum in Wenecja is situated at the foot of the ruins of the medieval castle built in the 14th century by legendary. Tourists can travel on the historic narrow gauge railway from Z.nin via Wenecja to Biskupin which is famous for a reconstruction of the Lusatian culture settlement and the Archaeological Museum.

Outeniqua Choo Tjoe

The Outeniqua Choo Tjoe was the last remaining continually-operated passenger steam train in Africa, ending operation in June 2009. The railway was completed in 1928, and links the towns of George and Knysna in the Western Cape, South Africa. The 3 hour journey also stops in the towns of Wilderness, Goukamma, and Sedgefield. The scenic 67-kilometre (42 mi) route hugs the rugged coastline of the Garden Route before ending by crossing a bridge over the lagoon in Knysna.

It was declared an officially preserved railway in 1992, carrying about 40,000 passengers per year at the time. A decade later, it carried 115,000 passengers per year, 70% of whom were foreign tourists.

The trains are usually pulled by SAR Class 19D steam locomotives, of 4-8-2 wheel arrangement with Vanderbilt-like "torpedo" tenders, although the task is occasionally handled by SAR Class 24 steam engines. When dry conditions in the summer increase the risk of wildfires, diesel locomotives (SAR Class 32s) are used instead.

During August 2006 the line was damaged due to heavy flooding. From November 2006 is has be rescheduled to run between George and Mossel Bay (with a stop at Hartenbos) until further notice.

In 2008, the train and the Kaaiman's River Bridge were featured in a television advertisement for Stella Artois. In 2007, the train's owners, Transnet Limited, announced that the train was not regarded as part of its core business. Transnet initiated a tender process to dispose of the train to a new owner/operator. However, on August 19th 2010 Transnet announced that, following unsuccessful attempts to find such a new operator, the train would cease operating. Nonetheless, the Western Cape Province's Finance, Economic Development and Tourism Minister, Alan Winde, says he is resolved to keep this heritage tourism asset operational.

Azpeitia Railway Museum

The Azpeitia Railway Museum (Basque Railway Museum) in Azpeitia, Basque Country, Spain, has a collection of steam locomotives and other rolling stock as well as other items, connected with the Basque Narrow gauge railways. The museum is located at the station in Azpeitia.

The museum railway between Azpeitia and Lasao, is not any longer connected with the rest of the Basque railway net. The museum and the museum railway to Lasao is run by Euskotren. Azpeitia is located 45 km from San Sebastian and 75 km from Bilbao.

Rigi-Bahnen

Rigi Railways (Rigi-Bahnen) is a group of railways on Mount Rigi, located between two of the arms of Lake Lucerne, in Switzerland. They include two standard gauge rack railways, the Vitznau-Rigi Bahn (VRB) and the Arth-Rigi Bahn (ARB), along with the Luftseilbahn Weggis-Rigi Kaltbad (LWRK) cable car.

Upsala-Lenna Jernväg

Upsala-Lenna Jernväg (ULJ) (literally: Upsala-Lenna Railway) is a 32.6 km long 891 mm (3 Swedish feet) narrow-gauge heritage railroad in Uppsala County, Sweden. 891 mm is the most common narrow-gauge in the country, but has only been used in Sweden and in a mine in the Norwegian island of Spitsbergen. The railroad, run by the SRJmf society, is one of a few remaining lines of a greater network of narrow-gauge railroad lines in the area called Stockholm-Roslagens Järnvägar (SRJ).

Alishan Forest Railway

The Alishan Forest Railway is an 86 km network of 2 ft 6 in (762 mm) (narrow gauge) railways running up to and throughout the popular mountain resort of Alishan in Chiayi County, Taiwan.

Lézard rouge

The lézard rouge (French for "red lizard") is a historic Tunisian train, once the property of the Bey of Tunis but now used for tourists. It runs from Metlaoui to Redeyef and passes through the Selja Gorge, taking some 40 minutes for the journey. The track was originally used by mining trains carrying phosphates.

Alderney Railway

The Alderney Railway in Alderney is the only working railway in the Channel Islands. It opened in 1847 and runs for about two miles (3 km), mostly following a coastal route, from Braye Road to Mannez Quarry and Lighthouse. The railway is run by volunteers and usually operates during summer weekends and bank holidays.

Bibliography

• Heritage Tourism (Themes in Tourism) by Dallen J. Timothy and Stephen W. Boyd, published by Prentice Hall in 2003, ISBN 0582369703, 9780582369702, Pages 327

• Beaver, Allan (2002). A Dictionary of Travel and Tourism Terminology. Wallingford: CAB International. p. 313. ISBN 0851995829. OCLC 301675778.

• International Association of Scientific Experts in Tourism. "The AIEST, its character and aims".

• "Recommendations on Tourism Statistics". Statistical Papers. M (New York: United Nations) (83): 5. 1994.

• "UNWTO Tourism Highlights, 2009 Edition". World Tourism Organization. 2009. http://www.unwto.org/facts/menu.html. Retrieved 2009-10-04. Click on the link "UNWTO Tourism Highlights" to access the pdf report.

• Muhammad Abdullah Chaghtai Le Tadj Mahal D'Agra (Hindi). Histoire et description (Brussels) 1938 p. 46.

• 'Abd al-Hamid Lahawri Badshah Namah Ed. Maulawis Kabir al-Din Ahmad and 'Abd al-Rahim u-nder the superintendence of Major W.N. Lees. Vol. I Calcutta 1867 pp384-9 ; Muhammad Salih Kambo Amal-i-Sal\lih or Shah Jahan Namah Ed. Ghulam Yazdani Vol.I (Calcutta) 1923 p. 275.

• Begley, Wayne E. (March 1979). "The Myth of the Taj

Mahal and a New Theory of Its Symbolic Meaning". The Art Bulletin 61 (1): 14.

- "taj-mahal-travel-tours.com". taj-mahal-travel-tours.com.. http://www.taj-mahal-travel-tours.com/garden-of-taj-mahal.html.
- Wright, Karen (July 2000). "Moguls in the Moonlight - plans to restore Mehtab Bagh garden near Taj Mahal". Discover.
- Allan, John (1958) (edition = First). The Cambridge Shorter History of India. Cambridge: S. Chand, 288 pages. p. 318.
- "Taj Mahal". World Heritage List. UNESCO World Heritage Centre. http://whc.unesco.org/en/list. Retrieved 28 September 2007. "The World Heritage List includes 851 properties forming part of the cultural and natural heritage which the World Heritage Committee considers as having outstanding universal value."
- Baidyanath, Saraswati (2006). "Cultural Pluralism, National Identity and Development". Interface of Cultural Identity Development (1stEdition ed.). New Delhi: Indira Gandhi National Centre for the Arts. xxi+290 pp. ISBN 81-246-0054-6.
- "The Jantar Mantar, Jaipur - UNESCO World Heritage Centre". Whc.unesco.org. 2010-07-31.
- "History - British History in depth: Edward VII: The First Constitutional Monarch". BBC. 2009-11-05.
- "World Weather Information Service".
- Top 50 Emerging Global Outsourcing Cities, Global Services-Tholons Study, 2008
- De Souza, Teotonio R. (1990). Goa Through the Ages: An economic history. Goa University publication. 2. Concept Publishing Company. ISBN 9788170222590.
- Sakshena, R.N. (2003). Goa: Into the Mainstream. Abhinav Publications. ISBN 9788170170051.

- Isadora Tast: Mother India. Searching For a Place. Peperoni Books: Berlin 2009, ISBN 978-3-941825-00-0

- Massey, Reginald (2004-01-01). India's dances: their history, technique, and repertoire. Abhinav Publications, 2004. ISBN 8170174341.

- Mohammada, Malika (2007). The foundations of the composite culture in India. Aakar Books, 2007. ISBN 8189833189.

- Arnett, Robert (2006-07). India Unveiled. Atman Press, 2006. ISBN 0965290042.

- Sharma, Shaloo (2002). History and Development of Higher Education in India. Sarup & Sons, 2002. ISBN 8176253189.

- Mark Kobayashi-Hillary Outsourcing to India, Springer, 2004 ISBN 3-540-20855-0 p.8

- Nikki Stafford Finding Lost, ECW Press, 2006 ISBN 1-55022-743-2 p. 174

- "45". What Is Hinduism?: Modern Adventures Into a Profound Global Faith. Himalayan Academy Publications. 2007. p. 359. ISBN 1934145009.

- "Non Resident Nepali - Speeches". Nrn.org.np. http://www.nrn.org.np/speeches/rmshakya.html.

- "Religions of the world: numbers of adherents; growth rates". Religioustolerance.org.

- "Religions Muslim" (PDF). Registrat General and Census Commissioner, India.

- Eugene M. Makar (2008). An American's Guide to Doing Business in India. ISBN 1598692119.

- Peter H. Marshall Nature's web: rethinking our place on earth M.E. Sharpe, 1996 ISBN 1-56324-864-6 p. 26

- "Tandoori Village Restaurant Brisbane". AsiaRooms.com. http://www.asiarooms.com/travel-guide/australia/brisbane/what-where-to-eat/indian-restaurants-in-brisbane/tandoori-village-restaurant-brisbane.html.

- "Indian food now attracts wider market.". Asia Africa Intelligence Wire. 2005-03-16.
- Louise Marie M. Cornillez (Spring 1999). "The History of the Spice Trade in India".
- "Elephant Festival Jaipur - Elephant Festival Jaipur Rajasthan - Elephant Festival in Rajasthan India". Rajasthantourism.org.

Index